ADVANCE PRAISE FOR

Gaming SEL: Games as Transformational to Social and Emotional Learning

"Games can provide a context for exploration, experimentation, and perspective-taking—a playground for human development that can help us better understand ourselves and each other. In this timely and thoughtfully researched book, Farber presents rich evidence that games build resilience and emotional well-being, and provides a robust catalogue of ideas, examples, and references to explore."
—Michael Preston, Executive Director,
Joan Ganz Cooney Center at Sesame Workshop

"Matthew Farber's book gives the reader a compelling and nuanced tour of a very important subject—social and emotional learning and the role that games can play in supporting it. I would encourage anyone looking for a comprehensive and accessible introduction to this topic to read this book! I particularly appreciate Farber's broad knowledge of game design efforts in this area, as well as his grasp of related literature."
—Katherine Isbister, Professor of Computational Media, University of California, Santa Cruz; author of *How Games Move Us: Emotion by Design*

"Matthew Farber delivers a much-needed resource for those interested in finding ways to meet youth where they are. Games are undeniably a meaningful part of young people's lives, and identifying ways games can offer pathways to growth and self-awareness is gold! His understanding of social and emotional learning and the games industry provides a unique insight into how games can contribute to the development of thriving global citizens."
—Susanna Pollack, President, Games for Change

"Kudos to Matthew Farber for synthesizing so much research, contemporary evidence, and expert voices into a book that is both relevant, provocative, and thoughtful. Emotions are the gatekeepers of attention, motivation, and cognition; through technology, young people make sense of and contribute to their world. This book explores the present and possible roles for technology to play in this space."
—Mark Sparvell, Education Marketing Director, Microsoft

"*Gaming SEL* takes us into a fascinating and resourceful journey exploring the development of social and emotional skills (more specifically in children) and the ways in which games can support social and emotional learning (SEL). Matthew Farber summarizes the results of empirical research and gathers the expertise of dozens of academics, researchers, educators, and game designers to digest it all in a very approachable way for the reader. Using a multitude of examples from board games to video games, he also offers a compelling guide for harnessing the emotional and engaging power of games for SEL. This book is a must-read for teachers, parents, and anyone interested in understanding *why* and *how* games can foster a growth mindset, allow us to experiment with emotions and interpersonal relationships safely, and support our overall emotional well-being."

—Celia Hodent, PhD in psychology, game UX consultant; author of *The Gamer's Brain* and *The Psychology of Video Games*

Gaming SEL

This book is part of the Peter Lang Education list.
Every volume is peer reviewed and meets
the highest quality standards for content and production.

PETER LANG
New York • Bern • Berlin
Brussels • Vienna • Oxford • Warsaw

Matthew Farber

Gaming SEL

Games as Transformational
to Social and Emotional Learning

PETER LANG
New York • Bern • Berlin
Brussels • Vienna • Oxford • Warsaw

Library of Congress Cataloging-in-Publication Data

Names: Farber, Matthew, author.
Title: Gaming SEL: games as transformational
to social and emotional learning / Matthew Farber.
Description: New York: Peter Lang, 2021
Includes bibliographical references and index.
Identifiers: LCCN 2020057132 (print) | LCCN 2020057133 (ebook)
ISBN 978-1-4331-8642-4 (hardback) | ISBN 978-1-4331-8595-3 (paperback)
ISBN 978-1-4331-8596-0 (ebook pdf) | ISBN 978-1-4331-8597-7 (epub)
ISBN 978-1-4331-8598-4 (mobi)
Subjects: LCSH: Educational games—Social aspects. | Social learning. |
Affective education.
Classification: LCC LB1029.G3 .F38 2021 (print) | LCC LB1029.G3 (ebook) |
DDC 371.33/7—dc23
LC record available at https://lccn.loc.gov/2020057132
LC ebook record available at https://lccn.loc.gov/2020057133
DOI 10.3726/b18044

Bibliographic information published by **Die Deutsche Nationalbibliothek**.
Die Deutsche Nationalbibliothek lists this publication in the "Deutsche
Nationalbibliografie"; detailed bibliographic data are available
on the Internet at http://dnb.d-nb.de/.

© 2021 Peter Lang Publishing, Inc., New York
80 Broad Street, 5th floor, New York, NY 10004
www.peterlang.com

All rights reserved.
Reprint or reproduction, even partially, in all forms such as microfilm,
xerography, microfiche, microcard, and offset strictly prohibited.

Table of Contents

List of Figures   ix
Foreword by Anantha Kumar Duraiappah, Founding Director, UNESCO MGIEP   xi
Acknowledgments   xiii

Introduction   1
    About This Book   4
    Links, Lessons, and Games   5
    References   6

Part I
Chapter One: How Mister Rogers Taught Us to Feel   9
    Co-viewing and Joint Media Engagement   10
    The Emotional Intelligence of Fred Rogers   14
        Social and Emotional Play in the Neighborhood of Make-Believe   16
        Rogers's Six Principles of Learning Readiness   17
        Playing in Daniel Tiger's Neighborhood   20
    How Are You Feeling Today?   23
    Mood Management Theory   26
        Mood Management and Video Games   28

Links, Lessons, and Games	30
References	31
Chapter Two: An Exploration of Social and Emotional Learning	35
CASEL's SEL Framework	37
Critiques of SEL	40
Attack of the Frameworks!	42
SEL Kernels and Brain Games	44
UNESCO MGIEP's EMC² Framework for Social and Emotional Learning	47
Prosociality and the Greater Good	52
Links, Lessons, and Games	54
References	54
Chapter Three: How Games Give Players "The Feels"	59
Affordances and Emotions	61
"Game Feel"	62
"Where Special Rules Obtain"	65
Games as Curriculum	70
From Mechanics to Meaningful Situations	72
Links, Lessons, and Games	76
References	76

Part II

Chapter Four: Empathy Games	83
Can a Video Game Teach Empathy?	85
Content Warnings	87
On the Appropriateness of Role-Play	89
Paired Texts and Impossible Field Trips	97
Links, Lessons, and Games	99
References	100
Chapter Five: Mindful, Kind, and Compassionate	105
The Mindful Knight	107
Play Deliberately: A Mindful Walk in the Virtual Woods	109
Kind Words: A Game About Being Nice	114
SEL in the Game of School	119
Compassion Games: Survival of the Kindest	122
Extra Life and the Children's Miracle Network	124
Links, Lessons, and Games	126
References	127
Chapter Six: Ethics, Perspective-Taking, and Teen Identity	131
Can a Video Game Teach Ethics?	132

Quandaries, Perspectives, and Dilemmas	137
Awkward Moments and Implicit Biases	138
iThrive Games and the Teen Brain	141
Can Video Games Transform Behavior?	145
Links, Lessons, and Games	148
References	149
Chapter Seven: Co-op Play, Teamwork, and Relationship Skills	**153**
Games of Kinship and Interdependence	155
"We Broke Out!"	157
Lessons from Recess	160
Scholastic Esports and Cyber Wellness	163
Tilt Malleability and Growth Mindset	165
Games of Love and Self-Discovery	168
Links, Lessons, and Games	171
References	172
Chapter Eight: How Making Games Supports Self-Awareness	**175**
The Games for Change Student Challenge	177
Global Game Jam NEXT: A Global Game Jam for Youth	180
Anti-Defamation League Game Jams	182
Autopathographical Game Design	184
Links, Lessons, and Games	189
References	189
Index	**191**

List of Figures

Figure 1.   Screenshot from *GRIS*   2
Figure 2.   Peekapak's SEL Check-in Tool   24
Figure 3.   CASEL's SEL Framework   39
Figure 4.   EMC² Framework for Social and Emotional Learning   49
Figure 5.   Youth-designed *Immigrants and Border Patrol* Track Game   72
Figure 6.   Situational Game Design   74
Figure 7.   *Crystals of Kaydor* Emotion Identification User Interface (UI)   87
Figure 8.   Image of *The Mindful Knight* Book and Quill   109
Figure 9.   Floating Bedroom in *Kind Words*   115
Figure 10. Student Reflection After Playing *Kind Words*   118
Figure 11. Image of *Awkward Moment* Cards   139
Figure 12. Directional Lock in a Breakout EDU Digital Game   158

Foreword

Of Play and Games for Social and Emotional Learning

In one of the most viewed TED Talks to date, the late Ken Robinson illustrated how schools kill creativity. According to Robinson, a one-way instructional style—the "teacher knows best" approach—prevents learners from exploration, curiosity, critical thinking, and innovation, all the while making learning a mundane and boring activity. However, learning must be fun, and it must make one happy. As Roald Dahl, author of *Charlie and the Chocolate Factory*, eloquently stated, "Life is more fun if you play games." Now, imagine a world where we can infuse creativity in learning while making it fun and rewarding. Here is where this book comes in.

In *Gaming SEL*, Matthew Farber attempts to define how to achieve these two lofty goals—providing ways for learners to accomplish success through games while having fun in the process. However, Farber does not stop there; he has a bigger purpose, and this, I believe, is the unique contribution of this book to the education community.

This book focuses on games that build social and emotional learning (SEL) skills, what many call "soft skills." In actuality, these are the hardest skills to develop, and Farber does a brilliant job explaining how they can be cultivated with games.

The young of today are digitally native citizens. They are practically born with a screen console in their hands and are constantly connected with the virtual world of information, people, and places. Students today want to be involved, want meaning in their learning, and desire connection with others. They are more comfortable with digital learning than traditional printed textbooks. They are curious and are not so willing to just listen and take what is delivered as truth. In other words, students today want a dynamic learning environment where they feel challenged.

An important feature of this book is Farber's exploration of SEL frameworks. Although there is no one-size-fits-all approach, he does cover two very different frameworks: CASEL's SEL Framework, which many consider as one of the first, and the newer UNESCO MGIEP EMC^2 Framework for Social and Emotional Learning. The differences across SEL frameworks, their strengths and weaknesses, their uses—and the potentials for misuse—are well-elaborated. Furthermore, this book offers a narrative of SEL's origins and its changes over the past few decades.

It is well-documented that just playing games does not automatically stimulate and allow learners to achieve specific learning outcomes. This book illustrates and provides examples of how game-based curricula can be developed to achieve SEL outcomes. The many references to neuroscience, child psychology, and, of course, evidence-based studies are strengths of this book. *Minecraft: Education Edition*'s *The Mindful Knight*, *Kind Words*, and *Crystals of Kaydor* are shared as examples of games that teach empathy, kindness, and compassion in classrooms—they are new opportunities for teaching SEL with games.

I am confident that this book will be a seminal resource for the future use of games in education systems. It provides key insights into SEL and how to mainstream it within schools and curriculum with quality and rigor. It also offers guidance to teachers on how to use existing games for achieving SEL outcomes.

Increasingly, young people struggle with anxiety, stress, and depression. This is a book ahead of its time, yet urgently needed now. I hope the book is read and enjoyed by gamers within the education community as well as parents who are interested in children's well-being and flourishing.

Anantha Kumar Duraiappah, Founding Director, United Nations Educational, Scientific and Cultural Organization (UNESCO) Mahatma Gandhi Institute of Education for Peace and Sustainable Development (MGIEP)

Acknowledgments

I researched and wrote the entirety of this book during the COVID-19 pandemic. This book would not have been possible without the support of many people. I would like to thank my wife, Laura, and our son, Spencer, for their continued support. A special thank you is extended to my parents, Gary and Judith Farber, and my mother-in-law, Virginia Fisher.

I am grateful to my publisher for faith in my vision, and to the experts interviewed as part of my research. I would like to express my gratitude to my colleagues at the University of Northern Colorado, including the Technology, Innovation, and Pedagogy program, the School of Teacher Education, and the College of Education and Behavioral Sciences. Go Bears!

On a personal note, our beloved family pet dog Lizzie sadly passed away in October 2020. Throughout her long life, we took many mindful walks together. She was playful and loyal to the end. This book is dedicated to her memory.

Introduction

I tap "New Game" to begin. In beautiful watercolors, a woman in a red cape appears on my smartphone's screen. She suddenly collapses, then tumbles from the sky. Emotional orchestral music plays.

When she lands, her cape turns black. Her head tilts downward. I drag on the screen to pull her to move forward, but she walks slowly. The screen becomes foggy. She falls to her knees and weeps.

The gameplay is a two-dimensional puzzle-platformer, like *Super Mario Bros.* but darker in mood and tone. There are no pipes to climb into nor mushrooms to jump on. Instead, I traverse geometric objects scattered in a bleak, barren, and inhospitable landscape (see Figure 1).

I am playing *GRIS*, an award-winning game with no dialogue; the entire story is visual. The game's levels, color palette, and obstacles function as symbolic metaphors for the five stages of grief: denial, anger, bargaining, depression, and acceptance (Kübler-Ross, 1969).

At one point, wind pushes my avatar backward. The only way to proceed is not to fight the gust but to hide from it. I swipe down on my screen to shelter-in-place. When I do, my character's dress turns into some sort of shield. Hunkering down in *GRIS* represents my character's bargaining with waves of sadness. The only way my avatar can reach acceptance is to continue moving. I am confident that I can succeed.

Figure 1. Screenshot from *GRIS*. Source: Nomada Studio. Reprinted by permission of the publisher.

There is often no real way to lose a video game except if the player quits; nearly all games are presented as winnable (Toppo, 2015). Given enough try and practice, I know that I can defeat any monster or enemy.

An essential part of social and emotional learning (SEL) is the notion of *growth mindset*, the idea that if people keep trying, they can learn from their own mistakes and grow (CASEL's SEL Framework, 2020; Dweck, 1986; 2006). Having a growth mindset is more than failing and retrying; it is an attitude or belief that one's intelligence is malleable (Dweck, 2006).

Celeste is a video game that can promote growth mindset. Difficult to win, players control Madeline, a protagonist who climbs Celeste Mountain, a metaphor for her mental health challenges. Two years after the game's release, the designer confirmed to the *Celeste* player community that Madeline's tale is also a trans story (Thorson, 2020).

New York City educator Zachary Hartzman adapted *Celeste* to promote growth mindset with his high school English language learner (ELL) students. "How can we overcome adversity in our lives?" he asks his class after they play. "What is the game trying to teach us?"

I spoke with Hartzman about video games and SEL. In addition to *Celeste*, he also teaches with *GRIS*. "Most of my students fail the New York State Regents exam the first time, as they are ELLs," he told me. "*Celeste* helps teach them to be resilient and that difficulty is okay."

Why do we play games when we know we will fail? Game studies researcher Jesper Juul refers to this seeming contradiction as the *paradox of failure*. In his book *The Art of Failure* (2013), Juul mused how we, as humans, are wont to avoid failure—except when we choose to play games. The paradox of failure in games is explained in these steps:

1. We generally avoid failure.
2. We experience failure when playing games.
3. We seek out games, although we will experience something that we normally avoid. (Juul, 2013, p. 2)

I took comfort in *GRIS* because I could always pick myself up. Each time I failed, I tried a different solution. When I played *Celeste*, I died hundreds of times. Yes, hundreds—the game tabulates how many times players die with a "Death Count." (*GRIS* and *Celeste* are both rated "E for Everyone" in the United States by the Entertainment Software Ratings Board. Players respawn quickly and no graphic violence is depicted.) Although I failed repeatedly, I was encouraged to keep trying. At one point, my character received a supportive postcard. It read, "Be proud of your Death Count. The more you die, the more you're learning. Keep going!"

It may seem obvious why we watch movies, read books, and play games that make us happy. But why do we engage with media that can fill us with despair? Perhaps it is because we know that these experiences will end with catharsis, the Aristotelian term that describes the purging of negative emotions (Juul, 2013). When we watch scary movies or play zombie games, we feel catharsis after we escape our fears.

We consume media because it allows us to practice our emotions in spaces that are free from actualized consequences. Because *GRIS* and *Celeste* are games, I knew that I could confront any uncomfortable emotion, from sorrow to frustration. I also understood that my perseverance would lead to feelings of well-being and satisfaction.

Media literacy in the 20th century required an understanding of multimodal representation in comics, graphic novels, moving images (film, television), and information networks (telephonic systems, the internet) (Zimmerman, 2015). Comparatively, the 21st century is *ludic* (Greek for playful), an era where the multimodal media we encounter is often game-like, interactive, and playable (Zimmerman, 2015). Regarding gaming literacy in the *Ludic Century*, Zimmerman (2015) wrote,

> Literacy is about creating and understanding meaning, which allows people to write (create) and read (understand). New literacies, such as visual and technological literacy, have also been identified in recent decades. However, to be truly literate in the Ludic

Century also requires gaming literacy. The rise of games in our culture is both cause and effect of gaming literacy in the Ludic Century. (Zimmerman, 2015, p. 21)

Games function as a practice space for us to play with our emotions. In many games, players can perspective-take and develop virtual empathy through digital avatars. Games also *proceduralize* skills by breaking down competencies into discrete and mechanical steps (Bogost, 2007, 2008). *GRIS* modeled the stages of grief through video game levels. In *Celeste*, I learned how failure is part of goal achievement. We can also develop SEL skills through the self-expressive design of games.

I wrote this book during safer-at-home orders in the time of the COVID-19 pandemic—an interesting diversion for my own mental well-being. Stuck at home, my family played board games and video games together. Like many, we set up a private island in *Animal Crossing: New Horizons*, Nintendo's popular social simulation game. During scary and uncertain times, games were the glue that connected us.

Zimmerman (2015) wrote that gaming literacies gives us a lens to view the world as interconnected, and that doing so can help us to solve real-world problems. This book investigates how games help young people make sense out of the systems that they inhabit. As children cultivate SEL skills that relate to gaming, they can feel empowered, which can lead to positive changes in their own lives (Farber et al., 2020; Peppler et al., 2013; Senge et al., 2012).

About This Book

When I wrote this book, the video game *Among Us* was "viral" with children. Similar to other social deduction games, such as *Werewolf* and *Mafia*, in *Among Us*, players guess who the imposters are in a group. My 10-year-old son plays on his iPad but also at school on the playground. Using foam pool noodles to maintain physical distance, his friends play "IRL," slang for "in real life."

In *Among Us*, any player has a chance to win. It is social and online, engendering a sense of relatedness among players. Because players control the experience, a wide range of human emotions may be evoked (Isbister, 2016; Ryan & Deci, 2018). What's more, the game never excludes anyone; when voted out, players can still participate as "ghosts."

By the time you read this book, another game may usurp children's eyes and thumbs. Although games change, the pedagogy that undergirds "good" game-based learning holds steady (Gee, 2007). In "good" video games, players take on different identities to solve a series of well-ordered problems (Gee, 2007). Good video games also engage players in metacognition about games as designed systems

(Gee, 2007; Zimmerman, 2015). These principles hold true as much in *Minecraft* as they do in *Among Us*.

Like gaming, the field of SEL changes and advances rapidly. This book represents a snapshot of games that can cultivate social and emotional development. My research led me to speak with more than 50 experts, including cognitive psychologists, teachers, academics, and game designers. These conversations took place between March and October 2020; I completed this book in May of 2021.

In this book, research on social and emotional skills are first explored. Next, emotional affordances in games are analyzed. These parts are essentially the *why* and the *how* of teaching SEL skills with good games in transformational ways. Each chapter concludes with links to resources and games to play. Of course, websites change all of the time; if a link no longer works, try a quick Google search. Or, better yet, please visit this book's companion website, where you will find chapter discussion questions, my contact information, and other relevant materials: https://sites.google.com/view/gamingsel.

The games and frameworks in this book are from a decidedly American perspective, where I reside and teach. If you are from outside the United States, I suggest augmenting this book with *Rethinking Learning: A Review of Social and Emotional Learning for Education Systems* (2020), from UNESCO MGIEP. A free download, contributors (including me) represented different global regions. The publication is available here: https://mgiep.unesco.org/rethinking-learning.

I hope that this book helps contribute to your students' sense of well-being. Games can provide rich opportunities for social and emotional skill development. With thoughtful guidance, some games can help young people learn to manage emotions, perspective-take, demonstrate empathic concern, and exhibit prosocial behaviors. Game on!

Links, Lessons, and Games

Celeste: http://www.celestegame.com

Gaming SEL book companion website, which includes chapter discussion questions: https://sites.google.com/view/gamingsel

GRIS: https://nomada.studio

GRIS: Perception & Interpretation, UNESCO MGIEP's game-based course: https://framerspace.com/course/gris

Hey Listen Games, featuring free lesson plans for *Celeste* and *GRIS*: https://www.heylistengames.org/socialemotionallearning

How 'Among Us' Helps Students Master Argumentative Writing, by Angelique Gianas: http://edut.to/37n1EFp

Parents' Guide to Among Us: https://apps.apple.com/us/story/id1537448803

Rethinking Learning: A Review of Social and Emotional Learning for Education Systems, publication from UNESCO MGIEP: https://mgiep.unesco.org/rethinking-learning

UNESCO MGIEP's SEL Blog: https://medium.com/social-emotional-learning

References

Bogost, I. (2007). *Persuasive games: The expressive power of videogames*. MIT Press.

Bogost, I. (2008). The rhetoric of video games. In K. Salen & E. Zimmerman (Eds.), *The ecology of games: Connecting youth, games, and learning* (pp. 117–140). MIT Press.

CASEL's SEL Framework. (2020). *CASEL*. https://casel.org/wpcontent/uploads/2020/10/CASEL-SEL-Framework-10.2020-1.pdf

Dweck, C. (1975). The role of expectations and attributions in the alleviation of learned helplessness. *Journal of Personality and Social Psychology, 31*, 674–68.

Dweck, C. (2006). *Mindset: The new psychology of success*. Random House.

Farber, M., Williams, M. K., Mellman, L., & Yu, X. (2020). Systems at play: Game design as an approach for teen self-expression. *Journal of Games, Self, and Society, 2*(1), 40–84. Carnegie Mellon ETC Press.

Gee, J. P. (2007). *What video games have to teach us about learning and literacy* (rev. ed.). Palgrave Macmillan.

Isbister, K. (2016). *How games move us: Emotion by design*. MIT Press.

Juul, J. (2013). *The art of failure: An essay on the pain of playing video games*. MIT Press.

Kübler-Ross, E. (1969). *On death and dying*. MacMillan.

Peppler, K., Danish, J., & Phelps, D. (2013). Collaborative gaming: Designing board games to teach young children about complex systems and collective behavior. *Simulation & Gaming, 46*(9), 38–43. doi:10.1177/1046878113501462.

Ryan, R. M., & Deci, E. L. (2018). *Self-determination theory: Basic psychological needs in motivation, development, and wellness*. Guilford Press.

Senge, P. M., Cambron-McCabe, N., Lucas, T., Smith, B., & Dutton, J. (2012). *Schools that learn: A fifth discipline fieldbook for educators, parents, and everyone who cares about education*. Doubleday Currency.

Thorson, M. (2020, November 6). Is Madeline canonically trans? *Medium*. https://maddythorson.medium.com/is-madeline-canonically-trans-4277ece02e40

Toppo, G. (2015). *The game believes in you: How digital play can make our kids smarter*. St. Martin's Press.

Zimmerman, E. (2015). Manifesto for a ludic century. In S. P. Walz & S. Deterding (Eds.), *The gameful world: Approaches, issues, applications* (pp. 19–21). MIT Press.

PART I

CHAPTER ONE

How Mister Rogers Taught Us to Feel

As a young child, I was raised on a steadfast diet of schoolwork, family, friends, and television—lots and lots of television. I watched Mister Rogers talk about feelings and art and jazz. I learned about letters and numbers from the furry friends who lived on Sesame Street. I watched cartoons. I sang along to *Schoolhouse Rock!* and *Free to Be… You and Me*. I played dress up with Carole and Paula on *The Magic Garden*. I also read the collected works of Maurice Sendak and Judy Blume. In the book *Sunny Days*, David Kamp described this wave of children's programming as the "Age of Enlightenment Jr." (2020, pp. xx–xxi).

Children's television was the educational technology—and the screentime—of its day. Using television as a teaching tool actually began in American Samoa—"the bold experiment," as President Lyndon B. Johnson called it (Watters, 2015, para. 2). There, students sat in classrooms watching programs on math, science, language arts, and other instructional content. After viewing, worksheets were handed out and graded by the local Samoan teachers (Schram et al., 1981).

The War on Poverty was also launched during Johnson's term. It included social programs like Medicaid, which provided health coverage to low-income citizens, and Head Start, the early childhood education program. The goal of Head Start was (and still is) to end cycles of poverty. Head Start was founded by one of John F. Kennedy's relatives, Sargent Shriver; since its inception, it has served over 30 million children (Head Start History, 2018). As it happens, Sargent Shriver's son, Timothy P. Shriver, works as the current board chair of CASEL, the largest SEL initiative in the United States.

Of course, media nowadays is more than what is on our living room screens; it is ubiquitous and on-demand. This chapter shares current research and thoughts from several experts from the field of children's educational media. Our journey begins with a big bird and continues with a timid puppet named Daniel Striped Tiger.

Co-viewing and Joint Media Engagement

Produced by the Children's Television Workshop (now Sesame Workshop), and led by Joan Ganz Cooney, *Sesame Street* debuted on the newly established Public Broadcasting System (PBS) on November 10, 1969. Fast and frenetic, jumping from topic to topic, its songs and vignettes were patterned on commercial jingles, brief catchy songs about literacy and numeracy.

Cooney was a true innovator. She understood how lower socio-economic status children entered kindergarten lacking skills that their wealthier counterparts had. Unlike most other children's television shows of its day (*Howdy Doody*, *Lunch with Soupy Sales*), *Sesame Street* would be intentionally educational.

Sesame Street was conceived at a dinner party in 1966 as a way to "master the addictive qualities of television and do something good with them" (Davis, 2008, p. 8). The idea was to align the show's educational content to the latest academic research of the day. Cooney's approach continued in her other programs, including *Electric Company* and *3-2-1 Contact*.

An immediate hit with viewers, kids (and hip adults) flocked to *Sesame Street* to watch Jim Henson's Muppets—including Big Bird, Cookie Monster, and Grover—blend with a diverse cast of human actors, all set in an urban neighborhood. But did it work? Did *Sesame Street* fulfill Cooney's mission of educating those most in need? If so, how?

The short answer was, sort of. Researchers found that children were not able to fully make connections from the screen to the real-world without parent or caregiver facilitation (Reiser et al., 1984; Reiser et al., 1988; Salomon, 1977). Their findings suggested that shows like *Sesame Street* worked best when they were not used to babysit. Instead of being considered a teaching machine that passively transmitted knowledge to children, parents and caregivers were advised to join in and engage.

Watching and discussing educational television with supportive others is crucial to children's abilities to make meaning. This concept became known as *co-viewing*, "the occasions when adults and children watch television together, sharing the viewing experience" (Valkenburg et al., 1999 as cited in Takeuchi & Stevens, 2011). Co-viewing meant that children's media should not be solely responsible for learning outcomes.

Ideas around co-viewing persist to this day. Virginia public television station WETA recently published a set questions that parents and caregivers can ask young viewers:

- Tell me what happened in the show.
- What did the characters do?
- Do you agree with what the characters did? Why or why not?
- What did the characters talk about?
- How did you feel watching the show? Why?
- What was your favorite part? Why?
- What part didn't you like? Why?
- What questions do you have? (Co-viewing with Kids, 2019, para. 5)

The language around co-viewing is steeped in the era of educational television. These days, screens do more than broadcast entertainment or educational content; screens are hubs of information. They are interactive, dynamic, and connect us. Screens are the campfire of the modern age.

In 2011, discourse around co-viewing shifted and widened to include other forms of children's media. Now known as joint media engagement, co-viewing includes electronic books, webpages, mobile apps, streamed video, and video games (Takeuchi & Stevens, 2011). Sometimes called the "new co-viewing,"

> Joint media engagement is the spontaneous and designed experiences of people using media together. Joint media engagement can happen anywhere and at any time when multiple people are interacting together with media. Modes of joint media engagement include viewing, playing, searching, reading, contributing, and creating, with either digital or traditional media. Joint media engagement can support learning by providing resources for making sense and making meaning of a particular situation, as well as for future situations. (Stevens & Penuel, 2010 as cited in Takeuchi & Stevens, 2011, p. 9)

Joint media engagement is not something most parents and caregivers intuitively do. In a study, Fisch (2011) found that participants who facilitated conversations using prompts were "significantly more likely to make comments about characters' emotions, connect onscreen events to the children's own lives, encourage viewer participation with onscreen games and activities, and somewhat more likely to ask children to evaluate characters' actions" (Fisch as cited in Takeuchi & Stevens, 2011, p. 35). It was recommended that when prompts were not provided, additional supports should be in place to help facilitate learning transfer. Because of this, PBS KIDS, a block of children's programming, websites, and apps, shares guidance. It recommends a four-step approach: *watch, play, explore,* and *share.* Using *Molly of Denali* as an example—an animated series about a 10-year-old Alaskan Native girl whose family owns the Denali Trading Post—educator Elizabeth Bostwick wrote about how the show and online ecosystem can align to a joint media engagement model:

1. *Watch*: Watch the video, e.g., view a clip or episode of *Molly of Denali*.
2. *Play*: Play games, e.g., play *Fish Game Camp*, a *Molly of Denali* online game.
3. *Explore*: Engage in an activity, e.g., draw a map of Denali, Alaska.
4. *Share*: Communicate with your family; e.g., create a poster as a shared artifact. (Bostwick, 2020)

I spoke with early childhood literacy scholar Kathleen Paciga about social learning and joint media engagement. "We know from language learning that children learn when adults read books to them and then have a conversation back and forth that is socially contingent," she said. "We cannot appropriate language without a social component. Babies learn vocabulary through somebody pointing, followed by explanatory speech. That feeds into cognition."

Pointing and building vocabulary is a shared experience. How adults and children engage in media experiences can reinforce and build up emotions about the content onscreen or the experience itself. "When an adult and baby share by gazing and pointing at something, that brings the child joy," Paciga continued. "It is then mirrored in the adult's explanation—at least most times—reinforcing those same positive feelings cognitively."

The exchange of text to real-world connection can occur with games, too. Animals depicted in *Minecraft* can be compared to ones observed outdoors, in books, or at the zoo. Parents or caregivers can explain to children how minecarts run on tracks just like railroad trains and subway cars.

Joint media engagement can be a richer experience when children share with peers. "Every child does not need his or her own device for that device to be powerful," researcher Chip Donohue told me. Donohue is the founding director of the Technology in Early Childhood Center at the Erikson Institute. He is also a senior fellow at the Fred Rogers Center. "Engaging with digital media is not about learning letters or numbers. Devices are opportunities for children to explore their own world."

Everyone on a Chromebook does not necessarily lead to powerful learning. Technology is just one more thing in the classroom, just another tool to use. "But for some kids, it is a tool that might get them thinking, to become more open with sharing ideas with others," Donohue remarked.

Joint media engagement is not necessarily joint play. After all, parents and caregivers can't feasibly sit with children for every second of screentime. I can't join all of my son's *Minecraft* worlds. It is impractical to expect parents or caregivers to play with their children all of the time. However, the notion remains: experiences are richer when adults sit and discuss what children create and consume on screens.

Katie Salen Tekinbaş, researcher and co-founder of Raising Good Gamers, spoke with me about youth-driven gaming communities. "From a learning science and sociological perspective, the main thing is to engage with kids about their own interests," Tekinbaş said. "You don't actually have to be gaming with them. You just have to know enough about what they are doing to ask them questions, and to legitimize their interests."

Variations of joint media engagement are part of BrainPOP's digital education platform, which includes videos and games. During the COVID-19 pandemic, BrainPOP created an ordered approach to learning on its portal. The intent was to provide a hierarchical model, from rote instruction to deeper learning opportunities. "We thought about how our features aligned to Bloom's Taxonomy," BrainPOP's Allisyn Levy explained. Common in lesson planning, Bloom's Taxonomy classifies learning outcomes by cognitive skill level, from rote knowledge acquisition to experiences that involve evaluation, synthesis, and content creation (Heick, 2020). "We didn't want students to watch a BrainPOP movie and take a quiz without getting to higher-level activities like creating," she remarked. Thus, BrainPOP's three-step process is:

1. *Discover*: Watch one of the 900 videos, then review the related readings.
2. *Play*: Play a game hosted on the platform.
3. *Create*: Show what you know through include concept mapping, coding, or movie-making tools. (Tools and Feature Support, n.d.)

In the white paper *Equity in Learning with BrainPOP: Fostering Access and Impact for All*, Hubert and Rosen (2020) explored how BrainPOP's SEL collection intersected with universal design for learning (UDL) and differentiated instruction (DI) practices. UDL is a set of design principles where students are afforded multiple means of engagement, representation, and action and expression (UDL Guidelines, 2020). DI describes how teachers can meet each students' diverse and individualized learning needs. Hubert and Rosen (2020) found that the intersection of UDL, DI, and SEL was a promising solution to supporting equity—also one of the original goals of Cooney's bold educational television experiment.

Next, insights from Fred Rogers, another early innovator in children's educational television, are shared. When interviewed, Rogers remarked that his show was the flip side of *Sesame Street*—"two sides of the same coin," as he often said (King, 2018, p. 249). Cognitive learning took place in the brownstones along 123 Sesame Street; social and emotional development resided in the Neighborhood of Make-Believe.

The Emotional Intelligence of Fred Rogers

In 1969, Fred Rogers, host of *Mister Rogers' Neighborhood*—a children's television show that would run for decades—testified before the United States Senate in defense of funding for public television. "I feel that if we in public television can only make it clear that feelings are mentionable and manageable, we will have done a great service for mental health," Rogers said.

Rogers remains a cultural force to this day. An icon, he was the subject of multiple documentary films, as well as a feature film starring Tom Hanks. Although *Mister Rogers' Neighborhood* went off the air almost two decades ago, it still can be streamed online. His spirit also lives on in the animated spinoff, *Daniel Tiger's Neighborhood*.

National Public Radio's Anya Kamenetz referred to Rogers as the "father of social and emotional learning" (2018, para. 1). Nearly two decades after his passing, why is Rogers—and SEL, for that matter—just now taking hold? I asked children's interactive media expert Warren Buckleitner his opinion. Like Donohue, he is a senior fellow at the Fred Rogers Center. "Why all of this sudden interest in Rogers?" I asked. "There is a real hunger for humanism, currently," he quickly replied.

Donohue shared a similar sentiment. "The most powerful thing I did at conferences was to quote Fred so people could see how intentional he was about childhood development," he said. "Educators need to be in the relationship business, intentionally thinking about SEL and opportunities to connect with kids." Next, Donohue shared an anecdote with me about Rogers,

> There's a famous story of a parent who ran into Fred in New York City in a high rise building somewhere. The parent broke into tears and talked about how he was failing because he couldn't do all the parenting things he wanted to do. Fred's response was, "Your child is so lucky to have a parent like you." That is so Fred. Though the parent said he was failing, Fred's reply was, "Because you know you are failing, your child is really lucky. You are thinking hard about this. You care about your child."

One of Rogers's gifts was how he spoke directly to his young viewers on the other end of the screen. This technique of breaking the fourth wall—the invisible line separating performers from the audience—remains a staple of children's and instructional television to this day. On *Dora the Explorer*, Dora turns to viewers when asking help. On *The French Chef*, Julia Child cooked cuisine while speaking right to the camera. Bob Ross spoke to all of us as he painted his "happy little trees." Breaking the fourth wall persists on new media platforms too: YouTube and Twitch vloggers and video game streamers often speak directly to their viewers and subscribers.

When the fourth wall is broken, there is an illusion of a one-on-one conversation between host and viewer. Some may even develop *parasocial relationships* with onscreen personalities, "one-sided symbolic relationship between the viewer and a media character" (Tolbert & Drogos, 2019, p. 4). On *Mister Rogers' Neighborhood*, Mister Rogers spoke to four-year-old me. He asked *me* how I was feeling, and then he validated *my* emotions. He told *me* that I was unique and special.

Children today can watch Daniel Tiger address audiences the same way Rogers did. Some may also form parasocial relationships with content creators on YouTube. In a recent study, children ages 9-12 reported experiencing friendship feelings with onscreen personas (Tolbert & Drogos, 2019). In another study, adolescent viewers of Twitch livestream videos reported that the platform helped them to cope when faced with difficult life experiences (e.g., problems at home, relationship issues) (de Wit et al., 2020).

Rogers respected his young viewers and he regarded television as a sacred space. He also understood the sheer number of children in the 1960s who spent hours watching television. "It is well documented that Fred didn't like the violent antics of *Howdy Doody*, where the actors threw pies at one another, and kids laughed at that," Paciga, also a Fred Rogers Center fellow, said. "The novelty of Fred was that he recognized the need that kids have to feel a social connection with somebody. He knew that someone needed to be a positive and empathetic friend."

Buckleitner concurred. "Rogers was genuine about how important it was to treat children with respect, to listen to children, and to incorporate their ideas," he said. "But Fred was a linear media person—he understood television. He did not understand digital. Interactive media is different, it's a transactional space. You take turns, and there is a psychology to that relationship."

Would today's YouTube generation grow impatient with Rogers's soft-spoken and deliberate delivery? One needn't look further than Bob Ross, a folk hero to many in Generation Z (folks born in the late 1990s through the 2010s). Shah (2018) credited Ross's *Joy of Painting* with starting the autonomous sensory meridian response (ASMR) genre of videos. Although ASMR is a pseudoscience, the popularity of watching relaxing videos is undeniable. When I searched "oddly satisfying" on TikTok, I found billions—yes, billions—of calming content. Co-viewing with my son, we found videos of people stirring bowls of soup, peeling bars of soap, and carving melted crayons. Interestingly, the crayon carving content led us to stream a classic *Mister Rogers' Neighborhood* episode, the one where he visited the Crayola crayon factory.

Social and Emotional Play in the Neighborhood of Make-Believe

On each episode of *Mister Rogers' Neighborhood*, viewers were transported to the Neighborhood of Make-Believe by following a small, model red trolley. Once there, social and emotional stories starring live actors and puppets played out. "Fred came in, greeted the children, and they then talked about things that were happening in Fred's immediate context," Paciga said. "He presented them with a problem, and then he brought them into the Neighborhood of Make-Believe. After, he talked with the children about the experience."

For Rogers, the Neighborhood of Make-Believe was sort of a live-action game, a play space free from real-world consequences where feelings could be explored. "If you think of Fred's programming as an analogy of learning, the game is when they are trying on feelings in a relatively low-risk context," Paciga continued.

In the Neighborhood of Make-Believe, King Friday XIII was pompous but caring; comparatively, Daniel Striped Tiger was tender. Rogers himself spoke *through* Daniel, his avatar-puppet who often struggled to manage emotions. "Some of the novelty in his approach was that he lived those experiences," Paciga said. "He reflected on himself in what was comforting to him as a growing child. Growing up, he was made fun of; he was bullied. For him, he turned to puppets. He wanted to be able to provide that opportunity to other children."

In one episode, Daniel confides to Lady Aberlin, who was portrayed by cast member Betty Aberlin. Through Rogers, Daniel tells her that he has realized that other tigers don't look like him or talk like him. Other tigers don't live in a clock or love people. "I've been wondering, am I a mistake?" he asks. "Sometimes I wonder, am I too tame?" Lady Aberlin then serenades Daniel, reassuring him that he is special, just the way he is. "I think you are just fine the way you are," she sings.

Paciga (2016) suggested that children can extend onscreen puppet stories in *Mister Rogers' Neighborhood* using digital puppetry apps, like Puppet Pals. Puppets these days may take the form of video game avatars, too. One example is Stampy Cat, voiced on YouTube by Joseph Mark Garrett. Child-friendly, his *Minecraft* channel has more than nine million subscribers. Just as Mister Rogers inspired children to play with their puppets, children may mimic Stampy Cat in their own *Minecraft* adventures, playacting stories of emotional curiosity and discovery.

Tuttle (2018) suggested that the ritualistic routines on *Mister Rogers' Neighborhood* may stem from church services, which regularly begin with the same liturgies. Tuttle (2018) studied Rogers's legacy through a theological lens, observing how his faith informed his being and his show. After all, Rogers was an ordained minister. Perhaps, his young viewers were his flock? According to Tuttle, the Neighborhood of Make-Believe could be seen as an allegory for the kingdom of heaven—"the perfect place for Fred to stage his own parables and work out his own theology of the kingdom of God" (2018, pp. 105–106).

No matter the lens, Rogers's Neighborhood of Make-Believe is powerful, as it was a space where children observed how stories, characters, and feelings could play out free from realized consequences.

Rogers's Six Principles of Learning Readiness

"And now here is my secret, a very simple secret: It is only with the heart that one can see rightly; what is essential is invisible to the eye" (de Saint-Exupéry, 1943, p. 64). This quote, from *The Little Prince* (de Saint-Exupéry, 1943), was one of Rogers's favorites. According to Paciga's research, it repeatedly appeared in the commencement speeches he gave, as well as in his many interviews with the press.

When his show aired, "SEL skills were invisible in school and in the media that children encountered," Paciga explained. "They were there, but they weren't shoving a pie in someone's face and then laughing about it."

To Rogers, social and emotional development were essential, but also often invisible. "For Fred, the 'whole child' meant that what we are focusing on now was not enough," Paciga continued. "We need to widen our lens and look deeper into the invisible, the things we cannot see in the child. Maybe that was Rogers's brilliance—he didn't have to put a label on it. He wanted kids to be kind, so he modeled kindness by showing children how kindness looks."

Rogers's personal expertise was in puppetry, music composition (his major in college), and television production. He was also smart enough to know what he didn't know—in this case, the then-nascent field of developmental psychology. So, Rogers decided to make himself an expert. He read famed pediatrician Benjamin Spock's bestselling book, *The Common Book of Baby and Child Care* (1946). He also met with Spock, who had founded the Arsenal Family and Children's Center in Pittsburgh, Pennsylvania, the city where his show was recorded. Child psychologist Margaret B. McFarland was a researcher there, as was, for a brief time, Erik Erikson. Erikson, who studied under Anna Freud, believed that children needed to be raised in healthy environments for them to later develop "in a normal way" (King, 2018, p. 132). Pediatrician T. Berry Brazelton, who studied mothers' and babies' feelings and behaviors—including unspoken communication during breastfeeding—was also at the Arsenal Center (King, 2018).

Rogers spent much of his time away from the television studio at the Arsenal Center learning firsthand from these experts. He considered McFarland to be his mentor. For nearly three decades, she met with Rogers, painstakingly reviewing his show's scripts, as well as the lyrics in the songs he composed (e.g., "Won't you be my neighbor?") (Flecker, 2014; King, 2018).

One of McFarland's favorite catchphrases was, "Whatever is mentionable is manageable" (McFarland as cited in King, 2018, p. 163). This quote, which Rogers shared in his 1969 testimony to the United States Senate, gave him a license to discuss ideas otherwise not mentionable on children's television. Over the years, episodes covered topics of death, divorce, and loss, each told using the puppets that resided in the Neighborhood of Make-Believe. Rogers then debriefed his young viewers with frank and honest conversation, looking directly at the camera. To Rogers, *Mister Rogers' Neighborhood* became a space to practice the developmental psychology he was learning. Rogers's biographer Maxwell King wrote,

> It was Fred Rogers who taught multiple generations of American parents how very critical the first few years of human life could be, and how social and emotional learning is more important at that age than cognitive learning. More than any other popular voice in American culture, Fred Rogers taught this powerful lesson to parents, teachers, and to children themselves through his gentle, slow-paced but richly textured programming. (2018, p. 134)

"Fred hung out with Erikson, and he did a lot of early childhood development stuff," Donohue said. "There was also something inherent in him to understand what kids needed to hear and see and experience that had payoffs downstream—but not 'quick turnaround' payoffs."

"Rogers learned how children are inherently social beings, and how those emotions are among the first visible thing to develop when children begin to make sense of their world," Paciga explained. "An infant just born shows emotion before cognition. Fred learned that. And he knew that was the space an early childhood audience needed to grow and explore in."

Through speaking with child development experts, Rogers learned how young children needed routines to feel comfortable and confident before they could be ready to learn. "You have to get through those things first," Donohue said.

On *Mister Rogers' Neighborhood*, the set routine was in the sequence of events. Each episode began with Mister Rogers entering the set the same way, every time.

He then removed his shoes and put on slippers. He always wore a cardigan sweater. He sang some of the same songs. Mr. McFeeley would come with the mail. As a result, young viewers—many of whom maintained a parasocial relationship with him—could predict and know what would happen next.

A set routine provides security and is emotionally reassuring, especially in an uncertain world—a world where children have little control or agency over their lives. Routines are a way for children to settle into new environments.

"Fred was a huge believer in routines," Donohue continued. "I go back to Maria Montessori and others who felt the same way. Routine is what gives children the capacity to make choices because they have power and agency over what is coming next."

In classrooms, teachers need to have routines. When thinking about game-based learning, it should not be, "We have some extra time today, you earned free time to play a game." The focus really needs to shift from games-as-reward to games-as-curriculum. Games, like books, movies, and other resources should be respected as teaching materials, part of a classroom's routine.

Playing games affords children opportunities to drive experiences. "Children want to be empowered at the individual level, in their relationships with others, but also in their larger communities," Paciga said. "And Fred realized this."

Paciga and Donohue (2017) suggest thinking about children's relationships to self, others, and the world. These levels of relationships can affect children's readiness to learn (Paciga & Donohue, 2017). For these reasons, CASEL's SEL Framework, covered in Chapter Two, surrounds SEL competencies with the systems and environments that children inhabit (CASEL's SEL Framework, 2020).

In 1983, Rogers and Barry Head developed Six Principles of Learning Readiness, a set of capacities children should possess to be emotionally prepared to learn. These principles, which emerged from Rogers's years of experience, state that children should have:

1. A sense of self-worth.
2. A sense of trust.
3. Curiosity.
4. Capacity to look and listen carefully.
5. Capacity to play.
6. Times of solitude. (Rogers & Head, 1983 as cited in Paciga & Donohue, 2017)

Rogers's Six Principles remain the focal point of continued research and work by the Fred Rogers Center for Early Learning and Children's Media at Saint Vincent College and at the Erikson Institute. These are foundational, bridging social and emotional development to cognitive learning, the S and E to the L—or, to paraphrase Rogers, the other side of the same coin (King, 2018).

The legacy of Rogers's Six Principles is echoed in a somewhat popular phrase amongst teachers, "Maslow before Bloom!" As mentioned earlier in this chapter, Bloom's Taxonomy is a classification system of cognition, sometimes illustrated as a triangle divided into six steps, ranging from recall, at the bottom, to creation, at the peak (Heick, 2020). Maslow's (1943) theory is also presented as a hierarchy, a five-tier model of fulfillment based on positive psychology principles. According to Maslow (1943), before humans can reach their full potential and self-actualize, their basic physiological and safety needs must be met.

Before academic learning takes place, teachers should consider students' learning readiness. One approach is to welcome students by name when they arrive to class. In a study on Positive Greetings at the Door strategies, Cook et al. (2018) found that student behavior, feelings of self-worth, and well-being improved when teachers greeted them. In other words, children were more ready to learn when teachers were attentive to their social and emotional needs. For additional strategies, read Tom Berger's blog on Edutopia, *How to Maslow Before Bloom, All Day Long*: http://edut.to/2ZmGtPl.

Playing in Daniel Tiger's Neighborhood

When Rogers began work on television, it was a new medium. Today, screens are on the computers on our desks, the tablets in our hands, and the smartphones in our pockets.

Rogers sometimes spoke about computers and how they could be harnessed to teach the next generation of neighbors about kindness, gratitude, and emotional management. He saw the utility in technology and how it could support these aspirations. But he also recognized limitations when compared to human interaction (Paciga & Donohue, 2017). In one of his commencement speeches, Rogers said, "I like to help children remember that, no matter what the machine may be, it was people who thought it up and made it, and it's people who make it work" (Rogers, 1969 as cited in King, 2018, p. 341).

Two decades after *Mister Rogers' Neighborhood* left the airwaves, new shows, apps, and games from Fred Rogers Productions continue his legacy. On any given day, children can watch *Daniel Tiger's Neighborhood*, an animated series starring Daniel Tiger, the four-year-old son of Daniel Striped Tiger, *Peg + Cat*, a cartoon about problem-solving skills, or *Odd Squad*, a live-action math-themed show. These programs adhere to Rogers's model of being slower-paced, honest, and authentic to young audiences.

Like Rogers's original show, *Daniel Tiger's Neighborhood* focuses on social and emotional development. One example is the episode Someone Else's Feelings (2014), in which Daniel gives his mother sunflowers. She thanks him, saying, "You were really thinking about me and what I would like. Now that's empathy!" Then she sings, "Think About How Someone Else is Feeling," reinforcing with song what was just modeled. Storylines and lessons like those in this episode led Robin Stern of the Yale Center for Emotional Intelligence to refer to *Daniel Tiger's Neighborhood* as "Mister Rogers 2.0" (Stern, 2017, para. 11).

On the Daniel Tiger Life's Little Lessons webpage, parents and caregivers can deepen learning through recommended joint media engagement activities. Lessons are sorted by themes, such as Separation, Mad Feelings, Alike and Different, Persistence, and Use Your Words. Under Mad Feelings, children can watch three videos and then take part in a letter writing activity, sharing feelings by writing them down.

There are mobile apps and games too, like *Daniel Tiger's Grr-ific Feelings*. A series of minigames and interactives, young children can sing along with Daniel about emotions, self-express by drawing on a digital easel, and take self-portraits ("selfies") in the Feelings Photo Booth. After taking a picture, children are asked to identify how they feel by matching their expressions to Daniel's.

Schell Games helped to bring the iconic characters of Fred Rogers into the 21st century. In addition to its games and apps, Schell Games developed Daniel Tiger's Neighborhood Ride, a trolley attraction at the Idlewild Park and Soakzone, a theme park in western Pennsylvania. Schell Games also happens to be headquartered in Pittsburgh, not far from Fred Rogers Productions.

How does one design a Fred Rogers-aligned app or game? "The process is generally the same," Schell Games's founder and CEO Jesse Schell told me. "We watch *Daniel Tiger* episodes and ask, 'How can we adopt that topic in the interactive realm in a way that makes sense?'" The team then prototypes a design and playtests it locally, at the Children's Museum of Pittsburgh.

"An interesting constraint from Fred Rogers Production is not to 'ding' a kid for being wrong," Schell continued. "You're not wrong for being sad. We don't judge children. This means you have to take exploratory approaches."

Daniel Tiger apps and games are not timed and are all self-paced. *Tea Party* is one such example. An online game, *Tea Party* has a first-person camera perspective, putting children at the table's head, facing Daniel. Like the animated show, Daniel breaks the fourth wall by greeting players and guiding the interactions. Players pick out the tablecloth pattern, the snacks, and the teapot. They can click on Daniel's friends and watch them eat cookies or take a drink. "And that's it—you are playing tea party, a classic children's activity," Schell said.

Tea Party may not look like there is a lot to do, but it is an SEL game, filled with opportunities for imaginative play. "It is the practice of a social situation. The characters are modeling appropriate behavior. Everyone says please and thank you. We don't teach you, 'Make sure to say please or thank you.' We put you in a situation where everything is engaged in polite behavior."

Young children likely will not notice the fine-print under the interactive on the PBS KIDS website—but parents and caregivers might. It reads, "Playing tea party is a way for children to work on important social skills, like thinking about the needs of others and taking turns. They also learn about getting along with friends, as children imitate grownup behavior with manners and caring conversation" (Tea Party, 2020, para. 1).

Games like those in the Daniel Tiger ecosystem are practice spaces for developing emotional intelligence. In *Playing Sandcastle*, young children build a digital sandcastle with Daniel Tiger. Open-ended and fun, the game is also about self-regulation and learning how to take turns. As children build their sandcastles, ocean waves occasionally come ashore, sometimes suddenly washing everything away. After the waves crash, Daniel models an appropriate response: "On no! Oh well. Let's try building a new one!" "Normally, we wouldn't put that in a game because it's frustrating," Schell said. "But we wanted to put in mild frustration so kids can practice dealing with it."

Daniel Tiger Stop & Go Potty is another app designed by Schell Games. Intended to transform behavior—to encourage young children to want to use the bathroom—it does not center on teaching toddlers how toilets flush. I spoke with Sabrina Culyba, formerly of Schell Games, about its design. Culyba did not personally work on the app, but she did check in with the team regularly, helping guide its creation.

"The big thing was that kids don't want to stop what they are doing," Culyba explained. "*Daniel Tiger's Stop & Go Potty* isn't about *how* to go to the bathroom. It's about how to believe that when you come back, your toys are still going to be there. It is about regulating the ability to stop an activity, set your toys down, and then go to the bathroom. To trust that when you come back, your friends and toys will be fine, and it's not a big deal."

What would Rogers think of today's ubiquity of screens? As it happened, Rogers didn't care for television when that first began entering people's homes. With computers, his philosophy remained the same. Donohue mused, "Fred would've said, 'We've got to take this thing on, to figure out how to make this a tool for good. After all, kids are going to be using it anyway!'"

On a segment of his show, he used a computer to show children that Mister Rogers could use a computer. "He then said the most important part of the segment was to show them how to turn it off and walk away," Donohue continued. "That's pretty powerful, and thoughtful."

How Are You Feeling Today?

As stated earlier, Fred Rogers championed Margaret B. McFarland's idea that feelings should be mentionable, which then makes them manageable. Recognizing and understanding one's emotions is the starting point of self-awareness.

Many teachers now embed emotional self-awareness into classroom routines. Some lessons begin with time afforded for students to stretch, breathe, and relax. New Mexico-based educator Jackie Gerstein has shared on her blog how she conducts "Share a Rose, Share a Thorn" activities with her middle school students. The class writes something positive from their day (the rose), followed by a not-so-good experience (the thorn) (Gerstein, 2020). These reflective activities are followed by teacher-led discussions around self-care strategies.

Some educational technology tools include emotional check-in features. Pear Deck, the guided slideshow tool, is one example. Teachers can copy pre-made slides from its SEL template webpage (https://www.peardeck.com/sel-templates) and add to their existing Google Slides or Microsoft PowerPoint lessons. One slide asks students to click on a "Stress Check" thermometer. "Are you in a good space to focus or can you not manage emotions today?" it asks. Another slide is more open-ended, asking similar questions as Gerstein's Share a Rose, Share a Thorn activity. Other educational technologies that offer social and emotional supports include NearPod and Microsoft Teams.

SEL tools have been integrated in some children's literacy platforms. Peekapak, a series of short stories and interactives, is an example. On Peekapak's SEL Check-in Tool, children click face icons on a mood board that match their feelings (see Figure 2). Teachers can then view what students self-report on a dashboard.

The Feelings Wheel (Wilcox, 1982) is a useful tool that goes beyond the brief spectrum of emotions on some mood board tools. Created by Gloria Wilcox in 1982, it was built around core emotions of sad, mad, scared, joyful, powerful, and peaceful. In the spokes that fan out, related emotions are listed. Connected to sad are guilt and shame. Guilt leads to remorse. On the opposite side of the Wheel, joyful extends to energetic and playful (Wilcox, 1982).

Plutchik's Wheel of Emotions is another visual representation of feelings. Resembling a flower, it includes different core emotions than Wilcox's wheel. Plutchik begins with joy, trust, fear, surprise, sadness, anticipation, anger, and disgust (Plutchik, 1962). It is tempting to go down an emotional rabbit hole of feelings wheel models, as there are many more in academic literature.

If some of these core emotions sound familiar, it may be because they influenced Disney Pixar's *Inside Out* (2015). *Inside Out* is a computer animated film about an 11-year-old girl named Riley who is navigating powerful emotions. Paul Ekman,

Figure 2. Peekapak's SEL Check-in Tool. Source: Peekapak. Reprinted by permission of the publisher.

author of the influential book *Emotions Revealed: Recognizing Faces and Feelings to Improve Communication and Emotional Life* (2003, 2007), served as a consultant. His firm, the Paul Ekman Group, advises video game publishers and movie studios using its proprietary Facial Action Coding System (FACS), a taxonomy of facial expressions that relate to emotions (Ekman, 2007).

Inside Out personified five core emotions that reside in Riley's head: Anger, Disgust, Fear, Joy, and Sadness. Joy is always lighthearted, looking for the silver lining whenever trouble appears. Comparatively, Sadness is less optimistic—her character is literally blue. At one point in the movie, Joy questions the purpose of Sadness. "Why is it important for Riley to ever feel sad?" she wonders. In an existential scene, Joy watches Sadness console Bing Bong, Riley's childhood imaginary friend. As Bing Bong cries, he begins to recover emotionally, feeling better. It is here that audiences discover Sadness's true power.

In an opinion piece for the *New York Times*, psychology professor Dachner Keltner, along with Ekman, wrote about Sadness, the unexpected star of *Inside Out*. They wrote, "*Inside Out* offers a new approach to sadness. Its central insight: Embrace sadness, let it unfold, engage patiently with a preteen's emotional struggles. Sadness will clarify what has been lost (childhood) and move the family toward what is to be gained: the foundations of new identities, for children and parents alike" (Keltner & Ekman, 2015, para. 12).

Inside Out is a powerful film on emotions and emotional regulation. It embodies abstract ideas through metaphors—Riley's train of thought is literally a train. Games can embody emotions, too. In the award-winning *Sea of Solitude*, a lonely woman's tears flood an entire city. In *GRIS*, the screen changes color as the protagonist makes her way through Kübler-Ross's (1969) five stages of grief.

To help parents, caregivers, and teachers, the Paul Ekman Group published *A Parents' Guide to Disney Pixar's Inside Out*, a joint media engagement resource for the film. After viewing, it advises adults to ask young viewers, "Why do we lose our temper? How does Sadness provide comfort? Why is it important to have sad memories as well as happy ones?" (Parents' Guide, n.d., para. 1).

Encouraging students to be self-aware and emotionally intelligent can help them to become happier and more connected human beings (Brackett, 2019). In addition to mood boards and joint media engagement opportunities, lots of educators and schools have embraced the RULER Approach, the Yale Center for Emotional Intelligence's acronym of emotional intelligence skills. RULER has been shown to improve student conduct (Cipriano et al., 2019; Reyes et al., 2012), which can lead to better learning outcomes and healthier peer relationships schoolwide. It uses emotional identification as a starting point for children (and adults) to become emotionally intelligent (Brackett, 2019). The five ordered steps in the RULER Approach are:

- **R**ecognizing emotions in oneself and others.
- **U**nderstanding the causes and consequences of emotions.
- **L**abeling emotions with a nuanced vocabulary.
- **E**xpressing emotions in accordance with cultural norms and social context.
- **R**egulating emotions with helpful strategies. (Brackett, 2019)

To move through the approaches in RULER, Yale Center for Emotional Intelligence's Marc Brackett suggests that children should become *emotion scientists*. In his bestselling book *Permission to Feel*, he writes, "An emotion scientist has the ability to pause even at the most stressful moments and ask: What am I reacting to? We can learn to identify and understand all our feelings, integral and incidental, and then respond in helpful, proportionate ways—once we acquire emotional skills" (2019, p. 50).

RULER's Mood Meter is a tool that can help with the identification of emotions. Not round or flower-shaped, the Mood Meter is square, with feelings listed in four color-specific quadrants. The red quadrant is for unpleasant, high-energy emotions, like anxiety, anger, and fear. Blue is where unpleasant feelings reside, from disappointment to sadness. The green quadrant is calm, relaxed. Being in the yellow quadrant means that you feel joy and elation (Brackett, 2019). The

Mood Meter can be found hanging on many classroom walls, on student handouts, and embedded in interactive slideshow presentations. There is also a Mood Meter mobile app—emotional self-awareness, on-the-go!

Mood Meter quadrants can help inform learning activities for students (Cipriano et al., 2019; Yale University, 2014). One approach is to provide students with a menu of choices mapped to colors on Mood Meter, essentially gamifying learning. Once students become emotion scientists, they can self-select an activity differentiated and aligned to their moods (Brackett, 2019; Yale University, 2014). Students who are in the yellow can be guided to creative problem-solving activities. Students who are in the red can engage in debates, building up their argumentative thinking abilities. Those in the blue may gravitate toward inquiry-based learning or empathy and perspective-taking lessons. Lastly, students who are in the green—those who feel calm and pleasant—might learn better when doing collaborative teambuilding work (Yale University, 2014).

Can students regulate their moods by playing a strategy game if they come to class excited? What quadrant should students be in to learn best by building in *Minecraft*? Could playing games alter someone's mood in the way that music and film sometimes do? Some researchers are studying just that. The Affective Computing group at the MIT Media Lab developed *Guardians: Unite the Realms*, a mobile game available on Apple and Android platforms. The game embeds a technique from cognitive behavioral therapy (CBT) known as *behavioral activation*. The concept is to ask participants to self-report by reflecting in journals on tasks and activities—in this case, digitally, in a video game. Early results suggest that the in-game reward system motivated players to consistently self-report (Taylor et al., 2019).

Mightier, from Neuromotion Labs, is a platform of video games that can be used as calming strategies for children who struggle regulating emotions. In addition to the games on its mobile app, players are also given a heart rate monitor band. Developed and tested at Boston Children's Hospital and Harvard Medical School, children who used Mightier technology and therapy showed "reduced symptoms aggression, oppositional behavior, and parent stress compared to children receiving control treatment" ("Mightier Scientific Overview," 2019).

In the next section, a theory on mood as it relates to our media diet is shared. From the field of psychology, it may explain why we engage with certain media and how that engagement can affect our emotions.

Mood Management Theory

Throughout this book, I explore how games can be transformational to SEL skill-building. In doing so, I map games to SEL frameworks, as well as highlight and share empirical research. Before proceeding further, let's take a moment to discuss why games are fundamental to emotional well-being.

"Games are great at reducing stress for a variety of reasons," Rachel Kowert told me. Kowert is the research director for Take This, a nonprofit organization that provides mental health resources to the gaming community and industry. She is also the author of several books on video games and well-being. There is quite a bit of research on how media and entertainment contribute to mood management and repair. Of note is a recent study from Johannes et al. (2020) that compared players of *Plants vs. Zombies: Battle for Neighborville* and *Animal Crossing: New Horizons* for their well-being, motivations, and need satisfaction during play. Results suggested that "players' in-game motivational experiences can contribute to affective well-being, but they do not affect the degree to which game time relates to well-being" (Johannes et al., 2020, p. 12).

Mood management theory is a theory about consumption in our media diet. It is not about screen time, but rather why we consume media and how it relates to our emotional state (Zillmann, 1988). Does media consumption make us more resilient and more emotionally aware?

Some of the media that we consume may be for entertainment purposes, a diversion from the real-world. We may watch science fiction to mentally transport us to worlds where magic is real. We might devour books about wizards and dragons and sorcery. We may play relaxing games when stressed or strategy games when bored. If we feel lethargic and want to be more energetic, we may listen to more upbeat music. "Entertainment media is an efficient coping strategy to bring negative moods and emotions back into balance," Kowert continued. "For example, bored individuals pick exciting television programs to watch, where stressed people prefer to watch relaxing programs."

It is, perhaps, obvious why we consume media that makes us feel good. After all, entertainment is a form of escapism. Why shouldn't the media we watch, read, and play make us feel "mentally occupied, or diverted" from real-world problems (Rigby & Ryan, 2016, p. 34)? But if that strictly were the case, then why do we watch scary movies or play horror games? Why do we seek out media that makes us sad? What about science fiction that makes us question humanity and its place in the universe (e.g., *2001: A Space Odyssey, Interstellar, Arrival*)? Why do we actively seek out media that makes us feel uncomfortable?

Media psychologists write about two forms of media: *eudaimonic*, a term coined by Aristotle about virtuous living, and *hedonic*, which stems from the Greek word for pleasure (hedonistic). Eudaimonia describes a deep sense of well-being beyond hedonic pleasure. Catharsis describes how we feel after difficult emotions are purged (Juul, 2013). Surviving a horror game or watching a movie set during wartime can be contemplative and can lead us to self-actualization. Experiencing awe, sadness, tenderness, and compassion in media of all kinds can inspire psychological growth (e.g., Reer & Quandt, 2020).

Mood management theory research suggests that we can't partake in too much of one or the other and stay balanced (Di Fabio & Palazzeschi, 2015; Reer & Quandt, 2020). "You can't just play *Animal Crossing*—you will also need something enriching," Courtney Garcia explained. Garcia hosts Screen Therapy, a YouTube channel of video game playthroughs through the lens of media psychology. "Conversely, you can't just play eudaimonic games either. You are going to need something to help you recover, emotionally," she said.

We are drawn to media that makes us cry because it allows us to tinker with our thoughts. Media can help us with catharsis, prepare us to cope, teach us how to grieve, and give us strategies to deal with loss (Reer & Quandt, 2020; Waterman, 2013). "We all know tragedy is going to strike us at some point, so we look for a blueprint on how to learn from others," Garcia continued. "We know we will cry with characters in a movie, and that it isn't happening to us. It is a safe practice space for coping with feelings. When we come out on the other side, we feel stronger."

We can be intentional with the media we consume. We may seek out media that challenges us to psychologically and emotionally grow. Or, we may consume media that optimizes our mood by inspiring recovery through positive feelings. As a media studies lesson, students can be asked to record and journal about the media they consume.

Mood Management and Video Games

In the early 1980s, video gaming often meant arcades, quick experiences designed to eat kids' quarters. These games provided quick thrills, little in the way of nuanced emotion. Similarly, film was also fairly basic when introduced at the turn of the 20th century. Famously (at least according to legend), in 1895, the French silent film *L'arrivée D'un Train en Gare de La Ciotat* (*The Arrival of a Train at La Ciotat Station*) frightened audiences who thought that the train flickering on the screen was real. What's worse, it appeared to be headed *through* the screen, about to run over viewers!

Modern cinema is more nuanced in ways that emotion is evoked. A horror movie may employ techniques afforded by the medium of film such as close-ups and jump scares. Tension and suspense may build through a combination of elements such as the narrative, musical score, and quick edits.

We tend to think of video games as being pure hedonic diversions, designed to evoke thrills and excitement. Parents may envision kids in *Fortnite* battle royale matches or themselves crushing candies on their smartphone screens. But like film, the medium of games has matured. Beyond *Pac-Man*, there are games about living with dementia, dropping out of college, dealing with grief, and coping with loss.

Let's look at the death positivity game *A Mortician's Tale*. Grim in tone, mood, and theme, as the title implies, players role-play as a young mortician named Charlie. Players-as-Charlie embalm and cremate the deceased while interacting with grieving families (graphics are cartoonish). The gameplay is slow and deliberate, with time afforded for contemplation and reflection.

Why would someone play a game like *A Mortician's Tale*? Why did people watch *Six Feet Under* for five seasons, a drama set at a family-owned funeral parlor? (Another game with a death positivity theme is *Spiritfarer*, where players role-play as a ferrymaster to the deceased.) Although I do play some games as escapist diversions, I also appreciate games with more profound themes. On my iPhone, I may switch between playing *Crossy Road*, a modern take on the arcade classic *Frogger*, and *Assemble with Care*, a more somber experience. In *Assemble with Care*, players fix objects for characters in the game, from old cameras to wind-up watches to tape recorders. Taking things apart and putting them back together becomes a metaphor for repairing the relationships between the game's characters.

Video games are different from the other forms of media that we consume because they are interactive. I am the one inserting embalming fluid; I am the person repairing and restoring people's lives. Good video games also engender feelings of competence, autonomy, and relatedness—three components of self-determination theory (SDT) that may be absent from people's everyday lives (Deci & Ryan, 2000; Ryan & Deci, 2018). At school, students are often assigned work, some of which can be boring, difficult, or frustrating. When playing games, children feel a sense of agency—they are in control, they drive the experience.

Using SDT as a framework, Kowert described how stay-at-home lockdowns during the COVID-19 pandemic made her feel less competent. "I can't be a worker and a mom and a wife under stress," she said. "I also have less autonomy—I can't go where I want to go. And I feel less relatedness because we are socially and physically distanced. Games at this time help us achieve those three things from the safety of our homes, six feet away from everyone."

Games have a great way of meeting our needs when they are not being met elsewhere. After remote learning, my 10-year-old son often watched *SpongeBob SquarePants* cartoons on television, a purely hedonic experience. He also played *Mario Kart 8 Deluxe* on Nintendo Switch as a mood repair strategy. In the *Mario Kart* go-kart series of racing games, Question Blocks (cubes adorned with question marks) appear on the track. Driving through one triggers a rotation animation, like a slot machine. But these are not randomized; prizes, which are power-ups, are not awarded by chance or happenstance. Instead, they level the playing field. Question Blocks for racers in tenth-place are stars and bullets, which propel players faster. Players ahead in the pack receive items that are less valuable, like coins or bananas. The game's system is coded to give players persistent feelings of competence.

Games have the potential to impact our well-being in a variety of positive ways, whether it's social modeling or mood management. "Play releases stress, and games have SDT elements that are designed to be engaging, which makes them good for our well-being," Kowert concluded.

In the next chapter, we move from emotional learning to social and emotional learning. Several frameworks are shared, as are strategies to develop skills and competencies through play.

Links, Lessons, and Games

Animal Crossing: New Horizons: https://www.animal-crossing.com
Assemble with Care: https://www.assemblegame.com
BrainPOP's SEL collection: https://go.brainpop.com/sel
Co-viewing with Kids (WETA): https://weta.org/kids/television/coviewing
Daniel Tiger online games and apps: https://pbskids.org/daniel
Feelings Wheel image: https://blog.calm.com/blog/the-feelings-wheel
Fred Rogers Center for Early Learning and Children's Media: https://www.fredrogerscenter.org
Guardians: Unite the Realm, from MIT's Affective Computing group: https://guardians.media.mit.edu
Hey Listen Games's game-based lesson plans: https://www.heylistengames.org
Joan Ganz Cooney Center at Sesame Workshop: http://www.joanganzcooneycenter.org
Microsoft Teams and OneNote SEL supports: https://educationblog.microsoft.com/en-us/2020/09/new-features-in-teams-and-onenote-support-social-emotional-learning-approaches
Mightier, a platform of video games and a heart monitor intended to affect mood and positive behavior change: https://www.mightier.com
A Mortician's Tale: http://laundrybear.com/a-morticians-tale
Mood Meter app: http://moodmeterapp.com
Mood Meter Overview (video): https://youtu.be/qj6AIczvDhg
NearPod: https://nearpod.com/social-emotional-learning
A Parents' Guide to Disney-Pixar's *Inside Out*: https://www.paulekman.com/projects/inside-out
Paul Ekman Group's Facial Action Coding System: https://www.paulekman.com/facial-action-coding-system
Pear Deck's SEL slide templates: https://www.peardeck.com/sel-templates
Peekapak, SEL literacy curriculum: https://www.peekapak.com
Puppet Pals, digital puppetry app: http://www.polishedplay.com/puppetpals1

RULER Approach: https://www.rulerapproach.org
Sea of Solitude: https://www.ea.com/games/sea-of-solitude
Screen Therapy, game reviews through a media psychology lens: http://screentherapyblog.wordpress.com
Spiritfarer, a spiritual game about being a ferrymaster to the deceased: https://thunderlotusgames.com/spiritfarer
Starting the Year with "All About Me" Activities, from Jackie Gerstein: https://usergeneratededucation.wordpress.com/2020/08/23/starting-the-year-with-all-about-me-activities
Test Your Emotional Intelligence, online quiz on reading people's faces: https://greatergood.berkeley.edu/quizzes/ei_quiz

References

Berger, T. (2020, September 23). How to Maslow before Bloom, all day long. *Edutopia*. https://www.edutopia.org/article/how-maslow-bloom-all-day-long

Bostwick, E. (2020, April 15). Engaging early learners using media. *PBS Teachers' Lounge*. https://www.pbs.org/education/blog/engaging-early-learners-using-media

Brackett, M. (2019). *Permission to feel: Unlocking the power of emotions to help our kids, ourselves, and our society thrive*. Celadon.

CASEL's SEL Framework. (2020). *CASEL*. https://casel.org/wpcontent/uploads/2020/10/CASEL-SEL-Framework-10.2020-1.pdf

Cipriano, C., Barnes, T. N., Rivers, S. E., & Brackett, M. (2019). Exploring changes in student engagement through the RULER approach: An examination of students at risk of academic failure. *Journal of Education for Students Placed at Risk, 24*(1), 1–19. doi:10.1080/10824669.2018.1524767.

Cook, C. R., Fiat, A., Larson, M., Daikos, C., Slemrod, T., Holland, E. A., Thayer, A. J., & Renshaw, T. (2018). Positive greetings at the door: Evaluation of a low-cost, high-yield proactive classroom management strategy. *Journal of Positive Behavior Interventions, 20*(3), 149-159.

Co-viewing with kids. (2019). *WETA*. https://weta.org/kids/television/coviewing

Davis, M. (2008). *Street gang: The complete history of Sesame Street*. Penguin.

Deci, E. L., & Ryan, R. M. (2000). Intrinsic and extrinsic motivations: Classic definitions and new directions. *Contemporary Educational Psychology, 25*(1), 54–67. doi:10.1006/ceps.1999.1020.

de Saint-Exupéry, A. (1943). *The little prince*. Reynal & Hitchcock.

de Wit, J., van der Kraan, A., & Theeuwes, J. (2020). Live streams on Twitch help viewers cope with difficult periods in life. *Frontiers in Psychology, 11*, 586975. doi:10.3389/fpsyg.2020.586975.

Di Fabio, A., & Palazzeschi, L. (2015). Hedonic and eudaimonic well-being: The role of resilience beyond fluid intelligence and personality traits. *Frontiers in Psychology, 6*. doi:10.3389/fpsyg.2015.01367.

Ekman, P. (2007). *Emotions revealed: Recognizing faces and feelings to improve communication and emotional Life.* Times Books.

Flecker, S. A. (2014). When Fred met Margaret. *Pittmed.* https://www.pittmed.health.pitt.edu/story/when-fred-met-margaret

Gerstein, J. (2020, August 23). Starting the year with "all about me" activities. *User Generated Education.* https://usergeneratededucation.wordpress.com/2020/08/23/starting-the-year-with-all-about-me-activities/

Head Start History. (2018, March 2). *U.S. Department of Health and Human Services.* https://eclkc.ohs.acf.hhs.gov/about-us/article/head-start-history

Heick, T. (2020, May 1). What is Bloom's taxonomy? A definition for teachers. *TeachThought.* https://www.teachthought.com/learning/what-is-blooms-taxonomy-a-definition-for-teachers/

Hubert, B., & Rosen, Y. (2020). Equity in learning with BrainPOP: Fostering access and impact for all. *BrainPOP.* https://cdn-about.brainpop.com/wp-content/uploads/2020/07/Equity-in-Learning-with-BrainPOP.pdf

Johannes, N., Vuorre, M., & Przybylski, A. K. (2020, November 13). Video game play is positively correlated with well-being. *PsyArXiv.* doi:10.31234/osf.io/qrjza.

Juul, J. (2013). *The art of failure: An essay on the pain of playing video games.* MIT Press.

Kamenetz, A. (2018, August 8). How the science of learning is catching up to Mr. Rogers. *NPR.* https://www.npr.org/2018/08/08/635354413/how-learning-science-is-catching-up-to-mr-rogers

Kamp, D. (2020). *Sunny days: The children's television revolution that changed America.* Simon & Schuster.

Keltner, D., & Ekman, E. (2015, July 3). The science of 'Inside Out.' *New York Times.* https://www.nytimes.com/2015/07/05/opinion/sunday/the-science-of-inside-out.html

King, M. (2018). *Good neighbor: The life and work of Fred Rogers.* Harry N. Abrams.

Kübler-Ross, E. (1969). *On death and dying.* MacMillan.

Maslow, A. H. (1943). Theory of motivation. *Psychological Review*, 50(4), 370-396. doi:10.1037/h0054346

Mightier Scientific Overview. (2019, November). *Mightier.* https://www.mightier.com/wp-content/uploads/2019/11/ScientificOverview.pdf

Paciga, K. (2016, March 2). Plugging in with puppets on-screen. *Fred Rogers Center.* https://www.fredrogerscenter.org/2016/03/plugging-in-with-puppets-on-screen/

Paciga, K. A., & Donohue, C. (2017). *Technology and interactive media for young children: A whole child approach connecting the vision of Fred Rogers with research and practice.* Fred Rogers Center for Early Learning and Children's Media at Saint Vincent College.

Parents' guide to Disney-Pixar's Inside Out. (n.d.). *Paul Ekman Group.* https://www.paulekman.com/projects/inside-out/

Plutchik, R. (1962). *The emotions: Facts, theories, and a new model.* Random House.

Reer, F., & Quandt, T. (2020). Digital games and well-being: An overview. In R. Kowert (Ed.), *Video games and well-being.* Palgrave Studies in Cyberpsychology. doi:10.1007/978-3-030-32770-5_1.

Reiser, R. A., Tessmer, M. A., & Phelps, P. C. (1984). Adult-child interaction in children's learning from Sesame Street. *Educational Technology Research & Development, 32*(4), 217–223.

Reiser, R. A., Williamson, N., & Suzuki, K. (1988). Using Sesame Street to facilitate children's recognition of letters and numbers. *Educational Communication and Technology Journal, 36*(1), 15–21.

Reyes, M. R., Brackett, M. A., Rivers, S. E., White, M., & Salovey, P. (2012). Classroom emotional climate, student engagement, and academic achievement. *Journal of Educational Psychology, 104*(3), 700–712. doi:10.1037/a0027268.

Rigby, C. S., & Ryan, R. M. (2016). Time well spent? Motivation for entertainment and its eudaimonic aspects through the lens of self-determination theory. In L. Reinecke & M. B. Oliver (Eds.), *The Routledge handbook of media use and well-being: International perspectives on theory and research on positive media effects* (pp. 34–48). Routledge.

Rogers, F. M. (1969, November 13). *Commencement speech.* Greenville, PA: Thiel College.

Rogers, F. M., & Head, B. (1983). *Mister Rogers talks with parents.* Family Communications, Inc.

Ryan, R. M., & Deci, E. L. (2018). *Self-determination theory: Basic psychological needs in motivation, development, and wellness.* Guilford Press.

Salomon, G. (1977). Effects of encouraging Israeli mothers to co-observe Sesame Street with their five-year-olds. *Child Development, 48*(3), 1146–1151.

Schram, W. L. (1981). *Bold experiment: The story of educational television in American society.* Stanford University Press.

Shah, A. (2018, February 7). Scientists have found out why voices like Bob Ross' is so soothing. *Star Tribune.* https://www.startribune.com/scientists-have-found-out-why-bob-ross-voice-is-so-soothing/472974813/

Spock, B. (1946). *The common book of baby and child care.* Dell, Sloan, and Pearce.

Stern, R. (2017, December 29). Mr. Rogers and the importance of social and emotional learning. *The Hill.* https://thehill.com/opinion/healthcare/476163-mr-rogers-and-the-importance-of-social-and-emotional-learning

Stevens, R., & Penuel, W. R. (2010). *Studying and fostering learning through joint media engagement.* Principal Investigators Meeting of the National Science Foundation's Science of Learning Centers, Arlington, VA.

Takeuchi, L., & Stevens, R. (2011, December). The new coviewing: Designing for learning through joint media engagement. *Joan Ganz Cooney Center at Sesame Workshop.* https://www.joanganzcooneycenter.org/wp-content/uploads/2011/12/jgc_coviewing_desktop.pdf

Taylor, S., Ferguson, C., Peng, F., Schoeneich, M., & Picard, R. W. (2019). Use of in-game rewards to motivate daily self-report compliance: Randomized controlled trial. *Journal of Medical Internet Research, 21*(1).

Tea Party. (2020). *PBS KIDS.* https://pbskids.org/daniel/games/tea-party

Tolbert, A. N., & Drogos, K. L. (2019). Tweens' wishful identification and parasocial relationships with YouTubers. *Frontiers in Psychology, 10,* 2781. doi:10.3389/fpsyg.2019.02781.

Tools and Features Support. (2020). *BrainPOP.* https://educators.brainpop.com/tools-features-support/

Tuttle, S. (2018). *Exactly as you are: The life and faith of Mister Rogers.* Eerdmans.

UDL Guidelines. (2020). *CAST.* http://udlguidelines.cast.org/

Valkenburg, P. M., Krcmar, M., Peeters, A. L., & Marseille, N. M. (1999). Developing a scale to assess three styles of television mediation: "Instructive mediation," "restrictive mediation," and "social coviewing." *Journal of Broadcasting and Electronic Media, 43*(1), 52–66.

Waterman, A. S. (2013). *The best within us: Positive psychology perspectives on eudaimonia.* American Psychological Association.

Watters, A. (2015, June 6). Teaching by television in American Samoa: A history. *Hacking Education.* http://hackeducation.com/2015/06/06/american-samoa-educational-tv

Willcox, G. (1982). The feeling wheel: A tool for expanding awareness of emotions and increasing spontaneity and intimacy. *Transactional Analysis Journal, 12*(4), 274–276. doi:10.1177/036215378201200411.

Yale University. (2014, June 16). *Yale Center for Emotional Intelligence: Mood Meter Overview* [Video]. YouTube. https://youtu.be/qj6AIczvDhg

Zillmann, D. (1988). Mood management through communication choices. *American Behavioral Scientist, 31*(3), 327–340.

CHAPTER TWO

An Exploration of Social and Emotional Learning

The Collaborative for Academic, Social, and Emotional Learning (CASEL) evidence-based SEL Framework has been used with millions of children in the United States. As it happens, both histories of SEL and CASEL are intertwined. In fact, the phrase "social and emotional learning" was coined at the same 1994 meeting that saw the formation of CASEL. Back then, it was known as the Collaborative to Advance Social and Emotional Learning (CASEL) (CASEL Milestones, 2020). In 2001, the A for "Advance" would become "Academic." More on that shift soon!

Since inception, CASEL has had prominent board members, including co-founder and chair Timothy P. Shriver, who also chairs the Special Olympics. Other members have included Linda Darling-Hammond and Eileen Rockefeller Growald. In 2010, Warren Buffett's NoVo Foundation became a major funder, thus enabling CASEL to become an independent nonprofit (CASEL Milestones, 2020). Other funders have included but are not limited to the following: The Allstate Foundation, the Chan Zuckerberg Initiative, the Rockefeller Foundation, the Bill & Melinda Gates Foundation, and the Institution of Education Sciences.

Initially housed at Yale University in 1996, CASEL soon moved to the campus of the University of Illinois, Chicago (UIC). There, co-founder and psychology professor Roger P. Weissberg led as its director from 1996 through 2020. Under his leadership, CASEL formed partnerships with other school-based organizations, notably the Association for Supervision and Curriculum Development (ASCD), a professional organization of principals, superintendents, and school leaders. In 1997, Elias et al. wrote the book *Promoting Social and Emotional Learning: Guidelines for Educators* for ASCD, the first text to describe the need for SEL in schools. Elias et al. (1997) defined SEL as "the ability to understand, manage, and express the social and emotional aspects of one's life in ways that enable the successful management of life tasks such as learning, forming relationships, solving everyday problems, and adapting to the complex demands of growth and development" (p. 2).

Promoting Social and Emotional Learning differentiated SEL from character education programs like those found at KIPP charter schools (Elias et al., 1997). Where character education programs tended to focus on aligning students to a school's core values (e.g., being honest, demonstrating resilience), SEL, they wrote, was different, as it more closely aligned with emotional intelligence (Elias et al., 1997). The connection to emotional intelligence stemmed from Daniel Goleman, one of CASEL's co-founders. Two years prior, *Emotional Intelligence: Why It Can Matter More than IQ* was published, a bestselling book where Goleman discussed how emotional intelligence could be taught and cultivated as a skill (Goleman, 1995).

Today, SEL skills are sometimes called "soft skills," competencies considered valuable to have when competing in the global workforce, such as collaboration, creativity, and critical thinking abilities (Aronica & Robinson, 2009; Wagner & Dintersmith, 2015; Wagner, 2014). More in line with the needs of 20th century economies, many schools today still persist in the emphasis of teaching "hard skills," such as the rote memorization of "tacit, academic" informational facts and knowledge (Baker-Doyle, 2017, p. 98). Are SEL competencies a new set of soft skills, supplanting the so-called 4 Cs (collaboration, critical thinking, communication, and creativity) of 21st century learning (Framework for 21st Century Learning, 2020)?

A newer field of study, some SEL research remains tethered to other fields, like assessment and special education. Early ideas of SEL were influenced by the social skills research work of Myrna Shure, creator of the I Can Problem Solve (ICPS) school-based SEL and violence prevention program. CASEL co-founder Mark T. Greenberg's Promoting Alternative THinking Strategies (PATHS) curriculum also informed research. PATHS is a set of alternative thinking skills about emotional regulation developed for children who are deaf or hard of hearing.

In December 2020, CASEL updated its SEL definition to be more explicit to the "identities, strengths and experiences of all children, including those who have been marginalized in our education systems" (Niemi, 2020, para. 2). CASEL now defines SEL as the process through which people "acquire and apply the knowledge, skills, and attitudes to develop healthy identities, manage emotions and achieve personal and collective goals, feel and show empathy for others, establish and maintain supportive relationships, and make responsible and caring decisions" (CASEL, 2020, para. 1). As mentioned, CASEL's influence is mainly in the United States, and its definition is one of many.

Why did it take nearly 25 years for CASEL and SEL to finally take hold in schools? Perhaps recent SEL adoptions were a reaction to bullying and violence in schools, increased political polarization in society, or as a backlash to the high-stakes testing regimes under No Child Left Behind and Race to the Top initiatives? The COVID-19 pandemic and current racial equity and social justice issues surely made SEL top of mind for many folks. Tate (2019) attributed the recent pique in SEL to factors such as increased youth anxiety about college and career readiness (Horowitz & Graf, 2019). Tate also suggested that SEL grew into the national education lexicon because of commonalities with other "buzzword" concepts in modern schooling, like "data-driven," "college and career ready," and "personalized learning."

As it happens, CASEL is not the only organization attempting to define the field. Crowded and somewhat fragmented, there are other frameworks in addition to CASEL's. Digging deeper, while the term SEL may sound like a buzzword, its underlying concepts surely are not. For millennia, humans have practiced empathy, perspective-taking, kindness, compassion, and self-efficacy. What's more, research on the brain's malleability are emerging, suggesting that these skills are, in fact, teachable.

CASEL's SEL Framework

In the past several years, CASEL has developed approaches to support educators who implement SEL programs. They offer a schoolwide toolkit, a districtwide toolkit, and a principal toolkit. CASEL also has certified partners.

In October 2020, CASEL's SEL Framework was updated. Sometimes just referred to as the "CASEL 5" or the "CASEL Wheel," there are five interrelated competency areas: self-awareness, self-management, social management, responsible decision-making, and social awareness. In more detail, the five core competencies in CASEL's SEL Framework are:

- *Self-Awareness*: The abilities to understand one's own emotions, thoughts, and values and how they influence behavior across contexts. This includes

- *Self-Management*: The abilities to manage one's emotions, thoughts, and behaviors effectively in different situations and to achieve goals and aspirations. This includes the capacities to delay gratification, manage stress, and feel motivation and agency to accomplish personal/collective goals.
- *Social Awareness*: The abilities to understand the perspectives of and empathize with others, including those from diverse backgrounds, cultures, and contexts. This includes the capacities to feel compassion for others, understand broader historical and social norms for behavior in different settings, and recognize family, school, and community resources and supports.
- *Relationship Skills*: The abilities to establish and maintain healthy and supportive relationships and to effectively navigate settings with diverse individuals and groups. This includes the capacities to communicate clearly, listen actively, cooperate, work collaboratively to problem solve and negotiate conflict constructively, navigate settings with differing social and cultural demands and opportunities, provide leadership, and seek or offer help when needed.
- *Responsible decision-making*: The abilities to make caring and constructive choices about personal behavior and social interactions across diverse situations. This includes the capacities to consider ethical standards and safety concerns, and to evaluate the benefits and consequences of various actions for personal, social, and collective well-being. (CASEL's SEL Framework, 2020)

Are there competencies that are more developmentally appropriate to learn at certain ages? Are some competencies foundational to others? To self-manage, the capacity to pay attention is required. To build up relationship skills, other basic skills may need to be cultivated, like emotional regulation.

Competencies in CASEL's SEL Framework are interrelated. Child psychologist Jean Piaget wrote about a set of mechanisms of change that are necessary but not sufficient conditions for child development. "The idea is that SEL competencies of self-management, self-regulation, and self-control are necessary but not sufficient to have empathy," CASEL board member Kimberly A. Schonert-Reichl explained. "But you do need those to build on the skill, as they are a precursor to other skills."

Brackett et al. (2015) suggested that social interactions within the systems and environments that children inhabit may influence SEL skills acquisition. Using the RULER Approach (see Chapter One), children can cultivate emotional intelligence within themselves. Next, other skills can be developed, including those that lead to prosocial behavioral change (Brackett et al., 2015).

Mahoney et al. (2020) codified this as *Systemic SEL*. Like the outer rings of a spoked wheel, Systemic SEL describes the "nested, interacting settings and processes involved in systemic SEL at proximal (classrooms, schools, families, communities) and distal (districts, states, national, international) ecological levels" (Mahoney et al., 2020, p. 1). Bronfenbrenner (1979/2006) had similarly proposed a model on how children develop as a function of their interactions with people, objects, and symbols across several nested and interactive contexts (home and family, school, parents' workplaces, mass media, laws, cultural ideals, etc.) over time. Illustrated as a wheel, CASEL's SEL Framework (see Figure 3) adapts Systemic

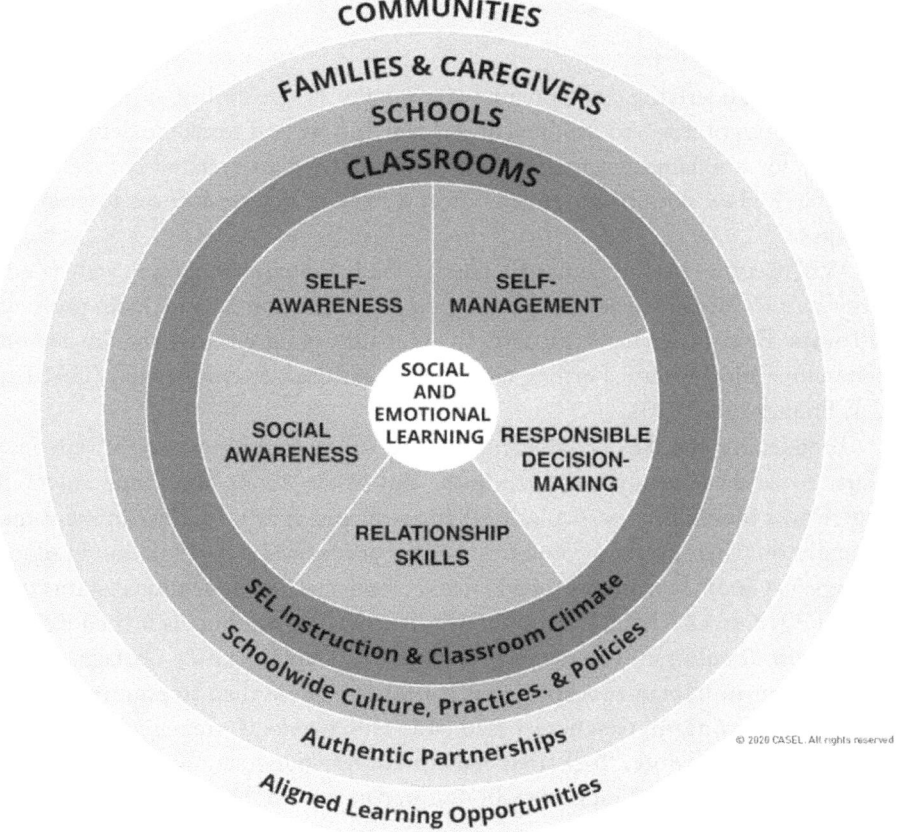

Figure 3. CASEL's SEL Framework. Source: CASEL. Copyright © 2020 CASEL. All rights reserved. www.casel.org/what-is-SEL

SEL with Bronfenbrenner's (1979/2006) ecological systems theory model, where SEL learning extends outward to homes and communities.

Games, which are ubiquitous in children's lives, are played through the proximal and distal systems that children inhabit. Seventy-one percent of children play video games; 65% of adults play games with their children as an opportunity to socialize with them ("Essential Facts," 2021). Children play educational games in classrooms, schoolwide at recess, at home with their families, and in communities, with friends, in sports leagues, and online. When playing games in these systems, SEL skills—like self-regulation, goal-setting, and growth mindset—are taught and reinforced by peers, adults, and coaches. When video games are played and discussed in online communities, cultural and social capital peer mentorships with other community members can be developed (Rafalow, 2018).

Critiques of SEL

One of the underlying components of empathy is the ability to project one's emotions onto others—to feel how others feel. But what if someone demonstrates empathy for a villain or a tyrant? What about other interrelated competencies, like ethics? How does being ethical affect a person's responsiveness to another's feelings?

Whereas the 2017 version of CASEL's SEL Framework simply stated "empathy" as a social awareness competency, the 2020 iteration now includes prosocial outcomes. Beyond having a capacity for empathy, children now should demonstrate empathic concern. Further, empathy should lead to compassion (CASEL's SEL Framework, 2020).

Broadening the SEL competencies in 2020 to include prosocial outcomes seems to address many past critiques. But what about the implicitness of frameworks themselves, particularly when social and emotional development may be taught only because of the link to academic success? Is self-regulation in school settings just another word for "obedience to the social and educational status quo" (Mirra, 2018, p. 12)? If SEL does not address social oppression, is it then just another form of cultural hegemonic miseducation (Camangian & Cariaga, 2021)? Isn't it better to humanize learning with a focus on care than to require students to adhere and conform to school-based SEL frameworks (Camangian & Cariaga, 2021)? Simmons wrote, "SEL that fails to address our sociopolitical reality and combat racial and social injustice will not prepare our young people for the world they will inherit" (2021, p. 30).

Can SEL fit in already crowded academic curriculum? What if CASEL could show that SEL programs could not only advance students' social and emotional competencies but could also lead to increased academic success? As mentioned at the beginning of this chapter, in 2001, the "A" in CASEL was changed from "Advance" to "Academic"—"a significant change that reflects the intimate link between academic learning and SEL" (CASEL Milestones, 2020, para. 13). "CASEL decided early on as a rationale for being that the only way for many people to pay attention to SEL was to connect it to academic achievement," Schonert-Reichl remarked.

A meta-analysis is featured prominently on the CASEL website, linking SEL outcomes to an 11-percentile increase in observed student academic achievements (Durlak et al., 2011). "But what this may have done, to the detriment of the SEL field, was to make it seem as one central purpose of SEL was to increase academic achievement," she continued. "The ends to SEL is then seen as increased academic achievement, and not about making good persons and full human beings."

"Therein lies a problem," Erikson Institute founder Chip Donohue told me. "SEL got us thinking about social and emotional. Executive function and growth mindset confound this. Social and emotional development became social and emotional learning when we hung the word 'learning' on the outside edge as SEL. Do the S and E lead to L?"

Donohue is also an advisor to the Fred Rogers Center for Early Learning. As shared in Chapter One, his work focuses on emotional readiness in young children. "We fell in love with the phrase SEL because the learning helped sell it. But what Fred [Rogers] was really talking about was human development—how we learn in our early years, how to get along with others, and how to understand someone else's thinking, needs, and feelings."

Aristotle famously remarked, "Educating the mind without educating the heart is no education at all." Schonert-Reichl concurred. "I believe that teaching social and emotional development skills has been around since education began," she said. "There has also been a rise in understanding how important these skills are for getting along with others, such as self-regulation."

SEL needs to be in a supportive context that affords students' voice and promotes positive teacher relationships. Competencies should not be taught as standalone subjects, and educators should not devote time solely for lessons on empathy and perspective-taking (Farber & Rivers, 2020; Mirra, 2018). Schonert-Reichl continued,

> SEL has to be on the floors, in the doors, in the pores. When kids walk into the school, SEL should be in every interaction. It's that hidden curriculum, how are you valued, what do we value? Students may see a poster on the wall about SEL, but they may pass by a trophy case on one side of the hallway and an honor roll plaque on the other side. Those things say, "Here's who really matters to us."

Schonert-Reichl later shared innovations about the neuroplasticity of the human brain. As we see in later chapters, the brain is malleable and SEL is teachable. "All this research on the brain has filtered down to education. The malleability of these skills means that we can teach these competencies and that they can be cultivated through experiences."

Attack of the Frameworks!

Finn and Hess (2019) wrote that SEL skills could be, at times, ambiguous and, therefore, overly subjective to assess. In 2019, William Merchant, a colleague in the Applied Statistics and Research Methods department at the University of Northern Colorado, and I discovered that firsthand. We happened to be co-investigating the effectiveness of an SEL digital literacy platform in afterschool sites in a large school district. We had taken over the study from another researcher who had medical issues and could no longer continue with data analysis.

Pre-treatment and post-treatment student data on SEL outcomes were collected from 2018 through 2019. We then used a quasi-experimental design with nonequivalent treatment/control groups. Groups were assigned at the site level with individual students as the unit of analysis (Farber & Merchant, 2020).

We found no significant change in the studied group (n = 1,726). Upon digging deeper, we found something problematic: The school district was tethered to a subscribed measurement suite, in this case, Teaching Strategies (TS) GOLD. GOLD is designed to assess children from birth through grade three on social, emotional, cognitive, physical, and language development and learning. However, the curriculum we studied did not neatly map or align with these measures (Farber & Merchant, 2020).

Specific to SEL, GOLD has three assessment areas, scored by teachers throughout the school year on a rubric. Children in these three areas should: (1) Regulate their own emotions and behaviors; (2) Establish and sustain positive relationships; and (3) Participate cooperatively and constructively in-group situations ("GOLD Teaching Strategies," n.d.). Only some of these areas aligned with SEL frameworks like CASEL's. GOLD does not measure empathic concern or ethical responsibility—two competencies in the CASEL Framework.

We suspect that this is an example of something that may be occurring regularly: Not great alignment between SEL instruction with school district measures (Farber & Merchant, 2020). We are not the first to confront this issue. CASEL board members Timothy P. Shriver and Roger P. Weissberg wrote that there might be as many as 100 SEL frameworks (Shriver & Weissberg, 2020). In 2017, Berg et al. identified 136 frameworks across 14 SEL domain areas! More clarity in the field is undoubtedly warranted (Singh & Duraiappah, 2019).

The fragmentation of terminologies, differences in competencies, and the sheer number of frameworks impedes the science needed to advance the field of SEL. Stephanie M. Jones, a developmental psychologist at the Harvard Graduate School of Education, explores just that: the science and practice of SEL frameworks and curriculum. Jones also studies the link between experience, stress, strain, vulnerability, adversity, and growth patterns and change in social and emotional behavior over time.

Jones leads the Ecological Approaches to Social Emotional Learning (EASEL) Laboratory, where she studies social and emotional behavioral development from early childhood through adolescence. She spoke to me about the current state of SEL and the three pillars of work that comprise the EASEL Lab. The first pillar is research. At the EASEL Lab, this is mainly longitudinal—long-term studies that evaluate the strategies and practices implemented in preschools, elementary schools, and middle schools, conducted as community-based randomized trial research. "These projects are about what happened, what worked, and what do we do about it," Jones said.

EASEL Lab's second pillar is to disseminate its work to the practitioners of SEL: teachers in the field. Part of this dissemination includes the Taxonomy Project, one of the EASEL Lab's hallmark initiatives. The Taxonomy Project aggregates competencies from other frameworks and connects them. "Now people can be more transparent, precise, and coordinated in how they talk about SEL," Jones said.

One issue that Jones observed was an inconsistency in language between frameworks. About confusion around terminologies, Zhou (2020) wrote, "One school will focus on growth mindsets, another on restorative justice, another on the prevention of bullying, and so on" (para. 13). Jones and her lab similarly observed how the field of SEL itself was imprecise; having agreed-upon terminologies in scientific fields matter. "The imprecision—when things are not well-defined or explicit—is how you mix up what you know and what you do," Jones said. "We spend too much time in the field [of SEL] arguing about what is important, or we are too loose about what things mean. What does it look like in a kid to show you they can X—whatever X is? We need real science to make the practice more effective."

Self-management is a competency in some frameworks, while in others, it is self-control or self-regulation. But self-control is not quite self-management. Self-control is "an umbrella construct" bridging "concepts and measurements from different disciplines (e.g., impulsivity, conscientiousness, self-regulation, delay of gratification, inattention-hyperactivity, executive function, willpower, intertemporal choice)" (Moffitt et al., 2011, p. 2693 as cited in Jones et al., 2016, p. 4). This convolution of language interrupts the process of learning from science to practice and learning from practice to build science.

As a solution, the EASEL Lab created and shared the Explore SEL tool (http://exploresel.gse.harvard.edu). Free and web-based, it aggregates and compares 39 SEL frameworks, including ones from CASEL, Head Start, and Character Lab. A few nations (e.g., Haiti, Kenya, Singapore), some states (e.g., Connecticut), and some cities (e.g., Anchorage) have SEL frameworks, as does Sesame Workshop, LEGO, and the World Health Organization. UNICEF has not one, but two frameworks!

Frameworks were selected based on certain conditions. First, they needed to represent a wide range of disciplines and they should be widely adopted. Further, the competencies listed should be easily describable, that way, they could be efficiently coded. "We created visuals to show how they overlap or are distinct," Jones said. "We also tried to go deep inside existing programs to describe them in more detail, with more objectivity and accuracy about what they actually do." Using Explore SEL, I was able to compare frameworks, domains, and terms visually. Just click on links, and the tool instantly produces easy-to-read, color-coded infographics!

The third pillar of the EASEL Lab is to design, pilot, and implement (and, to gather data, ultimately) the strategies and practices that work in actual, real-world classrooms. In other words, where, when, and how do teachers embed SEL in lessons? "We've done that in a whole variety of ways, starting about eight years ago, rethinking how programs that support SEL are designed and executed," Jones explained. "Our first response to that challenge was to make a new and better program. When we did that, we learned a few things that led us to our current work."

SEL Kernels and Brain Games

Based on educator feedback and research findings, Jones's team found that teachers did not want to implement a long-form SEL curriculum—prescribed scope and sequence, multi-day lessons that detail strategies and practices to follow. After all, teachers already grapple with a crowded curriculum, a laundry list of standards they must meet each school year. As a result, they decided to meet teachers' needs by creating bite-sized SEL activities that could be easily inserted into existing lessons.

After reviewing 25 SEL programs and 436 activities, a curricular overlap was discovered (Shafer, 2016). For example, several programs included mindfulness activities, like guided breathing strategies to reduce stress. Jones's team teased out

212 specific strategies, which were then sorted into categories: deep breathing, positive self-talk, step-by-step procedures, yoga and exercise (Shafer, 2016). These categories became known as SEL Kernels, small-scale standalone activities that take about five-minutes to complete. Modular and adaptable, SEL Kernels are like ingredients on a social and emotional activity menu. Using them, teachers can select and remix SEL into existing lessons. "The idea was to give more agency to teachers with SEL," Jones said.

The EASEL Lab also published 30 games based on executive function and self-regulation. Known as Brain Games, each game helps children to grow skills that they can carry into other settings. "The reason we designed them was because of the neuroscience that highlighted executive function and self-regulation, linking those skills—for good or ill—to experiences of stress and vulnerability," Jones explained.

Each of the Brain Games target working memory, attention control, and response to inhibition. The EASEL Lab team calls them "brain powers," skills centered on children's abilities to "focus, remember, and stop and think" (Shafer, 2016, para. 4). As with the SEL Kernels activities, Brain Games became another opportunity to move away from scope and sequence curriculum to quick activities on routines and practices. "The games we created can be used at any time of the school day. They are fun activities teachers can do with kids."

Brain Games can be printed on index-sized cards (all of the SEL Kernels and Brain Games are linked at the end of this chapter). On each card is a brief descriptor of how to play and why. "We wanted to make the skill explicit to the teacher," Jones said. Cards also illustrate a theory of change, shown with three interconnecting circles, followed by rules and steps for each game, plus a set of recommendations to play in different ways. There are also debrief questions that encourage discussion and reflection.

Most Brain Games are variants of folk games, playground games passed down generationally. For instance, *Simon Says* and *Stop-and-Think* are classics that also help with response-inhibition. To play, children receive an increasingly complex set of steps and must remember what to do. Other games include *Remember*, a concentration game about working memory, and *Focus*, which challenges attention control. *Silly Stories* is about self-control. Children make silly motions as words are said in stories, such as drumming with their fingers or strumming an invisible guitar. But they can only do so as a response and cannot share out of turn. Debriefing questions ask players to reflect on their capacity to stop and think and control impulses.

Brain Games's approach is similar to some lessons in CASEL founder Mark Greenberg's PATHS curriculum. For instance, PATHS's *Stop Light* activity mirrors Brain Games's *Red Light, Green Light* game. Both remix classic children's games to become practice spaces for executive function and response-inhibition skills. To play, children respond to color: red means stop, take a moment; yellow indicates to slow down and think about feelings; and green signals that it is okay to proceed (PATHS Curriculum, 2012; Weissberg et al., 1988).

Researchers at the EASEL Lab conducted randomized trials using SEL Kernels and Brain Games in several schools. "We found that kids exposed to the program did better in math, reading, and a bunch of areas closely tied to executive function and self-regulation," Jones said. "They were less impulsive, and their attention was more direct and focused over long periods."

After these findings, Brain Games were iterated for use in different settings. "We did a quasi-experimental study in South Carolina and observed positive results for kids: classroom practice improved. We did a randomized trial recently in Massachusetts and found that executive function and self-regulation across the board improved. Since then, we have adopted the concept to toddler, preschool, and adolescence."

Emerging neuroscience research on response-inhibition tasks suggest that these skills are teachable. Delalande et al. (2019) studied self-control using classic game-like psychological tasks. In the study, an experimental group (adults and children) played the Stroop Test and the Stop-Signal-Task. Findings were compared to a control group who answered trivia questions.

The Stroop Test, which dates back to the mid-1930s, measures cognitive load and attention (Delalande et al., 2019; Hodent, 2017). Cognitive load refers to how our working memory can store small bits of information at any one time. Cognitive load theory is why phone numbers in the United States are grouped in three and four digits. It is vital, as we don't need to remember certain things for very long. When I follow GPS instructions, details go into my working memory, then can be forgotten; I may never need to remember that route again. Other information, such as how to drive a car, is more important, and is, therefore, retained.

To play the Stroop Test, participants are asked to read lists of words out loud; the first set is written with matched colors, the next set is misaligned. Round one includes the word "red" written with red ink. In round two, "red" is written in blue. Word aside, the task is to say blue and not red out loud. This task becomes difficult because the misalignment of color creates mental friction.

Celia Hodent considered the effects of the Stroop Test when designing the video game *Fortnite*. "You must direct players' attention to relevant information while minding their cognitive load to avoid overwhelming their working memory," she wrote (Hodent, 2017, p. 56). But sometimes, for fun, players intentionally add complexity to gameplay. In the social deduction game *Among Us*, some players have modified ("modded") the game in Color Mode. In this player-created variant, "every player is named after a color that doesn't match their avatar, leading to brain gymnastics and misidentification during emergency meetings" (Peel, 2020, para. 14). (Emergency meetings are when players discuss and vote out imposters from the group.)

The Stop-Signal-Task is the second task in the Delalande et al. (2019) study. Another classic psychology test, it measures the ability to control the initiation of movement. It begins when participants see a flashing left or right arrow. When the indicator illuminates, participants must then press a button corresponding to its direction. However, from time to time, there is a beep, which means no button should not be depressed—the "Stop" in "Stop-Signal."

Grégoire Borst, professor of developmental psychology and cognitive neuroscience at Paris Descartes University, shared some of his research on inhibitory control and implicit bias. "The idea is that you play with the delay from the presentation of the arrow and the presentation of the stop signal," he explained. "The closer it is to response time, the more difficult it gets."

Borst next described the Delalande et al. (2019) findings in more detail, including observations from magnetic resonance imaging (MRI) of participants' brains. He also shared two of his published papers with me: one on structural aspects that showed changes in neural networks, and one on the functional aspects that did not show behavioral effects. "We found structural effects, but not behavior effects," he said. "Neuroplasticity was observed. There was a change in the cognitive control network—basically, the thickness and surface of some areas."

In addition to practicing self-control and self-regulation, there are also brain-based findings on people's ability to cultivate mindfulness, empathy, and compassion. As most educators and caregivers intuitively know, a changed behavior requires guidance and thoughtful facilitation.

UNESCO MGIEP's EMC² Framework for Social and Emotional Learning

United Nations Educational, Scientific and Cultural Organization (UNESCO) Mahatma Gandhi Institute of Education for Peace and Sustainable Development (MGIEP) is a category one research institute headquartered in New Delhi, India. Its mission is to focus on achieving the United Nations' Sustainable Development Goal (SDG) 4.7: "Education for building peaceful and sustainable societies across the world by developing programs that promote social and emotional learning with innovative digital pedagogies that empower youth" (UNESCO MGIEP, 2020). There are 17 SDGs, from eradicating poverty and hunger to boosting people's well-being. The achievement of these goals, adopted in 2015, is targeted for 2030. As of this writing, the world still has much work to do!

Many teachers take time to teach students about the SDGs. For instance, the website TeachSDGs features several projects connecting classrooms together using educational technology tools. Partners include Kahoot!, Flipgrid, Participate, and Empatico. I have integrated SDGs into coursework, having preservice teachers design projects using the goals as learning outcomes. Social studies teachers developed lessons on sustainable cities and communities (SDG 11); science teachers focused on life below water (SDG 14) compared to life on land (SDG 15). More ideas on integrating SDGs can be found on the World's Largest Lesson webpage.

On July 18, 2020, Nelson Mandela Day, *Rethinking Learning: A Review of Social and Emotional Learning for Education Systems*, was published by UNESCO MGIEP. A review of SEL and its impact on student health, school climate, and the potential for happier classrooms, CASEL board member Kimberly A. Schonert-Reichl contributed two chapters. With iThrive Games's Susan E. Rivers, I co-authored the chapter, Leveraging Technology for SEL Programs. Prior to iThrive Games, Rivers was a researcher at the Yale Center for Emotional Intelligence, where she published on the RULER Approach with Marc Brackett, Christina Cipriano, Tia N. Barnes, and others. Additional chapter contributors included Grégoire Borst, mindfulness professor Nimrod Sheinman, and SEL professors Patricia Jennings and Jennifer Kitil. Buddhist monk, photographer, and humanitarian Matthieu Ricard wrote the foreword. In total, the project had 23 contributors. CASEL board member emeritus Mark Greenberg and Greater Good in Education's Vicki Zakrzewski were among the reviewers.

Chapters of *Rethinking Learning* centered on the CASEL SEL Framework as a lens, as well as its own framework: UNESCO MGIEP's EMC^2 Framework for Social and Emotional Learning (Singh & Duraiappah, 2019; see Figure 4). A "whole-brain" framework, it includes four competencies: empathy, mindfulness, compassion, and critical inquiry (Singh & Duraiappah, 2019). Nandini Chatterjee Singh, who serves as UNESCO MGIEP's cognitive neuroscientist and senior project officer, developed the framework with the institute's founding director, Anantha Duraiappah.

To thrive in the 21st century requires empathy and the ability to problem solve. Because of this, some frameworks, such as the Framework for 21st Century Learning and Pratham's Life Skills Framework, focus on sets of skills informed by the needs of the modern workforce (Explore SEL, 2020). EMC^2 is different; it was founded on broad and aspirational notions of human flourishing. EMC^2 posits that "education systems need to move beyond a focus on economic growth and instead focus on building human flourishing, which requires an explicit focus on

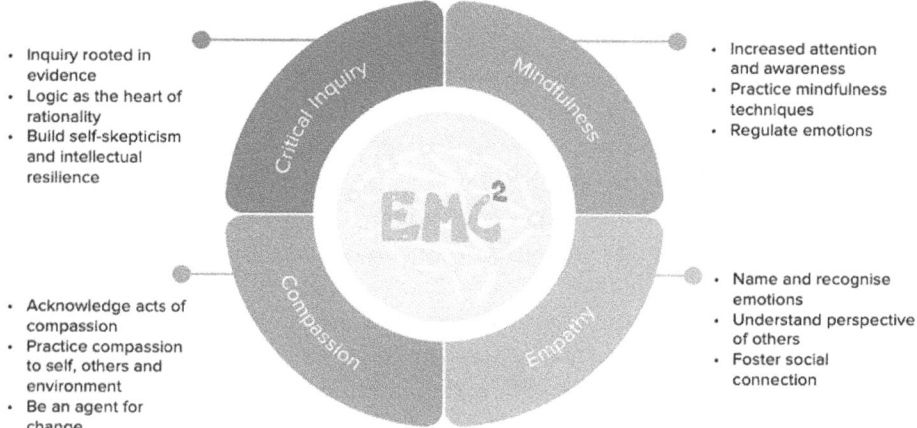

Figure 4. EMC² Framework for Social and Emotional Learning. Source: Chatterjee Singh, N., & Duraiappah, A. K. (Eds.) (2020). *Rethinking learning: A review of social and emotional learning frameworks for education systems.* New Delhi: UNESCO MGIEP.

promoting social and emotional skills in addition to rational thought" (Chatterjee & Duraiappah, 2020, p. 68). "Human flourishing is a wonderful idea," Singh remarked when we spoke. "It goes beyond well-being—which is a benefit for the self—to the idea that everybody can benefit. That is our conscious shift."

Of the four competencies in EMC², critical inquiry was the only one that came from a cognitive lens. The other three—empathy, mindfulness, and compassion—stem from neuroscience research. "This is one of the things that differentiates EMC² from other SEL frameworks: the embrace of neuroscience as an approach," Singh continued. "We [she and Duraiappah] looked at the attributes we wanted to consciously promote with kids, which were also competencies that could be taught."

EMC² is aligned to UNESCO—the central United Nations organization that MGIEP belongs to—and its mission, including strong notions of action. Hence, the framework's compassion piece consists of wording on children being change agents. "This is why experiential learning is so important," Singh said. "To put it simply, we want to ensure all of the four competencies we bring into classrooms should manifest in everyday behavior. Kids should be able to practice it. This was conscious for us. We want to ensure all of the four competencies are brought into classrooms and manifest in everyday behavior."

Compared to frameworks like CASEL's, EMC² focuses more on happiness and well-being than its link to academic outcomes. "Children should be less stressed and anxious," Singh said. Echoing Fred Rogers and his Six Principles of

Learning Readiness (see Chapter One), she continued, "When achieved, children will be ready to learn."

There is emerging research on how our brains are affected by experiential stimuli, such as gameplay and interaction with media. Kral et al. (2018) observed strengthened neural connections after adolescents played a video game where they were tasked to analyze emotions in alien faces (more on this in Chapter Four). Kidd and Castano (2013) published evidence how theory of mind, which relates to perspective-taking, improved among literary fiction readers. Findings such as these relate to how humans cognitively imitate others' emotions, which trigger or activate mirror neurons in limbic systems and the neocortex (e.g., Carr et al., 2003; Iacoboni, 2009). "Empathy and compassion come naturally for human beings," Singh continued. "Especially young children. We seek to nurture these natural abilities."

Like empathy, neuroplasticity has been observed with mindfulness training games—the "M" in EMC^2 (e.g., Davidson et al., 2003; Patsenko et al., 2019). "The noise of our lives can be difficult to tune out," she remarked. "Mindfulness takes some training because the world is distracting, so you want to bring attention to what you are doing." Mindfulness training "activates a brain network that includes the frontal and parietal cortex, which controls voluntary deployment of attention and a network which is responsible for reorienting attention, namely the frontal cortex primarily in the right hemisphere and temporoparietal junction" (Singh & Duraiappah, 2019, p. 9).

Compassion is the first "C" in EMC^2, another SEL skill that can be taught and cultivated. Absent from the 2017 version of CASEL's SEL Framework, it is now included in the 2020 update under social awareness. Both CASEL and EMC^2 connect empathy to compassion. Like empathy, this link is supported in neuroscience: Compassion training affects the limbic and neocortex systems related to prosocial outcomes from developing empathy (e.g., Jazaieri et al., 2014).

The second "C" in "C^2" is critical inquiry, the framework's cognitive competency. Critical inquiry connects to empathy and civics—our place in society (Mirra, 2018). In addition to compassion as an outcome, empathy should be linked to critical thought. "This competency is included because of Anantha [Duraiappah]," Singh said. "After all, what good is having empathy, compassion, and mindfulness if it is misdirected?"

As a standalone construct, empathy tends to focus on the individual and not the various social groups that people inhabit. About critical thinking and empathy, Mirra (2018) wrote,

> Taking a critical perspective on empathy encourages us to interrogate what we each bring to the table when we seek to empathize with others and to acknowledge the fact

that the ways in which we are privileged (or marginalized) in public life inevitably influence how we interpret the experiences of others. (Mirra, 2018, pp. 7-8)

There are moments in history (and currently) where people empathize with dictators and terrorists because they lack critical empathy (Mirra, 2018). Known as *selective empathy*, this describes how people sometimes empathize with those who are morally corrupt (Breithaupt, 2019). Mirra (2018) calls this *false empathy*, when ideological rhetoric is used to manipulate people for political gain.

"Sometimes, being purely logical can take you down a less empathetic or compassionate road," Singh said. "Empathy, mindfulness, and compassion need to interplay with rational and logical thinking." Brain research supports this relationship: people's decision-making is tied to emotion (e.g., Habib et al., 2015).

Interestingly, EMC^2 does not talk about society in the ways that CASEL's framework does. As Singh explained, children don't grow up in isolation; people always surround them. Where society is explicit in frameworks like CASEL's, it is implicit in EMC^2.

An emphasis on the self was a critique sometimes leveled on Fred Rogers. On his television show, he famously sang, "You are special." How do those ideas situate in collectivistic societies? "The culture of family structures in India has changed in the past 30 years," Singh replied. "Families used to be larger and you weren't special, you were one among many. You grew up thinking, 'Whatever I have will be shared amongst other people.' But Indian culture also is about the need to look within. This is ingrained in most Indian homes and in societies you find within India. You feel this in rural areas too, where the sense of community is very strong."

Prosociality undergirds EMC^2, as it suggests that children should mechanically pause and think how they feel, which can help them get in touch with their feelings. "If you make this into a habit—consciously pause and reflect—you then may automatically reach out to help those in need. Make it a habit, like memorizing multiplication tables. This can improve both human flourishing and well-being."

Singh practices EMC^2 throughout her daily life, like when she prepares dinner for her family. Cooking a meal focuses her on being in-the-moment. Further, meal preparation is an empathetic and compassionate act, as she must consider the feelings of those who will be eating. Critical inquiry is the cognition required during food preparation.

She also practices the framework at academic conferences. She asks audiences, "When your child comes home, will you ask, 'What marks did you get on your math or English test?'" Then she switches the paradigm: "Wouldn't it be nice if we moved to a time when your child came home and instead you asked, 'How many people did you help today?' That might be easier for the child to answer. Helping others is a natural trait; you don't even have to teach it. Whereas getting marks on an exam is an effort and is dependent on the instruction they get, asking if they helped anyone today puts no pressure on the child. Not everyone in the audience agrees with me. But I hope to increase that little by little."

Prosociality and the Greater Good

"A prosocial world is all about relationships—generosity, altruism, gratitude, and relationship-building skills," Vicki Zakrzewski began. Zakrzewski is the education director for Greater Good in Education (GGIE). "We believe that starts with the individual, cultivating their prosocial qualities. Based on our deep dive into the research, character education gives a sense of ethics. What are we working toward? SEL helps put ethics into action."

Housed at the University of California, Berkeley, GGIE is part of the Greater Good Science Center. Its curricular focus is on building a kinder and more compassionate world through prosocial action, making it a perfect complement to frameworks like CASEL's and EMC².

The GGIE website is a treasure trove of activities, articles, and professional development for educators. There are resources on student and teacher well-being and tools for school leaders. What's more, all of the EASEL Lab's SEL Kernels and Brain Games are on the site!

GGIE's resources (https://ggie.berkeley.edu/practices) align with CASEL's SEL Framework but also with frameworks that include mindfulness and character education competencies. "We have the advantage of coming at SEL from research, and we have a bird's eye view of everything, to see how all of the pieces fit together," Zakrzewski continued. "We call it SEL+."

Early childhood SEL lessons tend to be about labeling and identifying feelings and ways of managing emotions. "We know from research that the younger years are when to teach about emotions. At early ages, emotions are identified so children can then think about what is an appropriate display. How do you resolve conflicts? How do you deal with negative thinking and negative thoughts you may have about yourself?"

Kindness Buddy is an example of an early childhood guided activity with steps and reflective questions. Developed by The Inner Resilience Program, children pick a buddy and then perform a kind act. After, everyone stands in a circle. They then take a ball of yarn and lightly wrap it around their wrists. After sharing their act of kindness, the ball of yarn is tossed to the next child in the circle. In the end, a web of kindness is constructed.

In middle school, there is a developmental shift, particularly in ethical and moral development. "That's where kids start to question the rules," Zakrzewski remarked. "In early grades, children follow what the teacher says. In middle school, they suddenly wake up and realize that these rules are arbitrary, that adults made them up. Children question, 'Why do these rules exist?'"

Middle school-aged children's SEL needs are more about the *whys* of the world. Children can be asked, "What is the difference between a rule and something harmful?" This question can connect to ideas around civil disobedience. For example, Mahatma Gandhi and Martin Luther King, Jr. challenged unjust laws. Civil rights icon John Lewis famously called this "good trouble"—law-breaking that is necessary to advance human rights.

The middle school lesson *People Who Made a Difference* aligns to these ideas. In this activity, students study historical figures who positively contributed to the world. After conducting and reporting research, students are asked to take part in a gratitude and mindfulness lesson where they express appreciation toward the person they studied. *Gratitude for Our Food* is another prosocial lesson. For middle school, students look backward in the food chain to consider all people who made efforts to get food to their table.

Developmentally, things change for older children. "Standalone SEL programs don't always work well in high school—kids can become cynical," Zakrzewski said. "Their job is to develop an identity, a sense of themselves, a sense of purpose. If you are going to teach SEL to high schoolers, it needs to be in the context of their lives."

GGIE's activities for high school children reflect this developmental shift. One such activity is *Encouraging Prosocial Actions in Students*, a self-study for teenagers that harness youth idealism. Students first consider and identify their values, which is guided by a handout. Next, they plan and follow through with a kind act, such as volunteering, donating blood, books, or clothes, or comforting those in need.

Earthrise: Bearing Witness to Our Planet is another high school lesson. In this activity, students learn about the famous Earthrise photograph from 1968, the image astronauts took of Earth from the lunar surface. Prosocial outcomes include fostering awe, bearing witness to the planet, being a global citizen, and having reverence for the earth.

Educators should take advantage of the resources on GGIE as they put SEL skills into action. What's more, the lessons are modular, remixable, and align to content. As a result, teachers can provide opportunities for students to practice SEL competencies in authentic and meaningful ways.

Links, Lessons, and Games

Building Social Skills with Books, lessons that align reading to CASEL's SEL Framework: https://education.byu.edu/buildingsocialskills

CASEL: https://casel.org

Centervention's SEL games and curriculum, including *Zoo U* for grades 2-4 and *Hall of Heroes* for middle school-aged children: https://www.centervention.com/social-emotional-learning-curriculum

EASEL Lab: https://easel.gse.harvard.edu

Earthrise: Bearing Witness to Our Planet lesson: https://ggie.berkeley.edu/practice/earthrise-photograph-bearing-witness-to-our-planet

Edutopia and SEL: https://www.edutopia.org/social-emotional-learning

Encouraging Prosocial Actions in Students lesson: https://ggie.berkeley.edu/practice/encouraging-prosocial-actions-in-students

Explore SEL: http://exploresel.gse.harvard.edu

Greater Good in Education: https://ggie.berkeley.edu

Kindness Buddy lesson: https://ggie.berkeley.edu/practice/kindness-buddy

People Who Made a Difference lesson: https://ggie.berkeley.edu/practice/people-who-made-a-difference

Rethinking Learning: A Review of Social and Emotional Learning for Education Systems, by UNESCO MGIEP: https://mgiep.unesco.org/rethinking-learning

SEL Kernels and Brain Games, from the EASEL Lab: https://ggie.berkeley.edu/wp-content/uploads/2020/02/Core_Kernel_Pack.pdf

Stop-Signal-Task: https://www.cambridgecognition.com/cantab/cognitive-tests/memory/stop-signal-task-sst

Stroop Test: https://www.math.unt.edu/~tam/SelfTests/StroopEffects.html

TeachSDGs: http://www.teachsdgs.org

UNESCO MGIEP: https://mgiep.unesco.org

World's Largest Lesson: https://worldslargestlesson.globalgoals.org

References

Aronica, L., & Robinson, K. (2009). *The element: How finding your passion changes everything*. Penguin.

Baker-Doyle, K. (2017). *Transformative teachers: Teacher leadership and earning in a connected world*. Harvard Education Press.

Berg, J., Osher, D., Same, M. R., Nolan, E., Benson, D., & Jacobs, N. (2017). *Identifying, defining, and measuring social and emotional competencies: Final report*. American Institutes for Research.

Brackett, M. A., Elbertson, N. A., & Rivers, S. E. (2015). Applying theory to the development of approaches to SEL. In J. A. Durlak, C. E. Domitrovich, R. P. Weissberg, & T. P. Gullotta (Eds.), *Handbook of social and emotional learning: Research and practice* (pp. 20–32). Guilford Press.

Breithaupt, F. (2019). *The dark sides of empathy*. Cornell University Press.

Bronfenbrenner, U. (2006). *The ecology of human development*. Harvard University Press (Original work published 1979).

Camangian, P., & Cariaga, S. (2021). Social and emotional learning is hegemonic miseducation: Students deserve humanization instead. *Race, Ethnicity and Education*, 1-21. https://doi.org/10.1080/13613324.2020.1798374

Carr, L., Iacoboni, M., Dubeau, M., Mazziotta, J. C., & Lenzi, G. L. (2003). Neural mechanisms of empathy in humans: A relay from neural systems for imitation to limbic areas. *Proceedings of the National Academy of Sciences of the United States of America, 100*(9), 5497–5502. doi:10.1073/pnas.0935845100.

CASEL (2020). *CASEL*. https://casel.org/

CASEL Milestones. (2020). *CASEL*. https://casel.org/casels-20-year-timeline/

CASEL's SEL Framework. (2020). *CASEL*. https://casel.org/wpcontent/uploads/2020/10/CASEL-SEL-Framework-10.2020-1.pdf

Davidson, R. J., Kabat-Zinn, J., Schumacher, J., Rosencranz, M., Muller, D., Santorelli, S. F., ... Sheridan, J. F. (2003). Alterations in brain and immune function produced by mindfulness meditation. *Psychosomatic Medicine, 65*, 564–570.

Delalande, L., Moyon, M., Tissier, C., Dorriere, V., Guillois, B., Mevell, K., ... Borst, G. (2019). Complex and subtle structural changes in prefrontal cortex induced by inhibitory control training from childhood to adolescence. *Developmental Science*, e12898. doi:10.1111/desc.12898.

Durlak, J. A., Weissberg, R. P., Dymnicki, A., Taylor, R. D., & Schellinger, K. B. (2011). The impact of enhancing students' social and emotional learning: A meta-analysis of school-based universal interventions. *Child Development, 82*, 405–432.

Elias, M. J., Zins, J. E., & Weissberg, R. P. (1997). *Promoting social and emotional learning: Guidelines for educators*. ASCD.

Essential Facts. (2021). *Entertainment software association*. https://www.theesa.com/esa-research/2020-essential-facts-about-the-video-game-industry/

Explore SEL. (2020). *EASEL Lab*. http://exploresel.gse.harvard.edu

Farber, M., & Merchant, W. (2020, November 19). *Measuring social emotional learning: What happens when things don't align?* 2020 National Council of Teachers of English Virtual Annual Convention. http://convention.ncte.org/2020-virtual-convention/general-info/program/

Farber, M., & Rivers, S. (2020). *Leveraging technology for SEL programmes*. In N. Chatterjee, A. Duraiappah, & R. Ramaswamy (Eds.), *Rethinking learning: A review of social and emotional learning for education systems*. UNESCO MGIEP.

Finn, C. E., & Hess, F. M. (2019, April). *What social and emotional learning needs to succeed and survive*. American Enterprise Institute.

Framework for 21st Century Learning. (2020). *Battelle for Kids*. http://www.battelleforkids.org/networks/p21

GOLD Teaching Strategies. (n.d.). *Teaching strategies*. https://teachingstrategies.com/solutions/assess/gold/

Goleman, D. (1995). *Emotional intelligence: Why it can matter more than IQ*. Bantam.

Habib, M., Borst, G., Poirel, N., Houdé, O., Moutier, S., & Cassotti, M. (2015). Socio-emotional context and adolescents' decision making: The experience of regret and relief after social comparison. *Journal of Research on Adolescence, 25*, 81–91.

Hodent, C. (2017). *The gamer's brain: How neuroscience and UX can impact video game design*. CRC Press.

Horowitz, J. M., & Graf, N. (2019). Most U.S. teens see anxiety and depression as a major problem among their peers. *Pew Research Center*. https://www.pewsocialtrends.org/2019/02/20/most-u-s-teens-see-anxiety-and-depression-as-a-major-problem-among-their-peers/

Iacoboni, M. (2009). Imitation, empathy, and mirror neurons. *Annual Review of Psychology, 60*(1), 653–670. doi:10.1146/annurev.psych.60.110707.163604.

Jazaieri, H., McGonigal, K., Jinpa, T., Doty, J. R., Gross, J. J., & Goldin, P. R. (2014). A randomized controlled trial of compassion cultivation training: Effects on mindfulness, affect, and emotion regulation. *Motivation and Emotion, 38*(1), 23–35. doi:10.1007/s11031-013-9368-z.

Jones, S., Bailey, R., Brush, K., Nelson, B., & Barnes, S. (2016). What is the same and what is different? Making sense of the "non-cognitive" 1 domain: Helping educators translate research into practice. *Harvard Graduate School of Education*. https://easel.gse.harvard.edu/files/gse-easel-lab/files/words_matter_paper.pdf

Kidd, D. C., & Castano, E. (2013). Reading literary fiction improves theory of mind. *Science (American Association for the Advancement of Science), 342*(6156), 377-380. https://doi.org/10.1126/science.1239918

Kral, T. R. A., Stodola, D. E., Birn, R. M., Mumford, J. A., Solis, E., Flook, L., ... Davidson, R. J. (2018). Neural correlates of video game empathy training in adolescents: A randomized trial. *NPJ Science of Learning, 3*(1), 13–10. doi:10.1038/s41539-018-0029-6.

Mahoney, J. L., Weissberg, R. P., Greenberg, M. T., Dusenbury, L., Jagers, R. J., Niemi, K., Schlinger, M., Schlund, J., Shriver, T. P., VanAusdal, K., & Yoder, N. (2020, October 8). Systemic Social and Emotional Learning: Promoting Educational Success for All Preschool to High School Students. *American Psychologist*.

Mirra, N. (2018). *Educating for empathy: Literacy learning and civic engagement*. Teachers College Press.

Moffitt, T. E., Arseneault, L., Belsky, D., Dickson, N., Hancox, R. J., Harrington, H., ... Sears, M. R. (2011). A gradient of childhood self-control predicts health, wealth, and public safety. *Proceedings of the National Academy of Sciences, 108*(7), 2693–2698.

Niemi, K. (2020, December 15). CASEL is updating the most widely recognized definition of social-emotional learning. Here's why. *The 74.* https://www.the74million.org/article/niemi-casel-is-updating-the-most-widely-recognized-definition-of-social-emotional-learning-heres-why/

PATHS Curriculum. (2012). *PATHS training.* http://www.pathstraining.com/main/

Patsenko, E. G., Adluru, N., & Birn, R. M. (2019). Mindfulness video game improves connectivity of the fronto-parietal attentional network in adolescents: A multi-modal imaging study. *Scientific Reports, 9,* 18667 (2019). doi:10.1038/s41598-019-53393-x.

Peel, J. (2020, October 30). Among us works because it's a board game in disguise. *PC Gamer.* https://www.pcgamer.com/among-us-works-because-its-a-board-game-in-disguise/

Rafalow, M. H. (2018). *Status: Developing social and cultural capital.* In M. Ito, C. Martin, R. C. Pfister, M. H. Rafalow, & K. Salen (Eds.), *Affinity online: How connection and shared interest fuel learning* (pp. 82–122). NYU Press.

Rogers, F. M., & Head, B. (1983). *Mister Rogers talks with parents.* Family Communications, Inc.

Shafer, L. (2016, August 29). Fun and (brain) games. *Usable knowledge.* https://www.gse.harvard.edu/news/uk/16/08/fun-and-brain-games

Shriver, T. P., & Weissberg, R. P. (2020, March 26). A response to constructive criticism of social and emotional learning. *Phi Beta Kappan.* https://kappanonline.org/response-constructive-criticism-social-emotional-learning-sel-shriver-weissberg/

Simmons, D. (2021, March). Why SEL alone isn't enough. *Educational Leadership, 78*(6), 30–34.

Singh, N. C., & Duraiappah, A. (2019). *EMC2: A "whole brain" framework for social and emotional learning—the key to human flourishing.* UNESCO MGIEP.

Singh, N. C., & Duraiappah, A. (Eds.) (2020). *Rethinking learning: A review of social and emotional learning frameworks for education systems.* UNESCO MGIEP.

Tate, E. (2019, May 7). Why social-emotional learning is suddenly in the spotlight. *EdSurge.* https://www.edsurge.com/news/2019-05-07-why-social-emotional-learning-is-suddenly-in-the-spotlight

UNESCO MGIEP. (2020). *UNESCO MGIEP.* https://mgiep.unesco.org

Wagner, T. (2014). *The global achievement gap: Why even our best schools don't teach the new survival skills our children need and what we can do about it.* Basic Books.

Wagner, T., & Dintersmith, T. (2015). *Most likely to succeed: Preparing our kids for the innovation era.* Scribner.

Weissberg, R. P., Caplan, M. Z., & Bennetto, L. (1988). *The Yale-New Haven middle school social problem solving (SPS) program.* Yale University.

Zhou, Y. (2020, April 27). Another education war? The coming debates over social and emotional learning. *Phi Beta Kappan.* https://kappanonline.org/another-education-war-social-emotional-learning-debates-zhao/

CHAPTER THREE

How Games Give Players "The Feels"

There is a kind of magic in watching children play *Candy Land*. A classic board game set on a winding path through the Peppermint Forest, the goal is to be the first player to reach King Kandy's Castle. The instructions are straightforward: Flip a card and move your token to the next space that matches that card's color.

During play, children learn the basics of turn-taking, self-regulation, impulsivity control, and goal-setting. The lack of written text and ease of rules means that parental supervision is often unnecessary. Some young players construct stories set in the game's toothsome world.

Although youngsters may revel in the colorful gameboard, *Candy Land* can be tedious for older kids and parents. Moving along a track by matching colors can be maddingly monotonous. Further, *Candy Land* lacks a leveled increase of challenge—it is as easy to play at the Lagoon of Lord Licorice as it is at Princess Frostine's Ice Palace.

Most games challenge players continually. Strategy games like *Chess* become more difficult as players move pieces. *Super Mario Bros.* adds more enemies through game levels. *A Theory of Fun for Game Design* author Raph Koster was one of the first to identify how level design in games happens to align with the zone of proximal development (Koster, 2005/2014). The zone of proximal development describes where learning is "matched in some manner to the child's developmental level" (Vygotsky, 1978, p. 85). Koster (2005/2014) also wrote that fun ceases for players—and learners—once mastery is attained.

As it happened, *Candy Land* was not designed to bore parents or irritate dentists. Prototyped on butcher block paper in 1949, retired teacher Eleanor Abbott made *Candy Land* while recovering from polio. Back then, polio was an incurable and highly infectious disease that threatened paralysis to anyone who caught it. Abbott saw *Candy Land* as a way to engender freedom to children who were restricted from playing outside (Joy, 2019; Kawash, 2010). Early editions of the game featured an illustration on the box "of a boy with lines on his legs that suggest the leg braces common to victims of the disease" (Kawash, 2010, p. 191).

In the late 1940s, there were few games made expressly for children. Thus, board games became a safe-at-home activity, away from swimming pools and ice cream parlors—public areas where polio was feared to spread (Kawash, 2010). With Abbott's game, children could now play together *without* adults. After she sold the game to Milton Bradley, millions of parents purchased copies for their children. Decades later, the game remains a household staple.

As I write this, history has repeated itself. In early 2020, the COVID-19 pandemic spread. Once again, children and grown-ups were locked indoors. But, while being physically distant, there was no need to be socially distant. To encourage people to play games online or at home while also staying safe, in the spring of 2020, the World Health Organization partnered with more than 40 game publishers to launch the #PlayApartTogether campaign.

We play games together to connect and to feel more human. Before the pandemic, playing games was already a social experience. More than half (55%) of frequent game players reported that games helped them to connect with friends and other people ("Essential Facts," 2018). At the onset of the pandemic, sales skyrocketed: consumers in the United States spent nearly $11 billion on video games in the first quarter of 2020—a new record ("Record First Quarter," 2020). The *New York Times* quickly dubbed Nintendo's social life simulator *Animal Crossing: New Horizons*, released on March 20, 2020, "the game for the coronavirus moment" (Khan, 2020, para. 1). Sales of jigsaw puzzles and board games—including the perennial classic *Candy Land*—also surged (Miller, 2020).

This chapter moves from King Kandy's Castle to Sleeping Beauty's Castle, where magic is real and imagination is limitless. As it turns out, there are many parallels between emotional experiences in good games and the mental transport afforded when we visit places like Disneyland. But first, let's explore exactly how games evoke "the feels."

Affordances and Emotions

Affordances are invitations to interact with physical or digital objects (Norman, 1988, 2013). A handle on a mug affords grasping. Chairs are shaped to invite sitting. Smartphone screens afford tapping, pinching, and swiping.

Our brains form mental models of how we expect objects to behave when we interact with affordances. For instance, as I type on my keyboard, I anticipate that text will appear on my laptop's screen. Expectations are reinforced by feedback: the sound of clicking keys, the appearance of letters and words.

Norman's (1988, 2013) definitions of affordances built on Gibson's (1977, 1979), who more generally considered how objects relate to perception. To Norman, affordances were specific to physical objects embedded with characteristics where users perceive function. For instance, when encountering a light switch, people toggle up or down. Toggling results in feedback that confirms (or denies) the user's mental model (lights go on or off).

Our mental models of affordances can sometimes be false. Norman (2013) shared an example of oven thermometers. Our mental model may assume that temperature in ovens are constant, when, in reality, heating elements go on and off, restarting when a threshold temperature is met (Norman, 2013).

Some objects do not indicate an interaction's consequence: Does one push or pull a door handle, or toggle a switch up or down? If a lavatory door has a protruding handle that affords pulling, how do we know if it is occupied? Without a clear indication, the only way to find out is through hypothesis and experimentation. Experimenting with affordances of objects in games may be fun, but not with real-world objects like bathroom door handles! Likely, there are no treasure chests of coins to be found in public lavatories. Therefore, *signifiers* may be needed on or near objects to guide use (Norman, 1988, 2013). In bathrooms, signifiers may also be color-coded; when locked by an occupant from the inside, a red "Occupied" sign may appear on the front of the door.

Hartson (2003) described four types of affordances as being dependent on what each accomplishes. First are physical affordances, like door handles and switches that invite pushing or pulling or toggling. Next are cognitive affordances, signs that indicate use, such as push or pull signs. Cognitive affordances are what Norman refers to as signifiers (1988, 2013). Sensory affordances are the third type, affordances that relate to perception. Font is an example, as it can be perceived as readable or legible or too small or poorly contrasted with backgrounds (Hodent, 2017). Finally, are functional affordances, when objects are used differently than how they were designed or intended (Hartson, 2003).

Objects can be designed to afford play. Sicart (2014) wrote, "Masks and disguises, merry-go-rounds, and computer controllers all point to the idea that play is possible in that context" (p. 7). Playgrounds are designed with playful affordances like slides, ropes, and swings. Holding dice affords rolling and throwing. Sometimes we can find play in everyday objects, like cups, rubber bands, and string.

Video games are often designed to provide signals and feedback to players. But sometimes affordances purposefully mislead players (Norman, 2013). This is more of an exception than rule. An example is the video game, *That Dragon, Cancer*, an empathy game about a young child with terminal cancer. In one vignette, the child is in a hospital room crying uncontrollably. In the room, players see a juice box and a stuffed animal. Interacting with these affordances fails; the child keeps crying. As a result, players feel a sense of hopelessness and despair (Tanz, 2016).

"A false affordance is when people understand a feature in a certain way intuitively, but it is not how it is used," Celia Hodent explained. Hodent is a cognitive psychology PhD and game user experience (UX) expert. "We want players to understand the affordance correctly because most of the time, we place the challenge elsewhere. But, depending on the game, it can make sense to create false affordances and mislead players by design."

Typically, there is an alignment of the functional affordances of objects in games. However, players can experience things differently than intended (Hartson, 2003; Upton, 2018). "A game may play around with people's perception," Hodent continued. "Or, in horror games, designers may want people to think something is dangerous when it's not so they can later scare them."

Regarding interacting with functional affordances, educational video games have a checkered history. Sometimes derided as chocolate-covered broccoli, in these games, learning is sugar-coated. In a chocolate-covered broccoli math game, players may be required to solve fraction problems before they can cast spells or shoot aliens. Comparatively, in a well-designed fraction game, gameplay may involve slicing blocks into smaller units. In this hypothetical "balanced design" game, player actions are aligned with learning goals—players learn about fractions by making fractions (Groff et al., 2015, p. 5).

"Game Feel"

Many video games embed discovery, novelty, and surprise in design to elicit emotions from players (Hodent, 2017). Lootboxes—prize crates that contain secrets—are an example. In video games, opening a lootbox is not like clicking a folder icon to retrieve a Word document file. Playful, these interactions are often pleasant, fun, and satisfying (Hodent, 2017).

Let's look at the lootbox in the massively popular game *Fortnite*. Instead of crates or treasure chests, players encounter llama piñatas. Yes, llama piñatas. Animated and interactive, their eyes move, gazing at the player's avatar. When the player hits the llama piñatas, there is a colorful reaction, replete with sounds and fanfare.

Celia Hodent helped design *Fortnite* when she worked as director of UX at Epic Games, the game's publisher. "You hit the llama and open it up just like a piñata, which is an interaction," she explained. "That emotional interaction is 'game feel.' It is not just the affordance. You see a chest, there is an affordance, and you understand that it opens if you click it. In *Fortnite*, the interaction is more—it's fun and emotional. The llama provides a narrative."

Game feel is the emotion players have when interacting with elements in a game's system, which can deepens the emotional connections players have to the overall experience (Hodent, 2017). There are three core components, or "3 Cs," to game feel: control, character, and camera (Hodent, 2017). First, let's discuss control in games. Control is important because it affects how players feel when moving through game environments (Hodent, 2017). In a first-person shooter game-like *Call of Duty*, players become intimately involved with how sensitive thumbsticks are when aiming weapons at enemies. Because of this, players need to sense that they are in control of characters. What happens when players release their finger while an avatar is running? Does that character come to a full stop? When that character jumps, what is the inertia in the animation? Is there leeway for players who make mistakes by consistently jumping too high or running too far? "Some players might overshoot or stop short, which doesn't feel good," Hodent said. "In the AAA industry [big-budget game publishing], there is a lot of work to nail those controls."

The next C is character, which includes avatars that players control, as well as the non-playable, computer-controlled characters (Hodent, 2017). If a character is supposed to be fast, it should look wiry or bouncy, like Sonic the Hedgehog. If a game has a monster, it should look scary, or at least dangerous (Hodent, 2017). *Nightmare: Malaria* is an example of a game with a social message about the need for mosquito netting for malaria prevention. The mosquito in the game is giant and terrifying, signaling danger to players. *Sea of Solitude* is another game where character design affords attributes to players. Filled with metaphors, a scary sea monster represents the protagonist's overbearing mother.

Design decisions are made when considering how control and character intersect to evoke game feel (Hodent, 2017). The controls in *Sea of Solitude* can feel stiff and constrained, likely symbolizing emotional obstacles the main character can't quite overcome. "A lot of platformers have what we call *coyote time*, where you can run beyond the platform but still be able to press to jump," Hodent said. "You have some space to make mistakes midair after overrunning," ("Coyote time" refers to Road Runner cartoon nemesis Wile E. Coyote, who often overran ledges of cliffs and mesas.)

Camera is the third C, describing players' emotions relating to visual perspectives (Hodent, 2017). "In a strategy game, you usually have a top-down camera with a larger view so that you can think about strategy," Hodent explained. "If you want to make a scary game, you might have a first-person camera to restrict field-of-view. All of that is going to have an impact on the way the player feels playing a game."

Chess and *Civilization* have a top-down camera. Many other games utilize a third-person or over-the-shoulder view, where players see their avatars throughout the experience. *Tomb Raider* and *Assassin's Creed* games are examples. By default, the building block game *Minecraft* uses a first-person perspective. *Fortnite* is usually played with a third-person camera. In addition to its shooter gameplay, part of the game's aesthetic appeal is the ability to change avatar costumes, or skins. Skins have a lot to do with player autonomy, which is part of self-determination theory (Ryan & Deci, 2018). "It is meaningful at the player's level to feel autonomy, but also meaningful at the relatedness level because other people see you being cool," Hodent remarked. "It's like fashion. It speaks to what you care about, your in-group, who you are rooting for in football. Teenagers care a lot about being part of a group, and *Fortnite* offers a space to do that." In *Fortnite*, children "learn to negotiate conflict, become independent, and explore what kind of person they want to be" (Squire & Gaydos, 2018, para. 5).

Dancing is a big part of *Fortnite*'s ecosystem. Hence, dance moves are in third-person camera, enabling players to see their character floss or breakdance. "If a game has a first-person camera, it would not be as meaningful to have different skins and dance moves," Hodent continued. "All of these elements need to interact with each other."

Games like *Fortnite*, *Overwatch*, and *Minecraft* have "emotes," brief animations—including dance moves, hi-fives, and hand waves—to convey character emotion. In *Super Mario Odyssey*, Mario emotes by spinning and backflipping midair when he jumps (Hodent, 2017). *Animal Crossing: New Horizons* embeds emotes as part of gameplay. As players proceed, they unlock "reactions." Reactions include joy, delight, and surprise, which can be selected when encountering villagers.

Emotes and reactions create bonds between players and games. But when games are in the first-person camera, it can present challenges to game feel. To ameliorate this, some games switch perspective. In *Overwatch*, when an emote plays, "the camera transitions to a third-person view, so you can see yourself being cool," Hodent said. "In *Overwatch*, as well as *Fortnite*, not only can you see yourself being cool, but others see you being cool."

The perspective of the camera is, of course, a primary convention of cinema. In the medium of film, seeing characters onscreen creates an invisible line, or "demarcation" (Murray, 2017, p. 147), bordering viewers from the experience. The first video game with a player-controlled camera was *Super Mario 64*. Designer Shigeru Miyamoto proposed that Lakitu, the character who rides a floating cloud, is following Mario, filming him the entire time. In other words, the camera would not be some random point in space; instead, it would mimic an actual camera. "Miyamoto's main point was that the camera was like another character," game designer Scott Rogers told me. Rogers also wrote about the 3 Cs in his book *Level Up: The Guide to Great Video Game Design* (2014). "The conceit was, 'The player won't see Lakitu the entire time, but he is filming you.' To me, that's a wonderful analogy because that is what a cinematic camera does." (I told my son this when he played a re-release of *Super Mario 64*. "When Lakitu appears on screen holding a camera, who is filming him?" he asked.)

Players may be less likely to perspective-take when in the first-person view as their game and real life identities blur (Darvasi, 2016)—what Gee (2007) calls the *hybrid identity* between player and avatar. To what extent does camera affect our ability to perspective-take? Aïete et al. (2016) designed a task where participants had to decide whether they thought an avatar was holding an object with the right or left hand. "We looked at whether participants could take a third-person perspective and whether they could control their egocentric bias," study co-author Grégoire Borst explained. Borst is a developmental psychology and cognitive neuroscience professor at Paris Descartes University. "We created a specific behavioral paradigm to ask people to go from a front-facing to back-facing avatar. We observed the cognitive costs from going from one to the other."

Findings suggest that player perspective matters. From childhood to adulthood, the ability to perspective-take was, in part, found to be related to the ability to control egocentric biases (Aïete et al., 2016). "We tend to respond from a first-person perspective, but sometimes we need to take a third-person perspective," Borst said. "In other words, you need to control your own biases to understand someone else's emotions."

"Where Special Rules Obtain"

I live in Disneyland. Okay, not literally. Actually, I live in Fort Collins, Colorado. Disney fans might recognize Fort Collins as the birthplace of Harper Goff, designer of Main Street, U.S.A., the first of many themed lands at Disneyland. As the story goes, in the 1950s, Walt Disney asked Goff to design an idealized version of his hometown of Marceline, Missouri. When he did, Goff discovered that Marceline—at least how Walt remembered it—changed considerably. So, Goff decided to revisit his hometown and photograph buildings in the Old Town district, including the bank, firehouse, cinema, and city hall—all of which were replicated in Disneyland ("Old Town," n.d.).

Before entering Disneyland's Main Street, U.S.A., guests pass a plaque that reads, "Here you leave today and enter the world of yesterday, tomorrow and fantasy." The engraving asks guests to willingly suspend disbelief, a concept first proposed by poet Samuel Taylor Coleridge in 1817. Like visiting Mister Rogers's Neighborhood of Make-Believe, when Disneyland guests read this plaque, they are magically transported to a faraway place. (Interestingly, there is a trolley in both the Neighborhood of Make-Believe and Main Street, U.S.A. Each were idealized versions of their respective creator's childhood hometowns.)

Mental transport can take place when visiting theme parks or when we interact with media. At the movies and in immersive video games, we believe that superheroes are real and that good triumphs over evil. In academic literature, the feeling of immersion into fictional worlds is known as *transportation theory* (Gerrig, 1993; Gerrig & Prentice, 1991). Transportation theory can depend more on a narrative's strength than elaborate set pieces (Murphy et al., 2011). Samuel Beckett's *Waiting for Godot* (1953) is often staged with few props; sometimes, just two actors with folding chairs. Beckett's script sets the sparse scene with five words: "A country road. A tree" (1953, p. 1). As audiences listen to Vladimir and Estragon's existentialist verbal sparring, they are no longer seated in a theater; they are transported to that country road. This effect is also not unique to plays; one century ago, performances of Wagner's operas were also considered immersive experiences by audiences (Vaitl et al., 1993).

The transition from going under the Disneyland Railroad train tracks to Main Street, U.S.A. embodies transportation theory. Guests are whisked from Anaheim, California to an imagined and designed experience.

Walt Disney grew frustrated with the architects who initially helped design the park because their ideas were not imaginative enough. He didn't want buildings—he wanted a massive set for an immersive experience. Walt soon turned to set designers for the type of designs he needed for Disneyland to take shape. Here is where Goff came in. A successful art director on classic Hollywood flims *Casablanca* and *20,000 Leagues Under the Sea*, Goff—like Walt—was a collector of vintage model trains. The rest is Disney history!

Disneyland is a place filled with emotions. The macabre theme of the Haunted Mansion permits us to explore mortality salience playfully. Cheating death is part of the Pirates of the Caribbean ride (Rogers, 2009). In Main Street, U.S.A., feelings of nostalgia may be evoked. Nostalgia is a powerful and complex emotion (Newman et al., 2020). When accessed daily, there can be negative effects; however, when "nostalgic memories are generated on request," it can be "predominantly positive," leading to a general sense of well-being (Newman et al., 2020, p. 325).

In addition to nostalgia, Disneyland is also the most magical place on earth. In 2018, Park et al. conducted an exploratory study on how emotions relate to locations in the park. Findings revealed "emotional hot spots" in each land—social spaces where guests gathered to share emotions (2018, p. 672). Social media analytics from 56,418 guest-shared tweets were reviewed, then text-mined for positive (n = 21,005) and negative (n = 4,500) emotive language. Common positive words included: happy/happiest, love, beautiful, thank, and fun. The word "magic" appeared in 1,069 of Disneyland guests' tweets (Park et al., 2018).

The goal of the work of Imagineers and cast members is to create the perfect guest experience. At Disneyland, park guests are more than tourists; they are actors in immersive lands (Kokai & Robson, 2019). As the legendary (and true) story goes, Italian literary theorist Umberto Eco once rode Disneyland's Jungle Cruise attraction, the boat ride through fictionalized jungles of Asia, Africa, and South America. After the ride, he stated, "Disneyland tells us that technology can give us more reality than nature can" (Eco, 1987, p. 44).

"In Disneyland, magic is real," Tracy Fullerton remarked to me. Fullerton is a game design professor who has also designed attractions for Disney Imagineering. "In Disneyland, imagination and believing in magic is valued." Once inside the park gates, all guests—not just children—are "expected to surrender to Disney's magic with childlike wonder" (Knight, 2016 as cited in Kokai & Robson, 2019, p. 8). Adults can be seen spinning in life-sized teacups, flying with Dumbo, and dodging Tie Fighters in the Millennium Falcon.

Actively taking on beliefs and arbitrary rules while in a special place is what we do when we play games. "That is one of the core similarities between Disneyland and the generic idea of a game: We are actively taking on a fantasy, a belief system, and a set of rules," Fullerton said. "Part of Disneyland's special rules is that it is okay to have pirate rides and jungle cruises close to each other. Part of the experience is that we can try on different fantasies, and we can also move on from those experiences. We leave the real-world behind and go to a place where 'special rules obtain.'"

"Special rules obtain" is a quote from philosopher Johan Huizinga, who wrote about how games transport us into a "magic circle," away from the real-world (1938/1955, p. 10). Huizinga wrote,

> The arena, the card-table, the magic circle, the temple, the stage, the screen, the tennis court, the court of justice, etc., are all in form and function playgrounds, i.e., forbidden spots, isolated, hedged round, hallowed, within which special rules obtain. All are temporary worlds within the ordinary world, dedicated to the performance of an act apart. (1938/1955, p. 10)

The magic circle in games is a fixed place; it can be a soccer field, a chessboard, a screen, or in the minds of players (Huizinga, 1938/1955; Salen & Zimmerman, 2003; Walther, 2011). In the magic circle, players are safe and free from actualizing real life "material consequences," making it a safe practice space to hypothesize and experiment (Huizinga, 1938/1955, p. 10).

Disneyland was constructed as a wheel-and-spoke system, with Sleeping Beauty's Castle at the center. Spokes from the Castle hub lead to Adventureland, Fantasyland, and Tomorrowland. Similarly, many video games use this system, transporting players to different lands. *Super Mario Galaxy* on the Nintendo Wii was set in Rosalina's Observatory, a central hub connected to kingdoms, galaxies, and worlds—each with different attributes. *Zelda: Breath of the Wild* and *Red Dead Redemption 2* have towns, camps, and villages where players craft materials, explore, and sleep. The missions or quests are typically set outside and around these bounded areas. Similarly, at Disneyland, shops and restaurants are located near Sleeping Beauty's Castle; adventures take place in the outer spokes. The social mobile game *Sky: Children of the Light* was designed using a wheel-and-spoke map, too. In this award-winning game, players can adventure together in seven explorable realms.

Disneyland is the Neighborhood of Make-Believe to the tenth power. Of course, not all theme parks are Disney parks—and not all games are *Sky: Children of the Light*. Many video games have simple maps with worlds that unlock as players progress. Similarly, some theme parks have simple maps that are rooted in a singular fantasy. For example, Knott's Berry Farm (California) is mostly set in the American West. Many more theme parks have inconsistencies, jumbles of overlapping fantasies. At Universal Studios Hollywood, Jurassic World: The Ride is located near Transformers: The Ride in the decidedly not-themed Lower Lot area.

Like video games, theme park dark ride attractions are designed experiences. Let's take the Haunted Mansion ride as an example. The adventure begins in the queue; waiting in line, guests move through a cemetery, then into the Stretching Room, a disguised loading room elevator. Many online multiplayer games have waiting rooms, too. Players of *Among Us* and *Fortnite* wait in a lobby before experiences begin.

After the Stretching Room, Haunted Mansion guests enter a Doom Buggy ride vehicle. The Doom Buggy has high-backed walls like a shell, intentionally isolating guests. The result is a limited field of vision, similar to a first-person camera in a video game. The Doom Buggy is part of a larger "Omnimover" ride system, where vehicles are pulled along a rail.

Game designer Scott Rogers is also a former Imagineer. In a talk at the 2009 Game Developer Conference, he shared lessons learned in game design from his time at Disneyland. For instance, lighting is used to encourage movement through environments in rides and games (Rogers, 2009). Rides and games may have companion narrators, too. In Doom Buggy vehicles, guests have the "Ghost Host," their personal phantom. In the *Halo* series of video games, Cortana guides Master Chief on adventures.

As Doom Buggy vehicles twist and turn, the audience's attention is focused to look at set pieces. Comparatively, in the Pirates of the Caribbean and It's a Small World dark rides, large groups of guests share a boat that is affixed to an underwater rail. "Those rides are about sensory overload, you get in the boat and get immersed in an environment," Rogers said. "In Pirates, you are in a cave filled with skeletal pirates and ships shooting at each other. You might miss the dog holding the jail key, but that doesn't matter. However, in Haunted Mansion, you won't miss the floating candle. Your attention is directed in the experience."

Many video games are designed as "on rails" controlled and curated experiences, much like theme park dark ride attractions. The narrative video games *Gone Home* and *What Remains of Edith Finch* are set in a large and empty house, with a story that is on rails. In *Gone Home*, the hub is the house's foreboding foyer and open staircase. *What Remains of Edith Finch* begins in the garage, then sprawls outward, branched like a metaphorical family tree. In both games, players freely explore houses. In doing so, they find objects in the environments, including diary entries, cassette recordings, and handwritten notes. As items are discovered, a nonlinear narrative is revealed. However, players cannot alter either games' narrative or outcome.

Can classrooms adapt a themed land or dark ride approach, where emotion and story combine to drive an experience? One approach is to wrap project-based learning in a narrative. This can be particularly effective when using inquiry as a hook, where student learning is driven by curiosity and discovery. *The Way Things Work*, a science curriculum unit at the Quest to Learn school in New York City, is an example. To "play," students are challenged to rescue Dr. Smallz, a doctor who shrunk himself while journeying into a human body. Challenges take place in game-like quests, a series of lessons that make up the larger mission, or unit (see the end of this chapter for the lessons).

Teacher John Meehan presents his lessons in nested, Disneyland-like lands. First, he creates movie trailers to pique student interest. Then he shares an interactive digital "park map," with lessons presented in themed lands (Meehan, 2019, p. 8). Instead of a straightforward unit on Ernest Hemingway or Henry David Thoreau, students enter *Dream Rush: The Race for the American Dream*. There, they see six lands to visit, including *Ernest Hemingway: The War Zone* and *Escape to Walden Pond*, each with lessons and activities created by Meehan.

When COVID-19 forced students to learn remotely, many teachers used the avatar creator Bitmoji to build virtual classrooms. My son's teacher published one for each content area, as well as a Calm Room. An SEL-aligned space, in the Calm Room, students practiced mindfulness. When they entered, they were greeted by the teacher's yoga-posed Bitmoji avatar. Once inside, there were clickable icons that led to videos on self-care and guided breathing.

Like theme parks, well-designed games are meaningful experiences for players. Theming in classrooms can also bring meaning to learning. In the next section, we explore how good games can go beyond being a series of transactions to being transformative.

Games as Curriculum

In the social deduction card game *Werewolf*, players (one or more) are randomly selected to be werewolves; the remaining players are villagers. Players close their eyes, and then peek or swap cards. When players open their eyes, they lie, bluff, and accuse each other of being the werewolf hidden amongst the villagers.

In games, players have agency to make choices and then experience consequences from those decisions (Isbister, 2016; Murray, 2017). During rounds of games like *Werewolf*, players may feel guilt, regret, joy, pride, or shame (Habib et al., 2015; Roberts et al., 2014; Treeby et al., 2016). Taking actions in *Werewolf* may enable students to feel like they are in a witch hunt—at least for a few minutes. I taught with *Werewolf* as a sort of experiential field trip in a social studies unit about the Salem Witch Trials. Students played, then I led a debrief, asking, "How did it feel to be falsely accused of being something you are not?"

Games are *interreactive* systems; when players take actions, games-as-systems change (Salen & Zimmerman, 2003; Smethurst & Craps, 2015). Moving pieces on a chessboard alters the game, thereby affecting the opponent's next move. The design grammar of games that puts these systems into motion consists of nouns and verbs (Koster, 2005/2014). The theme, or narrative wrapper, are the nouns; actions players take are the verbs (Koster, 2005/2014). In *Monopoly*, the names of properties are the nouns; building hotels and paying rent to landlords are the verbs. Some games get *reskinned*, like the many variants of *Monopoly*. Other games borrow and remix nouns and verbs. *Werewolf* and the video game *Among Us* share some of the same social deduction verbs. However, the nouns are different: Werewolves are imposters; villagers are crewmates. *Among Us* also adds in gameplay elements from *Tag* and *Hide-and-Seek*.

We design what we know, so it is not surprising that teachers often remake—or reskin—childhood perennials like *Monopoly* and *Candy Land*. One semester, a teacher preparation student shared a social studies-themed *Candy Land* remix with me. Instead of colors and candies, the board featured milestones from the Great Depression. Essentially a playable timeline, it was enjoyable to play. Board game spaces included Hoovervilles and shantytowns and it ended with Franklin D. Roosevelt's New Deal policies.

It is important to realize that not all curriculum maps to the nouns and verbs of *Candy Land*—or any game, for that matter. Not everyone thrived just because they lived through the Great Depression. Most social studies standards in the United States are written as "patriotic, triumphalist rhetoric," which implies that we are all better now than we were then (Mirra, 2018, p. 5). Historically, that triumphant march has been inequitable for many. For instance, when Black American veterans returned home from World War II, they received fewer G.I. Bill benefits than others (Blakemore, 2019). Progress for some, institutional and systemic setbacks for others.

Let's look at another reskinned track game, *Go Goals!*, free from the United Nations. Printable, it is available in multiple languages (https://go-goals.org). The gameplay is strikingly similar to *Snakes and Ladders*; however, the nouns were changed to be about the Sustainable Development Goals (SDGs), global priorities on quality education, gender equality, climate action, zero hunger, and clean water and sanitation. Board game spaces feature multiple-choice questions about the different SDGs. Roll the dice, then move that number of spaces on the board. The track ends at 2030, the year when SDGs should be met.

Does answering questions and moving along a track teach how to eradicate poverty or reduce inequities? Do we simply need to make it to 2030 to win? What if the verbs of track games were "hacked" or altered to align gameplay with learning outcomes or player emotions? In 2017, two of my students did just that. For a class project, they designed *Immigrants and Border Patrol*. Unlike *Candy Land* or *Go Goals!*, there is no end to the track; instead, it loops (see Figure 5). Rather than messaging progress, students used the game's board to model a broken system.

This game—designed by two 12-year-olds—has different goals for each player. The border patrol's objective is to catch the undocumented immigrant player by landing on their space. The undocumented immigrant player tries to avoid the other player while crossing to the other side of the board. Some spaces

Figure 5. Youth-designed *Immigrants and Border Patrol* Track Game. Source: Author.

had Fact Cards on them, which shared real immigrant stories. One read, "My parents emigrated to France from the West African island of Cape Verde, then later moved to Brooklyn" (Farber, 2017, para. 1). When landing on these spaces, players are instructed to read the Fact Cards out loud to the group.

Immigrants and Border Patrol's looped track restricted player movement—the border patrol almost always "catches" the other player. When this happens, neither player wins or loses. Instead, the rules require players to restart; the cycle simply continues. Thus, players of *Immigrants and Border Patrol* may end the experience feeling hopeless. There must be a better system. Maybe criminalizing undocumented immigrants isn't such a good idea.

Fun is not the antithesis of learning, nor is play. When teaching, it is key to align student activities with lesson objectives. This approach is true for games as well as pedagogical practices.

From Mechanics to Meaningful Situations

Some games use mechanics, or verbs, as symbolic metaphors to create meaning. For example, *Loneliness* is a game where players move a small square around a screen as other squares nearby react by scattering away. These interactions evoke feelings of loneliness and exclusion.

The Mechanics, Dynamics, Aesthetics (MDA) Framework (Hunicke et al., 2004) is a transactional, or cybernetic, game design framework. Fundamental is that games are systems, two-way interactions between game and player. The system starts when players interact with mechanics. Player interaction with systems then evokes emotions (Hunicke et al., 2004).

In the MDA Framework, mechanics refer to all of the component pieces of games, the tangible pieces, digital objects, and rulesets. Often, game designers speak about a game's *core mechanics*. These are different; core mechanics describe repeated loops of player action, like bluffing, guessing, or shooting.

Let's analyze *Werewolf* through the MDA Framework, a game where villagers try to root out the werewolf (or werewolves) hidden among a group of players. In *Werewolf*, the mechanics are the components—in this case, the role cards (villagers, werewolves) and the rules. Taking on roles and following rules creates the game's dynamic system. Players then sensate emotions as they lie, guess, and bluff in each round.

The party game *Happy Salmon* can also be analyzed through the MDA Framework. Each player's objective is to get rid of a deck of cards by matching theirs with other players' cards. The action of matching is done out loud while standing in a circle. Cards, which are the components, have actions written on them. "Pound-it" means that players fist bump; "Switcheroo" indicates that players need to switch standing positions. Shouting creates the game's manic dynamic system, which often results in players feeling happy.

Is there a recipe of component ingredients that will create emotions in dynamic systems? Just like learning is more than the input and output of knowledge, games are more than mechanics and systems. Cybernetic frameworks like MDA may oversimplify how design and emotion interplay. Game designer Eric Zimmerman once remarked that thinking about games in terms of parts is akin to thinking about food only in its nutritive sense, ignoring the aesthetic experience of enjoying cuisine (Zimmerman, 2019, 8:41). Gameplay, and learning, is not a series of transactional acts. Game design, and teaching, is an art.

"Games, by their nature, problematize things," Tracy Fullerton told me. In addition to teaching at the University of Southern California, she has also created several games for learning. "The creation of play is slippage in a system. Games do not lead you directly to learning—*on purpose*. They take an inefficient playful route to get to the learning. And that *is* the learning. We need to acknowledge that games' benefits are often the opposite of what most learning games specialists think the benefits of games are."

It is foolhardy to assume that players will "learn" because they clicked the right buttons or pulled the correct levers. We need to start thinking about games as experiences and situations, not as vending machines that dispense knowledge and skills.

At the 2019 Connected Learning Summit, Fullerton spoke about her game, *Walden, a game*, and how it was built around situations, not choices. A slow-paced experience about exploration and discovery, players become Henry David Thoreau at Walden Pond. The decisions players make do not always have immediate consequences.

Sid Meier—designer of *Civilization* and other world-building games—famously and succinctly defined games as a "series of interesting choices" (Meier, 2012 as cited in Isbister, 2016, p. 2). In her Connected Learning talk, Fullerton modified Meier's definition. Hers was based on Brian Upton's (2018) *situational game design* framework, "a methodology that takes into account how play unfolds when the player either isn't interacting or isn't trying to win" (p. 5). Games, Fullerton surmised, "were a series of meaningful situations" (2019, 32:06).

Of course, there are emotions from making choices in games. But there are also emotions that are evoked from the situations that lead up to those choices (Upton, 2018). In a 1994 interview, Fred Rogers said, "The white spaces between words are more important than the text because they give you time to think about what you've read" (Rogers, 1994 as cited in King, 2018, p. 314). Situational game design is similar because it is about players' attitudes *between* interactions (see Figure 6). Through a situational game design lens, there are heuristics in players' minds about the uncertainty of what may or may not happen next. Upton (2018) refers to these as *passive constraints* and *anticipatory play*.

It is much easier to extract student mastery of game mechanics in balanced games, especially when player actions are aligned to learning goals. In a hypothetical math game, if players slice enough objects to move from level one to level two, the implication is that they have mastered fractions. Games like these can report

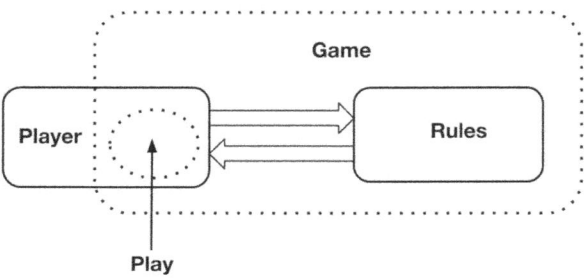

Figure 6. Situational Game Design. Source: Brian Upton. Reprinted by permission of the author.

psychometrics on teacher dashboards. Situational games are different, as some of the action occurs in players' minds.

Working with UNESCO MGIEP, we applied a situational game design framework to inform our study of the interactive fiction game *Bury Me, My Love*. The narrative is about Nour, a refugee trying to find her way from Syria to Europe. On behalf of her husband, Majd, the player chooses replies from a chat-based interface where texting options are presented. It can be an intensely emotional experience for players to speak with Nour as she faces various obstacles and has a lot of doubts in her journey.

Bury Me, My Love was designed to be played in real-time to mimic the anxiety of waiting for responses. Anticipatory play occurs in these moments, the expectant pauses when players think and contemplate before considering which responses to make. In our pilot study, instead of aggregating tallies about choices players made, we used pre- and post-test questionnaires. Our goal was to understand changes relating to content knowledge and empathic concern from participants.

I asked Fullerton to share a personal moment of situational gameplay with me. Without hesitation, she replied, "To me, *Journey* is the ultimate example of a situational game." Developed by thatgamecompany, a studio led by her former MFA student Jenova Chen, *Journey* was published in 2012 and won BAFTA, Games for Change, and Game Developers Choice awards. Mapped to Joseph Campbell's (1949/2008) hero's journey cycle, players join online strangers (who cannot speak) on a quest. *Journey* happened to be the example Upton (2018) used in his situational game design book. The game's image also adorns the front cover of Isbister's 2016 book, *How Games Move Us: Emotion by Design*.

There are, of course, game mechanics in *Journey*; players can run and fly and interact online with other players. "But it is how we feel about those mechanics, and how we interpret every situation we are in," Fullerton remarked. "That is what makes that game so special. It isn't that there is a flying mechanic. It isn't that there is another person there. What makes it powerful is how we feel about all of it."

Fullerton shared an anecdote about crossing a bridge with an in-game companion. During play, the other online player suddenly disappeared from the experience. "The wind blew my companion off, but I stayed on," Fullerton recalled. Did the other player die in the game? Was there an internet connection break? "I looked for ways to get down to help or save this person. I didn't hear her cry back; I only heard the wind. I will never know, and I've lost her forever. The only thing I can do is go onward. With the heaviest heart, I decided to cross the bridge and leave."

None of that happened, except in Fullerton's mind. Feelings of companionship were based on Fullerton's in-game situation, not from interacting with mechanical affordances. By the absence of design, by adding some risks, and by a situation put together by the other online person, the overall experience evoked an array of emotions. "This was one of the most powerful and minimal situations I have ever experienced in any form of media," Fullerton concluded. "And I will remember it always."

Links, Lessons, and Games

Among Us: http://www.innersloth.com/gameAmongUs.php
Bury Me, My Love: http://burymemylove.arte.tv
Bury Me, My Love: Identity in Crisis, UNESCO MGIEP's game-based course: https://framerspace.com/course/bmml
Educators Turn to Bitmoji to Build Community and Engagement, on Edutopia: https://www.edutopia.org/article/educators-turn-bitmoji-build-community-and-engagement
Everything I Learned About Level Design I Learned from Disneyland, from Scott Rogers: https://gdcvault.com/play/1305/Everything-I-Learned-About-Level
Gone Home: https://gonehome.game
Journey: https://thatgamecompany.com/journey
Loneliness: https://www.necessarygames.com/my-games/loneliness/flash
Parents' Guide to Among Us: https://apps.apple.com/us/story/id1537448803
Reactions and Emotes in *Animal Crossing: New Horizons*: https://animalcrossingworld.com/guides/new-horizons/reactions-emotes-how-to-unlock-complete-list-by-personality
Sea of Solitude: https://www.ea.com/games/sea-of-solitude
Sky: Children of the Light: https://thatskygame.com
Werewolf: https://beziergames.com/products/one-night-ultimate-werewolf
That Dragon, Cancer: http://www.thatdragoncancer.com
Quest to Learn's game-like learning curriculum, developed by the Institute of Play, including *The Way Things Work*, Dr. Smallz's mission: https://clalliance.org/institute-of-play
Understanding the Success of Fortnite: A UX & Psychology Perspective, by Celia Hodent: https://celiahodent.com/understanding-the-success-of-fortnite-ux

References

Aïte, A., Berthoz, A., Vidal, J., Roell, M., Zaoui, M., Houdé, O., … Borst, G. (2016). Taking a third-person perspective requires inhibitory control: Evidence from a developmental negative priming study. *Child Development*, 87, 1825–1840.
Beckett, S. (1953). *Waiting for Godot*. Grove Press.

Blakemore, E. (2019, June 21). How the G.I. Bill's promise was denied to a million Black WWII veterans. *History*. https://www.history.com/news/gi-bill-black-wwii-veterans-benefits

Campbell, J. (2008). *The hero with a thousand faces* (3rd ed.). New World Library (Original work published 1949).

Darvasi, P. (2016). *Empathy, perspective and complicity: How digital games can support peace education and conflict resolution.* UNESCO MGIEP.

Eco, U. (1987). *Travels in hyperreality*. Picador.

Essential Facts. (2018). Entertainment software association. https://www.theesa.com/wp-content/uploads/2019/03/ESA_EssentialFacts_2018.pdf

Farber, M. (2017, April 13). Student-produced board games that promote empathy. *KQED*. https://www.kqed.org/education/457409/student-produced-board-games-that-promote-empathy

Fullerton, T. (2019, October 5). *Keynote with Tracy Fullerton, Connected Learning Summit 2019.* [Video]. YouTube. https://youtu.be/GznU1mJrYIY

Gee, J. P. (2007). *What video games have to teach us about learning and literacy.* Palgrave Macmillan.

Gerrig, R. J. (1993). *Experiencing narrative worlds: On the psychological activities of reading.* Yale University Press.

Gerrig, R. J., & Prentice, D. A. (1991). The representation of fictional information. *Psychological Science, 2*, 336–340. Gibson, J. J. (1977). The theory of affordances. In R. Shaw & J. Bransford (Ed.), *Perceiving, acting, and knowing* (pp. 67–82). Lawrence Erlbaum.

Gibson, J. J. (1979). *The ecological approach to visual perception.* Houghton Mifflin.

Groff, J., Clarke-Midura, J., Owen, V. E., Rosenheck, L., & Beall, M. (2015). Better learning in games: A balanced design lens for a new generation of learning games [white paper]. *MIT Education Arcade and Learning Games Network.* http://education.mit.edu/wp-content/uploads/2018/10/BalancedDesignGuide2015.pdf

Habib, M., Borst, G., Poirel, N., Houdé, O., Moutier, S., & Cassotti, M. (2015). Socio-emotional context and adolescents' decision making: The experience of regret and relief after social comparison. *Journal of Research on Adolescence, 25*, 81–91.

Hartson, H. R. (2003). Cognitive, physical, sensory, and functional affordances in interaction design. *Behaviour & Information Technology, 22*(5), 315–338. doi:10.1080/01449290310001592587.

Hodent, C. (2017). *The gamer's brain: How neuroscience and UX can impact video game design.* CRC Press.

Huizinga, J. (1955). *Homo ludens: A study of the play-element in culture.* Beacon Press. (Original work published 1938)

Hunicke, R., LeBlanc, M., & Zubek, R. (2004). MDA: A formal approach to game design and game research. *Workshop on Challenges in Game AI*, 1–4. doi:10.1.1.79.4561.

Isbister, K. (2016). *How games move us: Emotion by design.* MIT Press.

Joy, A. B. (2019). Candy Land was invented for polio wards. *The Atlantic*. https://www.theatlantic.com/technology/archive/2019/07/how-polio-inspired-the-creation-of-candy-land/594424/

Kawash, S. (2010). Polio comes home: Pleasure and paralysis in Candy Land. *American Journal of Play, 3*(2), 186–220.

Khan, I. (2020, April 7). Why Animal Crossing is the game for the coronavirus moment. *New York Times.* https://www.nytimes.com/2020/04/07/arts/animal-crossing-covid-coronavirus-popularity-millennials.html

King, M. (2018). *Good neighbor: The life and work of Fred Rogers.* Harry N. Abrams.

Knight, C. K. (2016). *Power and paradise in Walt Disney's world.* University Press of Florida.

Kokai, J. A., & Robson, T. (2019). *Performance and the Disney theme park experience: The tourist as actor.* Palgrave Macmillan.

Koster, R. (2014). *A theory of fun for game design* (2nd ed.). O'Reilly Media. (originally published in 2005)

Meehan, J. (2019). *EDrenaline rush: Game-changing student engagement inspired by theme parks, mud runs, and escape rooms.* Dave Burgess Consulting.

Meier, S. (2012). *Sid Meier's Interesting Decisions.* [Video]. YouTube. https://youtu.be/WggIdtrqgKg

Miller, H. (2020, April 5). Demand for jigsaw puzzles is surging as coronavirus keeps millions of Americans indoors. *CNBC.* https://www.cnbc.com/2020/04/03/coronavirus-sends-demand-for-jigsaw-puzzles-surging.html

Mirra, N. (2018). *Educating for empathy: Literacy learning and civic engagement.* Teachers College Press.

Murphy, S. T., Frank, L. B., Moran, M. B., & Patnoe-Woodley, P. (2011). Involved, transported, or emotional? Exploring the determinants of change in knowledge, attitudes, and behavior in entertainment-education. *Journal of Communication, 61,* 407–431. doi:10.1111/j.1460-2466.2011.01554.x.

Murray, J. H. (2017). *Hamlet on the holodeck: The future of narrative in cyberspace.* MIT Press.

Newman, D. B., Sachs, M. E., Stone, A. A., & Schwarz, N. (2020). Nostalgia and well-being in daily life: An ecological validity perspective. *Journal of Personality and Social Psychology, 118*(2), 325–347. doi:10.1037/pspp0000236.

Norman, D. A. (2013). *The design of everyday things* (Rev. and expanded ed.). Basic Books. (Original work published 1988).

Old Town and Disneyland's Main Street, U.S.A. (n.d.). *Fort Collins History Connection.* https://history.fcgov.com/legends/disney

Park, S. B., Jin Kim, H. J., & Ok, C. M. (2018). Linking emotion and place on Twitter at Disneyland. *Journal of Travel & Tourism Marketing, 35*(5), 664–677. doi:10.1080/10548408.2017.1401508.

Record First Quarter. (2020, May 15). *The NPD Group.* https://www.npd.com/wps/portal/npd/us/news/press-releases/2020/quarterly-u's-consumer-spend-on-video-game-products-reached-the--highest-total-in-us-history-in-first-quarter-of-2020/

Roberts, W., Strayer, J., & Denham, S. (2014). Empathy, anger, guilt: Emotions and prosocial behaviour. *Canadian Journal of Behavioural Science/Revue canadienne des sciences du comportement, 46,* 465–474. doi:10.1037/a0035057.

Rogers, F. (1994). *Charlie Rose Show* [Video]. YouTube. https://youtu.be/djoyd46TVVc
Rogers, S. (2009). Everything I learned about level design I learned from Disneyland. *Game Developer Conference.* https://www.gdcvault.com/play/1305/Everything-I-Learned-About-Level
Roger, S. (2014). *Level up! The guide to great video game design.* Wiley.
Ryan, R. M., & Deci, E. L. (2018). *Self-determination theory: Basic psychological needs in motivation, development, and wellness.* Guilford Press.
Salen, K., & Zimmerman, E. (2003). *Rules of play: Game design fundamentals.* MIT Press.
Sicart, M. (2014): *Play matters.* MIT Press.
Smethurst, T., & Craps, S. (2015). Playing with trauma: Interreactivity, empathy, and complicity in the walking dead video game. *Games and Culture, 10*(3), 269–290. doi:10.1177/1555412014559306.
Squire, K., & Gaydos, M. (2018, August 8). No, Fortnite isn't rotting kids' brains. It may even be good for them. *Education Week.* https://www.edweek.org/ew/articles/2018/08/08/no-fortnite-isnt-rotting-kids-brains-it.html
Tanz, J. (2016, January). A father, a dying son, and the quest to make the most profound videogame ever. *Wired.* https://www.wired.com/2016/01/that-dragon-cancer/
Treeby, M. S., Prado, C., Rice, S. M., & Crowe, S. F. (2016). Shame, guilt, and facial emotion processing: Initial evidence for a positive relationship between guilt-proneness and facial emotion recognition ability. *Cognition and Emotion, 30*(8), 1504–1511. doi:10.1080/02699931.2015.1072497.
Upton, B. (2018). *Situational game design.* Routledge.
Vaitl, D., Vehrs, W., & Sternagel, S. (1993). Prompts-leitmotif-emotion: Play it again, Richard Wagner. In N. Birbaumer & A. Ohman (Eds.), *The structure of emotion: Psychophysiological, cognitive, and clinical aspects* (pp. 169–189). Seattle: Hogrefe & Huber.
Vygotsky, L. S. (1978). *Mind in society: The development of higher psychological processes.* Harvard University Press.
Walther, B. K. (2011). Towards a theory of pervasive ludology: Reflections on gameplay, rules, and space. *Digital Creativity, 22*(3), 134–147. doi:10.1080/14626268.2011.603734.
Zimmerman, E. (2019, August 2). *Keynote: Games are not good for you* [Video]. YouTube. https://youtu.be/ic9prLftrMg

PART II

CHAPTER FOUR

Empathy Games

Upon release, the text-based poverty simulator *SPENT* received lots of accolades, including an award at the 2014 Games for Change Festival and praise on CNN and ABC News. As facts about homelessness float across the screen, players select where to spend their limited monthly funds. Should you buy health insurance from your employer, and if so, which plan? Do you splurge on things like ice cream or save money for shoes or childcare? What happens if you can't pay the minimum balance on a credit card?

Developed by brand awareness agency McKinney, *SPENT* was positioned as a shining example of how a video game could inspire empathy. Over the years, it has been played by millions of people and helped raise more than $70,000 for the Urban Ministries of Durham homeless shelter in North Carolina (Farber & Schrier, 2017; McKinney, 2011; Roussos, 2015).

Yale University researchers Roussos and Dovidio (2016) decided to test whether playing *SPENT* was actually making players empathetic. Their findings were surprisingly contrary: players who did not hold meritocratic beliefs began blaming the poor for not pulling themselves out of their situations. The choice-driven gameplay in *SPENT* implicitly messaged to some that poverty was the result of bad decision-making, regardless of outside systemic factors (Roussos & Dovidio, 2016).

Let's compare *SPENT* to another text-based game, *Depression Quest*. From Zoë Quinn, *Depression Quest* is based on her experience living with depression and social anxiety disorder. Unlike *SPENT*, which presents choices without context, Quinn's game is steeped in narrative. After paragraphs of text, some options can be clicked, while others are crossed out, visually illustrating how people with social anxiety disorder feel constrained. You know you should crawl out of bed and go to that party, but you can't.

In *Depression Quest*, the gameplay is slow and contemplative, affording reflection *between* choices. Different than *SPENT*, *Depression Quest* has a strong narrative, which supports mental transport of players to Quinn's world (Murphy et al., 2011). What's more, it is a situational game of passive constraints and anticipatory play, not a transactional system of button clicking (Upton, 2018).

Playing games enables us to perspective-take and make decisions based on the personas we actively inhabit (Isbister, 2016; Murray, 2017). In games, we may develop virtual relationships when we bond with seemingly sentient non-playable characters (Burgess & Jones, 2020; Harth, 2017; Isbister, 2016). In Telltale Games's zombie apocalypse game *The Walking Dead*, players have been observed exhibiting virtual empathy for the companion in their care (Smethurst & Craps, 2015). When researchers analyzed online discussion forums about the science fiction role-playing game *Mass Effect 2*, they found that some players had developed emotional attachments to Tali, a non-playable alien character (Burgess & Jones, 2020).

Empathy is the projection of thoughts and feelings onto another (Belman & Flanagan, 2010); this capacity relates to episodic memory and imagination (Gaesser, 2013). Nuanced, there are many different types of empathy (Schrier & Farber, 2019). Cognitive empathy describes the process of mentalizing other people's thoughts, emotions, and worldviews (Lamm & Majdandžić, 2015; Majdandžić et al., 2016). Affective empathy is when we feel how others feel—an emotional projection of self onto another (Batchelder et al., 2017; Batson, 2009). These are "partially dissociable constructs" (Batchelder et al., 2017, p. 2), linked together, difficult to untangle.

Complicating matters, we can have *selective empathy* when we favor the perspectives of those in in-groups over people in out-groups (Breithaupt, 2019). Bloom (2017) described a study where empathic concern clouded participants' ethical decision-making. Participants were shown a list of fictional people, each of whom needed a donated organ. Next, a backstory of a child on the list was shared. Participants who were empathetic to that child's circumstance began to move her up on the donor list, disregarding others' needs (Batson et al., 1995 as cited in Bloom, 2017).

There is not a straight line from having empathy to becoming prosocial; being empathetic does not automatically lead to compassionate or altruistic outcomes. As educators, we must be careful not to check the "empathy box" after a book is read, a film is screened, or a game is played. This chapter investigates the neuroscientific research of empathy games and shares best practice advice on cultivating empathic concern from children.

Can a Video Game Teach Empathy?

Imitative-observational behavior may be correlated to empathy and perspective-taking experiences in video games. In our brain's limbic system, there are mirror neurons that enable us to respond to stimuli of images such as facial expressions (Carr et al., 2003; Iacoboni, 2009). This process of meaning-making from action representation—"monkey see, monkey do"—describes how we react and imitate others' emotions. Mirror neurons may just illuminate part of the picture; affective empathy remains intertwined with cognitive empathy (Batchelder et al., 2017; Lamm & Majdandžić, 2015).

Researchers at the Center for Healthy Minds at the University of Wisconsin, Madison analyzed brain scans from adolescents who played the empathy-training game *Crystals of Kaydor*. Its game missions were designed to promote prosocial behaviors, such as cooperation and generosity, with 13-year-olds, the optimal age when brains are adept at rewiring following new stimuli. *Crystals of Kaydor* was the experimental intervention for randomized participants; the control group played the commercial role-playing game *Bastion*.

Gameplay begins as players crash land on the alien world Kaydor. Players control a robot explorer who encounters the local inhabitants, a species of plant-based humanoids. To survive, trust of the inhabitants needs to be gained. But there's one caveat: the only means of communication is nonverbal; the players' goal is to teach their robots how to interpret emotive facial expressions on alien faces.

After less than six hours of *Crystals of Kaydor* gameplay, participants demonstrated boosts in empathic accuracy—a task that involves mimicry of another's emotions (Kral et al., 2018). Next, the same participants underwent functional magnetic resonance imaging (fMRI) tests. Not only did empathic accuracy improve, participants' connectivity in neural networks increased (Kral et al., 2018).

I spoke with game designer Mike Beall, director of Gear Learning, to learn more. Among many others, he collaborated with Richard Davidson, founder and director of the Center for Healthy Minds, for this project. As it happened, a video game was not what was initially planned to be the intervention for the experimental group. Davidson had envisioned adolescents interacting with peers, learning empathy from human interaction. Beall decided to challenge Davidson to use a digital intervention. "Let's design a video game with robots and aliens," Beall declared.

Davidson agreed. Next, they worked on ideas about how players could "read" alien emotions through game mechanics. "We tried to find a game way to talk about emotions without saying 'emotions,'" Beall recalled. "So, we abstracted the concept; crystals substituted the word emotions by being color-coded. Red crystals caused negative emotions, and blue crystals were positive."

In the game, players move their robot avatar along (or over, as it appears to hover) Kaydor's surface by tapping on the screen. When local inhabitants approach players, they encounter the language barrier. Aliens emote, and players respond by dragging a slider up and down, from positive to negative. That core mechanic idea came from someone in Davidson's lab who read about an exercise on empathy in an academic paper. In it, two people—each with pen and paper—sat across a table from one another. Watching each other's faces, participants drew lines up and down based on observed facial expressions.

"We did this exercise over and over in the lab," Beall said. "I did this with about ten different people—one of us was the observer, and the other was the actor. This is what I wanted the game to do, to put empathy into slow motion. I see you, I observe you." This system of drawing lines led to the empathic awareness mechanic.

Regarding emotion identification, Beall and Davidson's team consulted with Rick Solis, who was trained in Paul Ekman's Facial Action Coding System (FACS), the taxonomy of human facial expressions and emotions discussed in Chapter One. Learning Games Network artist Adam Weins animated the alien's facial expressions by hand based on six emotions from FACS (this was years before motion capture technology became more widely adopted). Beall worked on the radial interface, which resembled the click wheel in the original iPod (see Figure 7).

Opposite emotions were listed across the wheel, not near one another. The purpose was to create some "friction," a cognitive pause to intentionally slow players down so they could read around the interface, choosing carefully. Happiness was across from sadness, disgust from surprise, anger from fear.

This study suggests the potential for using video games as an intervention to boost empathic accuracy with adolescents. Although *Crystals of Kaydor* was developed for research purposes and is not commercially available to play, there are other games that can be adapted to develop these sorts of skills with children. More importantly, the findings support the notion that empathy is a teachable and trainable skill (Kral et al., 2018).

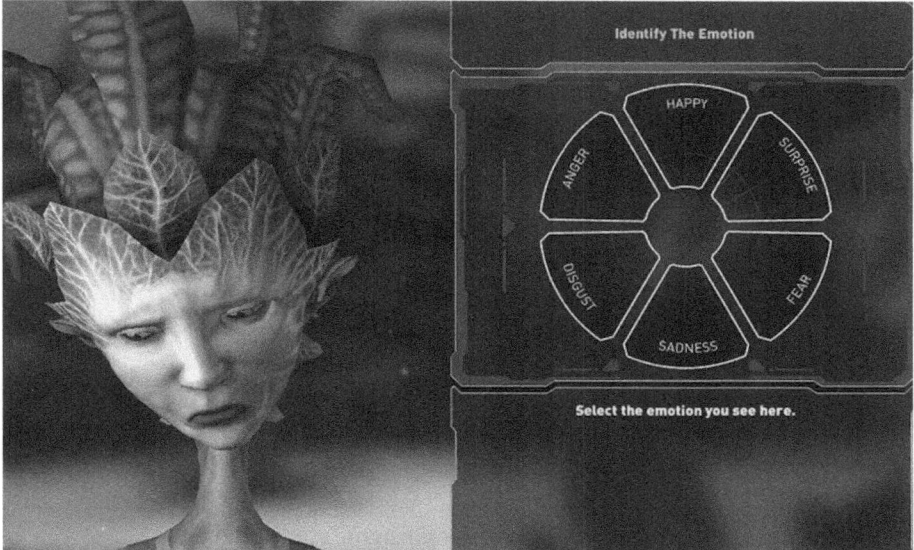

Figure 7. *Crystals of Kaydor* Emotion Identification User Interface (UI). Source: Gear Learning LLC. Reprinted by permission of the publisher.

Content Warnings

In addition to parental ratings systems, television shows, movies, and video games sometimes include warnings to audiences about potentially triggering or disturbing themes. Content warnings are often broadly written, while trigger warnings offer more detailed and specific alerts. An example of a content warning is, "This program depicts drug use." A trigger warning may read, "The following program includes a depiction of an eating disorder. Viewers discretion is advised."

Although more and more video games have content warnings, few include trigger warnings. The text-adventure narrative horror game, *the uncle who works for nintendo* (2017), is an example of a game that *does* have a trigger warning. The following is displayed on its start screen:

> This is a horror game. It does not make use of "screamers" or jump scares. Sound effects are used for tension and atmosphere. Some playthroughs may encounter plot points concerning a possible suicide. Thematically, many aspects of this game may recall the emotional abuse experienced by children at the hands of adults and, very often, other children. (Ztul, 2017, para. 1)

Confusing matters are inconsistencies about what warnings are shared with media consumers. On the Disney+ streaming service, some films have "Content

Advisory" warnings, alerting viewers about negative depictions of people and cultures. *Peter Pan* and *Dumbo* are examples. Yet, some films on the service lack trigger warnings. Disney Pixar's *Up*, rated PG for "parental guidance" by the Motion Picture Association of America, includes a scene about miscarriage. A trigger warning should be included, as some viewers of the children's film may not expect scenes of trauma, some of which may be triggering.

A maturing narrative media form, more and more video games tackle uncomfortable and difficult subject matter. One example is *That Dragon, Cancer*, a game based on Ryan and Amy Green's young child Joel, who had terminal cancer. Players take on multiple roles, playing as Ryan, but also as an onlooker. This game can help players cope with trauma and grief in their own lives, but scenes can also be triggering as emotions run high.

The explicitness of warning can vary depending on the game. *Hellblade: Senua's Sacrifice* is a Norse-set game with a hero who experiences psychosis. The game is about her hero's journey, not her psychological condition; having psychosis is part of her character. The trigger warning when the game starts reads:

> Warning: This game contains representations of psychosis. People with experience of psychosis, as well as professionals in psychiatry, have assisted in these depictions. Some may find these depictions disturbing, including those who, themselves, may have had similar experiences. If you would like to find out more about psychosis and mental health difficulties, visit: www.hellbladehelp.info. This game also includes violent scenes that some may find distressing. (Ninja Theory, 2017)

Life Is Strange is another game with powerful emotions. Borrowing tropes from young adult fiction, players may empathize with characters and situations. Set at a private school, it depicts teen relationships and peer pressure situations. The protagonist is Max Caulfield, whose last name is an apparent reference to *Catcher in the Rye*'s Holden Caulfield (Salinger, 1961). *Catcher in the Rye* is also set at a private boarding school.

With facilitation and thoughtful context, *Life Is Strange* could be used in a high school English language arts class as a paired digital text alongside Salinger's work. But teachers should know that the game also includes disturbing scenes that come without any warning at all. For instance, one central character dies by suicide after jumping from a school roof. The player can rewind time, either saving her, or not. When I played, I failed. I felt blindsided.

Night in the Woods is another game without an appropriately detailed trigger warning. A moving interactive narrative, the story centers on a cat named Mae who returns home after dropping out of college. Mae struggles with adulthood, anxiety, and relationship stressors. Rated T for Teen by the Entertainment Software Ratings Board, all characters are anthropomorphic (birds, dogs, bears). None of the content about anxiety is in the game's rating; only fantasy violence, drug references, language, crude humor, and alcohol and tobacco use are detailed (Night in the Woods, 2017).

Just as teachers should read books and screen films before using them in classrooms, it is best practice to review game content firsthand. Of course, teachers are busy; most—unless they are gamers—do not have hours to dedicate to video gameplay. YouTube can be a good resource, as is Common Sense Education, a website with detailed descriptions of games and other educational resources.

Importantly, students should always be afforded opportunities to opt-out of anything triggering. "When in doubt, add in a content warning," Kelli Dunlap advised. Dunlap holds a doctorate in clinical psychology and a master's degree in game design. She has presented at conferences about games, emotions, and content warnings. At a talk at the 2018 Games for Change Festival, she warned game developers that distress does not equal empathy and that someone else's trauma should be not a plot twist. "People need to know what they are getting into if there is a potential for harm," she continued. "It is ethical and respectful to that community to let people know what they are walking into. When in doubt, add in a content warning."

When preparing UNESCO MGIEP's curriculum around the Syrian refugee game *Bury Me, My Love*, my co-project investigators and I heeded Dunlap's advice. Although the game is text-based and not graphic, how the story unfolds in real-time is realistic and potentially jarring. The following warning was, therefore, added: "The game *Bury Me, My Love* and this course contain representations and discussions of war, violence, abuse, migration, and refugee crisis. Some may find these topics disturbing, including those who, themselves, may have had similar experiences" (Bury Me My Love: Identity in Crisis, 2020).

Dunlap shared a personal anecdote about *What Remains of Edith Finch*, an emotional video game where players experience death in an extended family. In one vignette, players are a baby playing in a bathtub; the baby's mother is heard across the room, arguing on the telephone. "When I played, I had a 2-year-old boy who loved the bathtub," she recalled. "I never had any personal trauma, but that scene was so intense, I had to hand over the controller and have someone else play because I physically couldn't. I wish I could've pushed a button and just skipped it. It was emotionally overwhelming, and I shut down."

On the Appropriateness of Role-Play

In 2018, I was on a panel at the Game for Change Festival about empathy and games. Moderated by Arana Shapiro, former co-executive director of the Institute of Play and current managing director at Games for Change, speakers included Daniel Braunfeld, Facing History and Ourselves's associate program director for special projects. Facing History is a website of lessons, activities, videos, and best practices in history education. On the panel, Braunfeld spoke about Facing History's approach to *Face the Future: A Game about the Future of Empathy*, a project completed with Jane McGonigal and the Institute for the Future. McGonigal is the author of several books on the power of games to promote well-being.

As authors Ibram X. Kendi (2019) and Robin J. DiAngelo (2018) wrote, it is not enough just to recognize racism; people need to become actively anti-racist. Facing History's mission is similar: To use history lessons to challenge teachers and students to stand up to bigotry and hate. "Standing up to bigotry and hatred speaks to the lens of how we do this work: People make choices, and choices make history," Braunfeld told me.

Facing History began in 1976 as an eighth-grade humanities class in a school just outside of Boston. The class was co-taught by two social studies teachers who later founded the educational nonprofit. The course did more than teach facts and dates; it challenged students to have real and difficult conversations about life in 1970s America. The questions asked in this classroom were both foundational and fundamental to what Facing History is as an organization today.

Back then, the Holocaust—a century-defining event—wasn't being discussed in many classrooms. What does it mean when schools aren't trusting students to have difficult conversations? "By difficult, we mean really wrestling with human behavior in the past and human behavior in the present," Braunfeld said. "Not difficult in the 'hard to talk about sense,' but asking why people turned on their everyday neighbors. How do adolescents think about obedience? How do they think about fitting into a social structure? These are questions innate to teenagers. They are the questions at the heart of democracy and genocide."

If we want students to become leaders in society after school, we need to engage them in those conversations during school. This foundation led Facing History to work with teachers, giving them the tools to have those conversations in ways that empower students.

Historical empathy is sometimes used in social studies classrooms as a way to bring the past to life. Historical empathy can be defined as the reconstruction of "others' beliefs, values, and goals, any or all of which are not necessarily those of the historical investigator" (Riley, 1998, p. 33). Like other forms of empathy, there are cognitive and affective processes that take place. Cognitive strategies may include ways to get students to think about how people in the past viewed their world and then made decisions based on those views. Imagining the perspectives of people from the past also means considering how those people felt, which relates to affective empathy. As mentioned earlier in this chapter, cognitive empathy and affective empathy are entangled and difficult to parse out (Batchelder et al., 2017).

It may seem implied that there is an ever-increasing trajectory—a ramp or spectrum of approaches—that teachers take when trying to evoke historical empathy from students. If writing a diary or journal or memoir is acceptable as a class assignment, does that mean it is then appropriate for students to write and perform skits about past events? If skits are fine, should reenactments also be done by students? If students perform reenactments, what's wrong with a simulation? Going further, what about games and virtual reality?

Suppose social studies or English language arts students are assigned to read *They Called Us Enemy* (Takei et al., 2019), a graphic novel about actor George Takei's childhood in a Japanese-American internment camp. Should students then write journals from the point-of-view of those who were interned? Should they play the next in the Mission US game series from WNET/Thirteen, *Prisoner in My Homeland*, which is set at a Japanese-American internment camp? What context do teachers need to give students when using new literacy tools like graphic novels and games?

In 2013, Denmark-based Serious Games Interactive published *Playing History 2: Slave Trade*. The description on the Steam gaming platform stated, "Travel back in time and witness the horrors of slave trade firsthand. You will be working as a young slave steward on a ship crossing the Atlantic. You are to serve the captain and be his eyes and ears. What do you do when you realize that your own sister has been captured by the slave traders?" Two years after its publication (yes—two years!), outrage swelled in the media, specifically about one of its minigames, *Slave Tetris*. In the commercial puzzle game *Tetris*, players turn tetrominoes as they cascade down the screen. *Slave Tetris* borrowed this mechanic; only this time, humans were objectified as game pieces. The goal: To fill in the bottom of a slave ship.

After controversy emerged in 2015, changes were made to the game. But as of this writing, *Playing History 2: Slave Trade* can still be purchased and played on the Steam platform. It is still something a teacher who searches online for educational games may encounter.

It is important that teachers not run up a ramp of teaching tools that may evoke historical empathy; there is not a straight line from journals and diaries to skits to reenactments and then simulations and games. Teachers need to pause, particularly as games and virtual reality allure in their ability to immerse learners. And this can be tricky for some teachers who look to trusted sources for educational games.

For Crown or Colony was the first educational game published in the Mission US series. In the game, students play as Nat, a boy witnessing the American

Revolution unfold in Boston. In a study, students demonstrated increased content knowledge and historical empathy for game characters and situations (Schrier et al., 2010). If a teacher uses this game in class, why not play the follow-up mission, *Flight to Freedom*? Here, players take agency of Lucy, a young enslaved woman in the American south. Should children "play" as the enslaved? Should people's trauma be gamified?

When is role-play appropriate in history class? What does reenactment look like? When do you ask students to embody a perspective and a voice? The Zinn Education Project, the website based on the work of Howard Zinn, offers advice on how to, and when not to, role-play in classrooms. First and foremost, context matters. Second, stereotypes must be avoided. Children should also not play as oppressors or victims (How to—and How Not to—Teach Role Plays, 2019). When role-playing in school:

- Explain complex social phenomena like white supremacy, settler colonialism, social class divisions, and wealth inequality, or environmental exploitation.
- Tell the truth about the past and present, including stories of events, groups, and individuals, too often erased, minimized, or oversimplified in corporate curricula.
- Increase students' capacity to act for justice by:
  o Growing their imaginative capabilities, the cornerstone of empathy and solidarity,
  o Exploring how systems affect people's choices, analysis necessary to solve, seemingly intractable problems,
  o Allowing time and space for democratic, participatory pedagogy,
  o Thwarting cynicism and resignation by emphasizing activism and resistance. (How to—and How Not to—Teach Role Plays, 2019, para. 7)

Again, it may not seem like a huge leap to go from classroom role-play or simulation to using games to evoke historical empathy—or any form of empathy, for that matter (e.g., cultural empathy, parallel empathy). After all, role-play and simulation are a part of many games.

Like film, television, and literary fiction, games are a powerful medium that can evoke empathy (Belman & Flanagan, 2010; Flanagan & Nissenbaum, 2014; Greitemeyer, 2013). Let's take the game *PeaceMaker* as an example. In *PeaceMaker*, players experience both sides of the Palestinian-Israeli conflict. In a study, participants' prejudice and negative stereotypes towards out-groups were shown to decrease (Kampf & Cuhadar, 2015). *That Dragon, Cancer* can also positively affect player empathy. As mentioned earlier, players take on multiple perspectives, at times controlling the father's actions, but sometimes seemingly removed, watching the characters as actions play out (Auxier, 2018). Timpane et al. (2017) suggest that these affordances could be used in medical training of palliative care.

Careful and thoughtful steps must be in place when considering the appropriateness of teaching with empathy games (Schrier & Farber, 2019). Braunfeld remarked,

> There is work teachers need to do in the beginning, asking themselves, "Is this even a thing we should be doing?" Not as a blanket statement, but ask, "When should we not be doing this?" Whether it is a skit, a simulation, or a video game, there are differences in format because of visualization. Because something can be lifelike, the attraction of using it heightens. But that also raises more questions, even though there are natural conclusions between them. If we can do X, why not do Y? Teachers should pause at this moment to consider the impact these activities can have on students' emotional safety and social and emotional learning.

A Class Divided, an expanded version of the PBS documentary *Eye of the Storm*, is a film Facing History has used with teachers. The film shares Iowa teacher Jane Elliot's "Blue Eyes, Brown Eyes" exercise, a simulation she conducted on her third-grade students in 1968—one day after Martin Luther King was assassinated. Elliot divided her class in half, telling the brown-eyed children that they would be in charge of the blue-eyed students. Then she watched how each group began to treat each other. Two days later, she switched the groups; now, the blue-eyed children were in charge.

In the first round, Elliot observed how blue-eyed students became convinced that they were not as smart as their brown-eyed counterparts. Then the reverse happened when she arbitrarily appointed the blue-eyed students to be superior. Her takeaway: Prejudice from racist beliefs is a learned behavior.

Having her young students experience discrimination led Elliot to become a public speaker and a sometimes-talk show guest. In 1992, she was on *The Oprah Winfrey Show*. As recent as 2018, she was on a panel with Angela Davis at the University of Houston, speaking about structural racism and privilege. Days after speaking with Braunfeld, I read about her legacy in the *New York Times*.

Was the Blue Eyes, Brown Eyes exercise ethical? Is it okay to conduct social experiments with students under the guise of calling it a simulation or a "teachable moment"? When I taught how the checks and balances system works in the United States government, I used simulation materials from iCivics that concluded with a bit of a "Gotcha!" moment. Students were split into three groups: lead chefs, menu writers, and nutrition inspectors. After redesigning the school lunch menu, it was revealed that their actions mirrored how bills become laws.

A school lunch menu/separation of powers simulation is not a social experiment. Students are embodying the government's mechanical actions, not the lived experiences of people, particularly those who were oppressed, marginalized, or victimized. "We use the Blue Eyes, Brown Eyes exercise with teachers with a very strong, 'We are going to look at what she did without ever endorsing that you do this,'" Braunfeld said. "It is similar to when we show teachers the Milgram experiment." In the famed Milgram experiment (1963), participants were told by an authority figure to give an electrical shock to someone unseen (but heard) in another room. The researcher, Stanley Milgram, was curious about the conditions that led followers in Nazi Germany to carry out atrocities. Most participants pushed the button; many were emotionally traumatized from the experiment (McLeod, 2017). The Milgram experiment is a classic example of a study founded on deception. Distress and harm were visible from participants during the experience (McLeod, 2017). And these were adults—Elliot's exercise was with young children.

For some teachers, game-like simulations may resemble psychological experiments. "Part of the inappropriateness is the gap between what teachers think they are doing and what some of the consequences are," Braunfeld continued. "When teachers want to do a simulation or reenactment, there is a belief that the activity is engaging and the kids will love it—the 'They will love it!' factor. Then there is the, 'They will learn something better' factor and the 'They are really going to get it' factor."

Braunfeld is describing the tempting allure of "Gotcha!" moments, the big reveal at the end of a lesson. But these can be dangerous and can cause psychological harm. Braunfeld shared a personal anecdote,

> I remember when I was a middle school student, we had a stations activity about slavery. The only station I remember was a reading posted under the desk about the Transatlantic slave trade. We had to lie on our backs under the desk and read it. There was a "Now you know what it felt like because it is dark and cramped!" idea behind it. I still do remember it—it was new and evocative and different. It checked off those boxes. But what ended up happening was that the wrong questions were asked, creating a false sense of understanding and minimizing the actual brutality of slavery. And I cannot imagine the trauma this activity inflicted on students whose identities were being minimized in this moment.

Children should not role-play as the oppressed or oppressors. "I often hear from teachers about simulations that involve manipulation, 'Well, kids like it!' But kids like ice cream, and we know better than to give it to them for dinner. 'Kids like it' should not be the only curricular-deciding factor."

As Braunfeld shared his middle school experience, I recalled an activity I conducted when I taught sixth-graders about the European Renaissance. Students were instructed to think of their favorite place. They were then given paper and tape and told to draw their illustration under their desks, lying on their backs.

This simulation may have evoked some historical empathy for Michelangelo, who spent years painting the ceiling of the Sistine Chapel. But it was also distinctly different than Braunfeld's experience, as Michelangelo was not a victim, nor was he a perpetrator.

Virtual reality (VR) experiences sometimes hijack people's life situations. Schrier and my UNESCO MGIEP working paper, *The Limits and Strengths of Using Digital Games as "Empathy Machines"* (2017) was written as a partial response to Chris Milk, whose 2015 TED Talk purported VR to be the "ultimate empathy machine." Milk's quote was a nod to Roger Ebert, who had extolled that virtue to the medium of film. But this may be an oversell. If I wear a VR visor and "experience" life in a Syrian refugee camp, I still know I am at home and not in any real danger. Comparatively, the *Anne Frank House VR* experience is more thoughtful in design. An authorized replica of the museum's attic tour, it engenders an "if you can't be in Amsterdam, you can now 'visit' the museum" sense of presence. Powerful and immersive, the viewer does not role-play as Anne Frank.

Regarding role-play and VR, game design professor Robert Yang cautioned against cultural appropriation—just because you can role-play does not mean you should, he warned. He wrote, "If you walk in someone else's shoes, then you've taken their shoes" (Yang, 2017, para. 1).

Speaking about lessons where students are asked to react to the past, "I push teachers not to ask students, 'What would you have done?'" Braunfeld said. "That question implies that you can understand all of the factors that go into a person's decisions."

We know that children are in an educational system where they are not given a complete story of people's experiences. We know the Black experience is not told in full in classrooms, nor are stories of Indigenous cultures. "You have a truncated history that is focused mostly on victimization," Braunfeld continued. "Then you ask kids to embody that. There is no way to set up safety to make it authentic, so kids get it. There is a false sense, which is worse."

The interplay between SEL and trauma is vital in this conversation. What does it mean to ask a child to take on the experience of a victim or an oppressor? And what about the trauma that can invoke in students? Author, activist, and former basketball player John Amaechi has worked with Facing History over the years. About emotional spaces in classrooms, he remarked, "Without safety there is nothing, there is no learning" (Amaechi as cited in Rappaport, 2014, para. 1).

The work at Facing History helps teachers to create classrooms where students have the safety to be brave. "Safety doesn't mean sterile," Braunfeld said. "It means that we are trying to have authentic conversations here, and that is going to take some risk."

There is a lesson about Jim Crow laws on the Facing History website, segregationist laws that followed the American Civil War. In a station rotation, students learn about lynching by viewing primary source images of faces in a crowd at a lynching site. There is no "Gotcha!" nor is there deception. Students are given a content warning explicitly stating that interacting with this folder is optional. "We don't want to shock and awe people into trauma. If you want to approach it, you are welcome to. We tell you in advance so that you can make the decision."

Again, to hammer this point home, manipulation through deception can be traumatizing—particularly when players are made to feel complicit. Let's examine Brenda Braithwaite's *Train* (2009), an art exhibit (not commercially playable) from her Mechanics is the Message series. The box included yellow pawns, railroad boxcars, and shards of broken glass. Players arranged yellow pegs in railroad boxcars only to learn the narrative during play: That the train's destination is Auschwitz, the Holocaust concentration camp. The mechanics here may work as an artistic statement, but that does not mean that it should be used in the safety of classrooms.

Braunfeld shared a shift in his teaching when using Facing History materials. He described an activity with composite profiles of people from the Weimar Republic (pre-Nazi Germany) right before the 1932 election. "I had students vote on the political parties without having the names of the associated political parties in them," he said. "I wanted kids to focus on the platform of the party and not have their pre-conceived notions of history influence their decision. My mindset was a "Gotcha! I will show them!" attitude. I stopped doing this because I don't want to manipulate kids into doing something—I want them to confront what they are doing."

The Weimar Republic lesson is not, "Did you vote for the Nazis?" The lesson actually asks, "If you think this person is going to vote for this platform, why? What was it about this person and the platform?"

I shared the gameplay of *Train* with Braunfeld. I prefaced that I had not personally played it, and that it was an example shared in books about games and emotion (e.g., Hodent, 2017; Isbister, 2016). Regarding feelings of complicity that *Train* engenders, Braunfeld commented, "There is also this: Did the people loading trains in Poland really not know what they were doing? I don't think that is historically accurate. I think people knew what they were doing. Many perpetrators were not tricked into doing something horrible. They made the choice to do so."

Nearly all games involve some sort of role-playing, which can connect to both empathy and perspective-taking. We must tread lightly and be thoughtful to not oversell games as some miracle solution to engendering empathy. How we position ourselves in stories shared in games is essential. Are we trying to become people from the past? Or, are we respecting the uniqueness of stories and people's voices so that we can draw out some universal questions? Let's hope the latter is true.

In the next section, I share how a teacher pairs a book along with an empathy video game. Her lessons cultivate empathy in safe and thoughtful ways. Using paired texts, particularly primary sources, is also an approach recommended by Facing History (Mai, 2018).

Paired Texts and Impossible Field Trips

Angelique Gianas has a unique approach to teaching her high school students about immigration issues: she pairs a video game with a book. Specifically, she uses *The Migrant Trail*, a single-player game inspired by the classic educational game *The Oregon Trail*, with Luis Alberto Urrea's novel *Into the Beautiful North* (2010). Her purpose is to evoke empathetic responses about others' plight through a multimodal approach. (*The Migrant Trail*, which was built with Adobe Flash, is no longer playable. Games with similar themes are shared at the end of this chapter, under Links, Lessons, and Games.)

Gianas teaches in La Mesa, California, which is in San Diego County, near where the novel is set. Like the characters in the book and the game, many of her students are immigrants from Mexico and other Hispanic countries in Central America. "They either experienced immigration themselves, their parents have immigrated, or sometimes, the students themselves or their parents are illegal immigrants," she told me. "This is an emotional and sensitive topic, shameful to some."

Into the Beautiful North is about Nayeli, a girl from a small town in Sinaloa, Mexico. As Gianas shared, Sinaloa's men left town to work in the North, to the United States. Each month, the men send some of their earnings home to their families. With the men gone, "narcos" drug cartels come in and take over the town. "Kids connected with that because some have experienced that in their lives," Gianas continued. "Also, there was the Pablo Escobar series on Netflix at the time, *Narcos*."

Nayeli, along with her friends—two girls and one boy who is gay—go to the North to find her father, who had stopped sending back money. Through their journey, they experience horrible things: they lose their bags on a bus, they get taken advantage of numerous times, they are robbed, and they have a run-in with border patrol.

Books engage empathetic responses from readers through a process known as theory of mind (Castano & Kidd, 2013). Theory of mind describes how readers of literary fiction interpret the author's words in their heads. Castano and Kidd (2013) attribute this effect only to literary fiction, not nonfiction. Bal and Veltkamp (2013) suggest that theory of mind may be dependent on the strength of narrative that mentally transports readers into fiction.

Through Nayeli and her friends, readers perspective-take about how some immigrants see America as a beautiful place—in this case, what they've seen on television about southern California and Hollywood. This is soon dispelled when Nayeli and her friends experience racism when they arrive. The beautiful north was not what they thought it was going to be.

"This is the opening unit in my class on overcoming adversity and resilience," Gianas said. The unit is framed around an essential question that maps to SEL. She asks students, "How do the adversities we face in our lives shape who we are?" "A lot of kids connect with the book in some way," she said. "Crossing the border is not like in the movies. It is not everyone running and jumping a fence. It is incredibly tragic and scary, a death sentence for many."

About halfway through the book, Nayeli and her friends get to the border. There they meet a "coyote," a person who is paid to smuggle in migrants. This is when Gianas introduces *The Migrant Trail*. But before they play, they look at an interactive map, which has crosses where migrant remains were found. *The Migrant Trail* was designed as a transmedia experience connected to the PBS documentary film, *The Undocumented*, and includes the faces and names of those in the documentary. The map and the game are affixed on *The Undocumented* website: https://theundocumented.com.

The gameplay is in two modes: Migrant Mode and Border Patrol Mode. In a part of Urrea's book, a border patrol agent's perspective is similarly shared. "A border patrol character in the book hates his job and wants to retire," Gianas said. "When he first catches Nayeli and her friends, he sends them back to Tijuana. He laughs at their story that they are going to get men to save their town. But by the end of the book, he ends up saving them and helps them cross into San Diego."

The game models how risky and challenging border crossing is. "I tell students that I don't condone crossing illegally, but you should understand why people do it," she said. "What is the situation they are escaping? Put yourself in their shoes. If you were in a town getting taken over by a drug cartel, would you leave? Of course, you would. I think *The Migrant Trail* opens up a lot of conversations to have with the class. Paired with the book, which has characters who are the same age as my students, they can talk about it."

Paired texts can help students build background knowledge, support reading comprehension, and promote critical thinking skills (Ciecierski & Bintz, 2016; Short et al., 1995). Defined as two texts that are "conceptually related in some way," paired texts can be from the same topic, genre, or theme (Ciecierski & Bintz, 2016,

p. 33). The most common pairing is a fictional narrative with a nonfiction text (Code & Runge-Pulte, 2007). In Gianas's class, Urrea's book is the fictional narrative, while *The Migrant Trail*, as it is a transmedia game based on a documentary film (Farber, 2019), is the nonfiction text. Video games are multimodal interactive texts, new media where narrative is represented with symbols and sounds and by embodied player actions (Cope & Kalantzis, 2015; Gee, 2007; Kalantzis & Cope, 2009). Is it possible that the affordances of games, when paired with the narrative structures in novels, can boost overall literacy and cultivate SEL skills?

In 2017, when I taught middle school, a reporter from WNYC, New York City's National Public Radio affiliate, observed my classroom. At the time, I paired *The Migrant Trail* with other readings to teach push and pull factors of immigration. Grouped in pairs, some of my students played in Migrant Mode, while others learned about border patrol agents. The lesson concluded with a compare and contrast chart and a journal reflection.

At one point in Migrant Mode, players have to decide whether to leave an injured person behind. I asked students how they felt when they had to make difficult decisions. "This is really hard," one of my students replied. She wasn't describing the mechanics; instead, she commented on the situation she was put in. (Students were given content and trigger warnings and opportunities to opt-out.)

Video games are new media, like podcasts or graphic novels, and can support student learning. "As much as I like reading, when I assign a book, it is like pulling teeth to get them to read," Gianas confessed. "Games help kids who struggle to engage with books."

When WNYC shared my use of *The Migrant Trail*, the reporter remarked that what I was doing was taking my students "on what would otherwise be impossible field trips" (Basu, 2017, para. 1). Games can do more than put us in other people's shoes—they can transport us to situations faraway from our own. Guided by thoughtful teachers, the possibilities of impossible field trips remain endless.

Links, Lessons, and Games

#ArmMeWithGames, a curated list of empathy games: https://www.literarysafari.com/armmewithgames
Anne Frank House VR: https://annefrankhousevr.com
Brené Brown on empathy: https://youtu.be/1Evwgu369Jw
Crystals of Kaydor: https://gearlearning.org/project-crystals-of-kaydor.php
Common Sense Education: https://www.commonsense.org/education
Depression Quest: http://www.depressionquest.com
Kelli Dunlap on content warnings in video games: https://dunlappsyd.com/2020/01/30/the-psychology-of-video-games-week-3-depression-in-video-games

Empathy through Game Play, from Facing History: https://www.facinghistory.org/resource-library/empathy-through-game-play

Empathy Village on *Minecraft: Education Edition*: https://education.minecraft.net/lessons/empathy-village

Facing History and Ourselves: https://www.facinghistory.org

Games and resources on local stories and immigrant voices: http://gamesforchange.org/studentchallenge/nyc/local-stories-immigrant-voices

Games for Change: http://www.gamesforchange.org

Games to Spark Empathy-building in the Classroom: https://www.kqed.org/mindshift/48233/4-games-to-spark-empathy-building-in-the-classroom

How to—and How Not to—Teach Role Plays, from Zinn Education Project: https://www.zinnedproject.org/news/how-to-teach-role-plays

Into the Beautiful North: http://luisurrea.com/books/into-the-beautiful-north

Learning, Education & Games vol. 3: 100 Games to Use in the Classroom and Beyond: http://press.etc.cmu.edu/index.php/product/learning-education-games-volume-3

Life Is Strange: True Colors is a sequel in the *Life Is Strange* series. In this entry, projecting empathy is the protagonist's superpower: https://lifeisstrange.square-enix-games.com/en-us/games/life-is-strange-true-colors

The Limits and Strengths of Using Digital Games as "Empathy Machines": https://unesdoc.unesco.org/ark:/48223/pf0000261993

Night in the Woods: http://www.nightinthewoods.com

PeaceMaker: http://www.peacemakergame.com

Practicing Empathy with Jane McGonigal: https://www.facinghistory.org/resource-library/video/practicing-empathy-jane-mcgonigal

Roots of Empathy: https://us.rootsofempathy.org

Teach with *Night in the Woods*: https://www.heylistengames.org/post/why-you-should-teach-with-night-in-the-woods

That Dragon, Cancer: http://www.thatdragoncancer.com

the uncle who works for nintendo: https://ztul.itch.io/the-uncle-who-works-for-nintendo

Using Digital Games—And Empathy—As Teaching Tools (WNYC): https://www.wnyc.org/story/using-digital-games-and-empathy-teaching-tools

What Remains of Edith Finch: http://www.giantsparrow.com/games/finch

References

Auxier, J. W. (2018). That Dragon, Cancer goes to seminary: Using a serious video game in pastoral training. *Christian Education Journal: Research on Educational Ministry, 15*(1), 105–117. doi:10.1177/0739891318759725.

Bal, P. M., & Veltkamp, M. (2013). How does fiction reading influence empathy? An experimental investigation on the role of emotional transportation. *PLoS One, 8*(1), 1-12.

Basu, S. (2017, June 19). Using digital games—and empathy—as teaching tools. *WNYC.* https://www.wnyc.org/story/using-digital-games-and-empathy-teaching-tools/

Batchelder, L., Brosnan, M., & Ashwin, C. (2017). The development and validation of the empathy components questionnaire (ECQ). *PLoS One, 12*(1), e0169185. doi:10.1371/journal.pone.0169185.

Batson, C. D. (2009). The definition of empathy. In J. Decety & W. Ickes (Eds.), *The social neuroscience of empathy* (pp. 3–16). MIT Press Scholarship.

Batson, C. D., Klein, T. R., Highberger, L., & Shaw, L. L. (1995). Immorality from empathy-induced altruism: When compassion and justice conflict. *Journal of Personality & Social Psychology, 68*(6), 1042–1054.

Belman, J., & Flanagan, M. (2010). Designing games to foster empathy. *Cognitive Technology, 14*(2), 5–15.

Bloom, P. (2017). Empathy and its discontents. *Trends in Cognitive Sciences, 21*(1), 24–31. doi:10.1016/j.tics.2016.11.004.

Breithaupt, F. (2019). *The dark sides of empathy.* Cornell University Press.

Burgess, J., & Jones, C. (2020). I harbour strong feelings for Tali despite her being a fictional character: Investigating videogame players' emotional attachments to non-player characters. *International Journal of Computer Game Research, 20,* 1. http://gamestudies.org/2001/articles/burgessjones

Bury Me My Love: Identity in Crisis. (2020). *Framerspace.* https://framerspace.com/course/bmml

Carr, L., Iacoboni, M., Dubeau, M., Mazziotta, J. C., & Lenzi, G. L. (2003). Neural mechanisms of empathy in humans: A relay from neural systems for imitation to limbic areas. *Proceedings of the National Academy of Sciences of the United States of America, 100*(9), 5497–5502. doi:10.1073/pnas.0935845100.

CASEL's SEL Framework. (2020). *CASEL.* https://casel.org/wpcontent/uploads/2020/10/CASEL-SEL-Framework-10.2020-1.pdf

Castano, E., & Kidd, D. C. (2013, October 3). Reading literary fiction improves theory of mind. *Science, 342*(6156), 377–380. doi:10.1126/science.1239918.

Ciecierski, L., & Bintz, W. (2016). Paired texts: A way into the content area. *Middle School Journal, 47*(4), 32–44. http://www.jstor.org/stable/44321069

Code, K., & Runge-Pulte, S. (2007). Economics and children's literature: The twin texts approach. *Southern Social Studies Journal,* 33 (1), 4–20.

Cope, B., & Kalantzis, M. (Eds.). (2015). *A pedagogy of multiliteracies: Learning by design.* Cambridge University Press.

DiAngelo, R. J., & Penguin. (2019). *White fragility: Why it's so hard for white people to talk about racism.* Beacon Press.

Farber, M. (2019). *The Migrant Trail.* In Schrier, K. (Ed.) *Learning, education & games vol. 3: 100 games to use in the classroom and beyond.* Carnegie Mellon ETC Press.

Farber, M., & Schrier, K. (2017). *The strengths and limitations of using digital games as "empathy" machines.* UNESCO MGIEP.

Flanagan, N., & Nissenbaum, H. (2014). *Values at play in digital games*. MIT Press.

Gaesser, B. (2013). Constructing memory, imagination, and empathy: A cognitive neuroscience perspective. *Frontiers in Psychology, 3*. doi:10.3389/fpsyg.2012.00576.

Gee, J. P. (2007). *What video games have to teach us about learning and literacy* (rev. ed.). Palgrave Macmillan.

Greitemeyer, T. (2013). Playing video games cooperatively increases empathic concern. *Social Psychology, 44*(6), 408–413. doi:10.1027/1864-9335/a000154.

Harth, J. (2017). Empathy with non-player characters? An empirical approach to the foundations of human/non-human relationships. *Journal of Virtual Worlds Research, 10*(2), 1–25. doi:10.4101/jvwr.v10i2.7272.

Hodent, C. (2017). *The gamer's brain: How neuroscience and UX can impact video game design*. CRC Press.

How to—and How Not to—Teach Role Plays. (2019, September 15). *Zinn Education Project*. https://www.zinnedproject.org/news/how-to-teach-role-plays/

Iacoboni, M. (2009). Imitation, empathy, and mirror neurons. *Annual Review of Psychology, 60*(1), 653–670. doi:10.1146/annurev.psych.60.110707.163604.

Isbister, K. (2016). *How games move us: Emotion by design*. MIT Press.

Kalantzis, M., & Cope, W. (2009). A grammar of multimodality. *International Journal of Learning, 16*(2), 361-426. doi:10.18848/1447-9494/CGP/v16i02/46137

Kampf, R., & Cuhadar, E. (2015). Do computer games enhance learning about conflicts? A cross-national inquiry into proximate and distant scenarios in global conflicts. *Computers in Human Behavior, 52*, 541–549. doi:10.1016/j.chb.2014.08.008.

Kendi, I. X. (2019). *How to be an anti-racist*. One World Press.

Kral, T. R. A., Stodola, D. E., Birn, R. M., Mumford, J. A., Solis, E., Flook, L., ... Davidson, R. J. (2018). Neural correlates of video game empathy training in adolescents: A randomized trial. *NPJ Science of Learning, 3*(1), 13–10. doi:10.1038/s41539-018-0029-6.

Lamm, C., & Majdandžić, J. (2015). The role of shared neural activations, mirror neurons, and morality in empathy—A critical comment. *Neuroscience Research, 90*, 15–24. doi:10.1016/j.neures.2014.10.008.

Mai, L. (2018, March 27). *Use historical empathy to help students process the world today*. Facing History and Ourselves. https://facingtoday.facinghistory.org/use-historical-empathy-to-help-students-process-the-world-today

Majdandžić, J., Amashaufer, S., Hummer, A., Windischberger, C., & Lamm, C. (2016). The selfless mind: How prefrontal involvement in mentalizing with similar and dissimilar others shapes empathy and prosocial behavior. *Cognition, 157*, 24–38. doi:10.1016/j.cognition.2016.08.003.

McLeod, S. A. (2017, February 05). *The Milgram shock experiment*. Simply Psychology. https://www.simplypsychology.org/milgram.html

McKinney. (2011). *SPENT*. http://playspent.org/

Milgram, S. (1963). Behavioral study of obedience. *Journal of Abnormal and Social Psychology, 67*, 371–378.

Milk, C. (2015). How virtual reality can create the ultimate empathy machine [Video]. TED. https://www.ted.com/talks/chris_milk_how_virtual_reality_can_create_the_ultimate_empathy_machine

Murphy, S. T., Frank, L. B., Moran, M. B., & Patnoe-Woodley, P. (2011). Involved, transported, or emotional? Exploring the determinants of change in knowledge, attitudes, and behavior in entertainment-education. *Journal of Communication, 61*, 407–431. doi:10.1111/j.1460- 2466.2011.01554.x.

Murray, J. H. (2017). *Hamlet on the holodeck: The future of narrative in cyberspace*. MIT Press.

Night in the Woods. (2017). *Night in the Woods*. http://www.nightinthewoods.com

Ninja Theory (2017). *Hellblade: Senua's Sacrifice*. https://www.hellblade.com/

Rappaport, J. (2014, November 10). Unlocking potential for student achievement. *Facing History and Ourselves*. https://facingtoday.facinghistory.org/unlocking-potential-for-student-achievement

Riley, K. L. (1998). Historical empathy and the Holocaust: Theory into practice. *International Journal of Social Education, 13*(1), 32.

Roussos, G. (2015, December 7). When good intentions go awry: The counterintuitive effects of a prosocial online game. *Psychology Today*. https://www.psychologytoday.com/blog/sound-science-sound-policy/201512/when-good-intentions-go-awry

Roussos, G., & Dovidio, J. F. (2016). Playing below the poverty line: Investigating an online game as a way to reduce prejudice toward the poor. *Cyberpsychology: Journal of Psychosocial Research on Cyberspace, 10*(2), 1–24.

Salinger, J. D. (1961). *Catcher in the rye*. Hachette.

Schrier, K., Diamond, J., & Langendoen, D. (2010). Using Mission US: For crown or colony? to develop historical empathy and nurture ethical thinking. In K. Schrier & D. Gibson (Eds.), *Ethics and game design: Teaching values through play* (pp. 239–261). IGI Global.

Schrier, K., & Farber, M. (2019). Open questions for games and empathy. *Connected Learning Summit 2018 Conference Proceedings*. Carnegie Mellon ETC Press.

Short, K. G., Harste, J. C., & Burke, C. (1995). *Creating classrooms for authors and inquirers (2nd ed)*. Heineman.

Smethurst, T., & Craps, S. (2015). Playing with trauma: Interreactivity, empathy, and complicity in the walking dead video game. *Games and Culture, 10*(3), 269–290. doi:10.1177/1555412014559306.

Takei, G., Eisinger, J., Scott, S., & Becker, H. (2019). *They called us enemy*. Top Shelf Productions.

Timpane, S. F., Zhang, M., & Yeh, I. M. (2017). New media: That dragon, cancer: An interactive video game. *Journal of Palliative Medicine, 20*(3), 38–308. doi:10.1089/jpm.2016.0555.

Urrea, L. A. (2010). *Into the beautiful north: A novel*. Back Bay.

Yang, R. (2017, April 5). "If you walk in someone else's shoes, then you've taken their shoes": Empathy machines as appropriation machines. *Radiator design blog*. https://www.blog.radiator.debacle.us/2017/04/if-you-walk-in-someone-elses-shoes-then.html

Ztul. (2017). *The uncle who works for nintendo*. *Itch.io*. https://ztul.itch.io/the-uncle-who-works-for-nintendo

CHAPTER FIVE

Mindful, Kind, and Compassionate

Mindfulness apps are seemingly everywhere these days. As I type this, the *Breathe* app on my Apple Watch chimes. On my wrist, a blue flower animates as I inhale and exhale. "Even a minute of breathing helps you think clearly," the notification reads.

A quick search in the Health and Fitness category in the Apple App Store leads me down a rabbit hole of dozens and dozens of self-care and meditation apps. Subscription-based *Headspace* and *Calm* are market leaders in this multimillion-dollar sector. I also find *Healthy Minds* in the App Store. From Richard Davidson's Center for Healthy Minds at the University of Wisconsin, Madison, *Healthy Minds* is a personalized meditative awareness podcast suite.

Some apps are game-based in approach. One example is *#SelfCare*, co-designed by artificial intelligence expert Brie Code. In this experience, players interact in a virtual bedroom where they light candles, read tarot cards, and breathe mindfully. Another game-based app is *SuperBetter*, a goal-setting self-care experience based on the work of game designer and futurist Jane McGonigal. Completing real-world challenges, like drinking water and walking outside, unlocks rewards. The companion website shares research: In a randomized control trial, playing *SuperBetter* decreased depressive symptoms with participants (Worthen-Chaudhari et al., 2017); in a clinical trial, concussion symptoms were reduced among teenage youth (Roepke et al., 2015).

Mindfulness, which has roots in Hinduism and Buddhism, has become somewhat of a cottage industry in the world of self-help. Beyond self-help and self-care, are mindfulness apps and games effective or are they "gimmicky" (Forbes, 2019, para. 1)? After all, mindfulness is part of ancient Dharmic practice; its onto-epistemological foundation should not be disregarded from its source tradition. (For a Dharmic approach to mindfulness in SEL, see UNESCO MGIEP's EMC² Framework for Social and Emotional Learning, described in Chapter Two.)

Can video games teach mindfulness? Like *Crystal of Kaydor* described in Chapter Four, researchers at the Center for Healthy Minds designed a game for an experimental study. The game developed, *Tenacity*, was an experience that promoted breath counting. Being present, or "in-the-moment," is a hallmark of mindfulness as a meditative practice; breath counting is an attention task that can create that state of awareness (Patsenko et al., 2019).

In *Tenacity*, tasks leveled-up in complexity through the experience. Players were first prompted to tap on an iPad screen once per breath for the first four breaths, then twice every fifth breath. As players progressed, the background on the screen changed, indicating a passage of time.

Tenacity was tested with a population of adolescents. The control group played *Fruit Ninja*, a game where players slice digital fruit with their fingers. Screen interactions in *Fruit Ninja* are similar but do not relate to breath counts the way they do in *Tenacity* (Patsenko et al., 2019). As with the *Crystal of Kaydor* study (Kral et al., 2018), functional magnetic resonance imaging (fMRI) measured neuroplasticity. Would adolescents' brains rewire based on digital stimuli?

Findings suggested that two weeks of *Tenacity* gameplay improved attention and mindfulness (Patsenko et al., 2019). Specifically, adolescent participants demonstrated "changes in the connectivity between their left dorsolateral prefrontal cortex and the left inferior parietal cortex in the brain, which are two areas critical for attention" (Patsenko et al., 2019; Spoon, 2019, para. 8). Like empathic accuracy (Kral et al., 2018), mindfulness was shown to be cognitively teachable.

Tenacity was designed as a proof of concept; for various reasons, it is not commercially playable. There are, however, mindfulness programs available for schools. Mindful Schools and Mind Yeti are notable examples of school-based curricular programs. Guided videos on the GoNoodle platform and on YouTube are options for individual classrooms.

Why is it important to be mindful? Mindfulness is a foundational skill that can lead to prosociality, particularly when connected to other SEL skills, such as empathy and compassion (Iwamoto et al., 2020; Singh & Duraiappah, 2019). Practicing mindfulness can also result in the reduction of stress, increased ability to focus, boosts in working memory, higher cognitive flexibility, lower emotional reactivity, and greater satisfaction of relationships (Davis & Hayes, 2012).

Where SEL is an approach that focuses on an "outside-in" approach, mindfulness takes an "inside-out" approach, focusing on cultivating qualities like kindness, empathy, and compassion (Iwamoto et al., 2020; "Mindfulness in Minecraft," n.d., para. 2). The capacity to be mindful also relates to emotional awareness centers in the brain that affect cognitive learning (Jazaieri et al., 2014; Zeidan, 2014).

It has been theorized that mindfulness—specifically, the extent to which one can be present in the moment—can lead to psychological well-being (e.g., Brown & Ryan, 2003). As such, in addition to mindfulness, this chapter investigates games that cultivate kindness, gratitude, and compassion. First, we visit *Minecraft*, the blocky world where children can build and create—and now, can meditate and reflect.

The Mindful Knight

Minecraft: Education Edition is more than a school-friendly version of the commercial video game—it is a robust website where like-minded educators can connect with peer mentors, download lesson plans, and access shared maps of community-generated worlds (Farber & Williams, 2019). Some of these lessons and worlds use the game as a practice space to develop empathy, perspective-taking, digital citizenship, and mindfulness.

"Like with so much else in *Minecraft*, the SEL curriculum emerged from the community," Deirdre Quarnstrom told me. When we spoke, Quarnstrom was the general manager of Minecraft Atlas at Microsoft, which focuses on initiatives like *Minecraft: Education Edition*; these days, she is VP of Education Experiences for Microsoft. "There was a demand for it, with classroom teachers telling us and showing us the potential to use *Minecraft* to explore SEL." One educator in this space was Stephen Reid, whose consulting company Immersive Minds developed SEL-themed worlds for teachers in the *Minecraft: Education Edition* community. Reid now works for Microsoft Education.

The *Minecraft: Education Edition* environment itself is naturally SEL—and not just because students can be grouped in teams solving problems together. Different than other digital learning platforms, *Minecraft* is a commercial game adapted for classrooms. As a result, children who play at home and also at school may need to bridge their school identity with their gaming persona. "Yes, there is a multiplayer aspect, but because students play at home too, there is another dimension to the learning opportunities," Quarnstrom said. "The game is about an actual digital identity that they are building on. This creates interesting scenarios for teachers and students to navigate together."

In terms of SEL lessons, of note is *The Mindful Knight*, a set of activities and a downloadable pre-constructed world. "*The Mindful Knight* started at a hackathon with Microsoft employees," Quarnstrom recalled. "They were interested in raising awareness around mental health and mental hygiene, and they saw *Minecraft* as a way to do that."

Hackathons (a portmanteau of "hacking" and "marathon") are part of the culture of Microsoft. At Microsoft Hackathons, employees produced Immersive Reader, a screen reading tool for children with dyslexia and dysgraphia, the Xbox Adaptive Controller, and a customizable digital assistant for the Microsoft Edge browser. *The Mindful Knight* won two Microsoft Hackathon awards: 1st Place for Mental Health Hack Challenge and 2nd Place for Hack for Modern Life.

"We had a game designer, Cole Phillips, orchestrate the project team," Quarnstrom continued. "Our secret sauce is to team game designers with educators. Great game designers know how to create 'hard fun' or 'serious fun.' They know how to create things that are challenging enough, so when students fail, they will still be motivated to come back." Teaming game designers with teachers was also the model used at Quest to Learn, a game-based school in New York City. When it opened, there was a room set aside called Mission Lab. In this space, teachers met with game designers from the Institute of Play to plan game-like learning experiences that felt playful and fun.

Quarnstrom's team did an initial build of the world and the lessons. She also brought in specialists from Microsoft Research to meet the game designers. Then it was playtested in classrooms. "We got a lot of feedback from teachers, places where it got to be too challenging or where it wasn't fun or where it was confusing."

The Mindful Knight is a set of quests introduced by Queen Serenity, a non-playable character who invites players to become a knight, which is achieved by collecting four relics. Players then travel through a courtyard to meet other non-playable characters, like Wizard, who instructs players to cast a Levitation Spell through focused breathing. As players breathe, their avatar levitates. Next, players meet Princess Breathany, who teaches them how to focus on their thoughts. Other moments of gameplay are set underwater, in the Pond of Presence, where all is serene. In the final challenge or boss level, players enter the dragon's lair. There, players are reminded that any feelings they experience are okay.

Student progress can be documented using the camera and the book and quill blocks (see Figure 8). Given to players by Queen Serenity, these blocks are unique to *Minecraft: Education Edition* and serve as a visual and written journal, a place where students can reflect. There are prompts, too. One is a pre-writing exercise asking, "How do you manage your emotions when you get upset by your experience at school?" Another asks students to share emotions associated with screenshots they took during their journey.

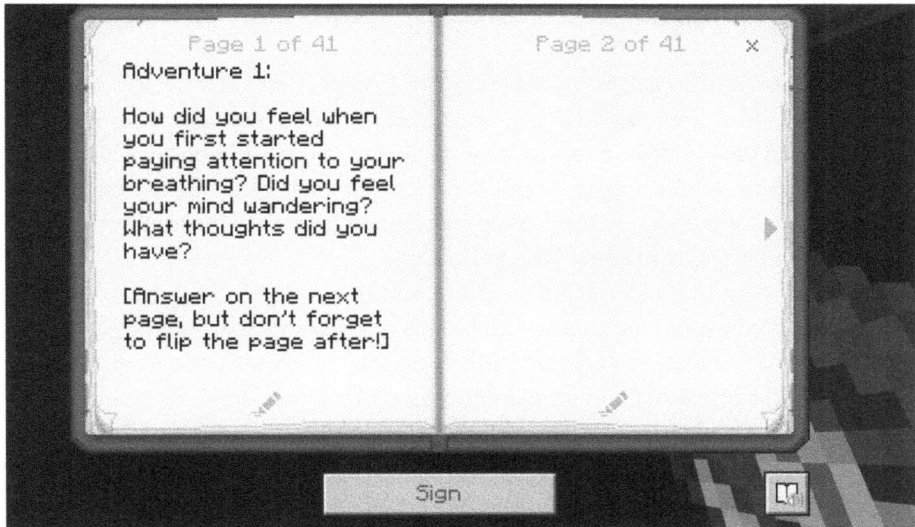

Figure 8. Image of *The Mindful Knight* Book and Quill. Source: Mojang Studios. Reprinted by permission of the publisher.

"Because we have game designers involved in all of our lessons and content, we can tap into the features in *Minecraft* in deep ways," Quarnstrom said. In other words, it is not superficially checking the SEL buzzword box. "Our game designers understand the underwater world in *Minecraft*, and how that can generate feelings of peace and meditation. That was something we used in *The Mindful Knight* world that we built up. There is a section where students go into the underwater world and then record what they see there as an exercise in self-regulation and mindfulness."

The Mindful Knight is just one of many SEL lessons on the *Minecraft: Education Edition* website. There is also an SEL Content Pack aligned to standards from the Committee for Children, a nonprofit based in Seattle. Educators can also take a free course on mindfulness, found in the Microsoft Educator Center. There are ten modules and a brief quiz, including an overview of mindfulness research and extension activities.

Play Deliberately: A Mindful Walk in the Virtual Woods

Walden, a game is an award-winning narrative exploration designed by Tracy Fullerton and developed by the University of Southern California Game Innovation Lab. Published in 2017, the game is based on Henry David Thoreau's

Walden; or, Life in the Woods (1854), the classic book about his two year experiment in self-reliance.

In the game, Thoreau is voiced by actor Emile Hirsh, star of the similarly themed 2007 film, *Into the Wild*. The arc takes place over the course of one year. The year is divided into four seasons that challenge players differently. The central core mechanic is environmental exploration; the story is told in the first-person camera. Players then explore and discover virtually through Thoreau's eyes, ears, and embodied movements—including walking.

Thoreau went to Walden Pond to "live simply in nature" (1854, p. 135). Thoreau was not a survivalist but had to survive; he was not merely experimenting whether he could live off of the 19th century grid; he wanted to learn from nature. His was a philosophical experiment about communing with nature's sublime beauty.

Walden, a game is part of a genre of games known as *walking simulators*, sometimes just called walking sims. Walking sims can involve environmental storytelling, where players uncover objects that reveal parts of a nonlinear narrative. I spoke about nonlinear environmental storytelling with game designer Steve Gaynor (*Gone Home*, *Tacoma*) back in 2015. In his game, *Gone Home*, players explore the Greenbriar house. Empty of people, it is filled with objects (diaries, cassette tapes) that reveal a story of family dysfunction. According to Gaynor, "*Gone Home* is a clear demonstration of how much the narrative process happens in your head, as opposed to on the page or on the screen" (as cited in Farber, 2015, para. 15). This metacognitive process lends the walking sim readily to English language arts classrooms.

As part of my case study ethnographic dissertation research, I observed *Gone Home* adapted for a high school class. Since then, I have been on a curriculum writing team creating lessons around a similar walking sim, *What Remains of Edith Finch*. And as I write this, I am part of a small team adapting *Walden, a game* for classrooms. That team also includes Fullerton, along with Matthew Hamilton, one of her PhD students.

There are many affordances for mindfulness in *Walden, a game*. After all, it was Thoreau who famously wrote, "I went to the woods because I wished to live deliberately, to front only the essential facts of life, and see if I could not learn what it had to teach, and not, when I came to die, discover that I had not lived" (1854, p. 52). The tagline for Fullerton's digital adaptation riffs on Thoreau's quote. On the game's website, players are invited to "Play deliberately."

What makes *Walden, a game* a walking sim? And, what exactly is a walking sim? Walking sims often lack points to accumulate, badges to achieve, ways to level-up characters, and win or loss conditions. Are walking sims games or interactive stories? "Walking sims are almost always differentiated from a normal first-person game because of the reduction of threat," Fullerton explained. "Classically, we think of the walking simulator as something about walking, but so are first-person shooters, which have walking and running. The real differentiation is the reduction of threat and the emphasis on exploration rather than threat assessment."

As a player of open-world games who sometimes ignores goal-focused missions in favor of virtual world exploration, this explanation resonated with me. When playing the aesthetically beautiful *Red Dead Redemption 2*, I sometimes wander through campsites and rustic towns in the American West landscape. I am not alone in these pursuits: In 2019, the Audubon Society published a list of rare migratory bird species that players can discover while exploring in the game (Lund, 2019).

Walking sims describe any game where players can explore but not be harmed. Crafting and exploring in *Red Dead Redemption 2* between missions is not much different from doing that in *Animal Crossing: New Horizons*. In *Animal Crossing*, players can catalog wildlife, converse with non-playable characters, and stargaze. *Minecraft* can be played like a walking sim, too; in the start menu, select Peaceful Mode, and the blocky world becomes yours to discover!

The full version of *Walden, a game* takes about six hours to play. Subdivided into eight half-seasons, players cycle through summer, fall, winter, and spring. Missions are a fairly open-ended affair: as long as Thoreau's basic needs are met (survival as well as an appreciation of nature), players can freely explore the environment and choose which goals they would like to take on. An immersive experience, its lengthy gameplay with few elusive goals can be a tough sell to traditional classrooms. That's not to say that teachers are not using the game; in fact, thousands are, using a curriculum guide published by Journeys in Film. But again, this is for the full version.

As a result of many teacher workshops, Fullerton applied for an extension grant from the National Endowment for the Humanities, supporters of the initial project. With this new support, Fullerton led in the development of an educational adaptation, one that now consists of "mini-episodes" that take about 30-minutes each to play. Mini-episodes were updated to have focused goals and can be streamed on lower-end computers, requiring no installation or high-end graphics technology. The educational version can now run on most Chromebooks. What's more, these new modules are totally free to access and play.

"The full version was meant to give an open-ended, user-set goal from the outset," Fullerton said. "It is a six hour long experience that is guided only by time—the day cycle, the season cycle, and the challenges within that changing world. Other than that, players are free to do whatever they want within the constraints of each day and each season."

As stated earlier, Fullerton recruited Hamilton and me to assist in developing a curriculum around the newly produced mini-episodes. The first set of lessons were on the book's and game's theme of self-reliance. "You are going to the woods. What will you bring?" we ask students. Subsequent lessons are on environmental studies, civil disobedience, and mindfulness. The curriculum is modular and can be taught and played in any order that fits a particular teacher's needs.

The mini-episode on mindfulness, and the lessons that support it, utilize what Fullerton calls "Wander Mode." "You can wander openly with no restraints," she explained. "You don't have to do upkeep on your character or your house—but of course, we will let you. You are free to do these things if that is what makes you peaceful. But, you won't need to do them."

As a walking sim, care was taken to ensure that the player's experience would be situational, not mechanical (Upton, 2018). Much of the game is about passive constraints, anticipatory play, and slow, reflective, and contemplative thought (Upton, 2018). This engenders a different experience than in *Tenacity*, the breath counting game from the beginning of this chapter. The goal of *Tenacity* is to hone attention skills, which relates to mindful presence, being in the moment. Different in approach, affordances for mindfulness in *Walden, a game* were inspired by Thoreau's experiment of living deliberately in the woods.

The game's immersive quality is fine-tuned to the player's experiences. When you walk as Thoreau, the camera slightly bobs up and down in tune with your footsteps. Further, the environment itself responds to the character, as does the soundscape. If a player stops at a location in the woods, wind can be heard passing through trees. Water skaters glide across the surface of the pond. In other words, as the player inhabits Thoreau in this world, a sense of presence is engendered. "As you walk, you feel the steps," Fullerton said. "The actual steps are heard, and the visual is in beat. Like real-world walking, our virtual world walking is built to feel as embodied as possible."

This connection of virtual walking to Thoreau's musings on real-world walking intrigued Fullerton. In her keynote talk at the 2019 Connected Learning Summit, Fullerton quoted Thoreau, who wrote an essay just before his death, simply titled, *Walking* (1862). Posthumously published, Thoreau wrote, "Two or three hours' walking will carry me to as strange a country as I expect ever to see" (1862, para. 15).

In her talk, Fullerton shared more on Thoreau's connection to walking. "Thoreau was a naturalist, an activist, a philosopher, a writer—and also a teacher," she said. "And his best classroom was the woods." Thoreau sometimes split his days walking, then writing. She then quoted from author Rebecca Solnit, who wrote, "The rhythm of walking generates a kind of rhythm of thinking" (2001, p. 5). According to Solnit, the pace of walking—around three miles per hour—may equal the speed of human thought (Solnit, 2001 as cited by Fullerton, 2019). (Fullerton's entire talk is linked at the end of this chapter.)

I asked Fullerton what she meant by this and how it related to mindfulness in walking sims like *Walden, a game*. "The simulation of walking is important to mindfulness," she replied. "Beyond its utility for human beings, there is a nonutilitarian aspect that involves mindfulness, and the absorption and tilling of ideas. Being mindful is part of that physicality we feel when we are walking from place to place."

Walden, a game and the mindfulness app *Headspace* were part of a comparative qualitative case study of user experiences at Georgia Tech. Professor Betsy DiSalvo and her master's students collected data, then Hamilton analyzed and wrote up findings. When we talked, they remarked on connections from Upton's (2018) ludic semiotics to mindfulness. "There is an epistemological cycle of testing things and receiving feedback," Hamilton said, referring to how humans tend to confirm their cognitive schemas. "We seek information that affirms our knowledge. Interestingly, when we play games, it becomes pleasurable to expand those schemas. Games can support us being uncomfortable with goallessness or the lack of telos or the obvious endpoint of life, which is *Walden*'s theme. Mindfulness is the leap into this unknown."

Mindful by Design author Caitlin Krause recommends journaling as essential to reflective practice. In her book, she refers to student journals as their "garden space," where ideas begin and are later cultivated (Krause, 2019, p. 38). In fact, journaling is built into many role-playing video games: *The Mindful Knight* in *Minecraft: Education Edition* has students recording thoughts on mindful practice in a journal; in *Red Dead Redemption 2*, protagonist Arthur Morgan records events in a digital, leather-bound journal. *Walden, a game* also tracks and records players' experiences. "One of the things we heard from teachers was that they would like students to journal alongside the game's journal," Fullerton said. In the educational mini-episodes, the game still journals. But now, there is a space for students to journal next to that. "The in-game journal functions as a prompt, a reminder of what you did, so you can write about your own feelings and experiences, and respond after the fact."

The *What I Lived For* module was designed to cultivate mindfulness. It models a contemplative walk around the pond with special spots marked with stone cairns that prompt students to stop, reflect, and breathe with Thoreau. Students are asked to design a reflective journal with prompts framed to encourage students to think of the land, animals, and plants encountered more like active characters in the experience, rather than seeing the environment as a backdrop or setting.

Walden, a game's Wander Mode and *Minecraft: Education Edition*'s *The Mindful Knight* lessons are just two examples of mindfulness opportunities in video games. *Alto's Adventure*, an endless downhill skiing mobile game, may also afford mindfulness. In the settings, players can toggle to "Zen Mode," a mode that removes challenges, threats, and loss conditions. On the developer's website, a letter from a thankful Zen Mode player is shared:

> *Alto's Adventure* doesn't make me more stressed than I already am. Skiing down a mountain is calming (especially helped by the music, props to your music maker!). It makes me feel as if I'm professing and being productive without the frustrations of getting to that next level in narrative game [*sic*.] or other mobile games.
>
> *Alto's Adventure* has become something I use as a coping mechanism when I need it, so thank you again for developing it. And well done, it's a bloody work of art. (Relax with Zen Mode, 2016, para. 2)

Games published by thatgamecompany may also cultivate contemplative thought. Its games include *flOw*, an experimental game in flow theory that Jenova Chen first created for Fullerton as part of his master's thesis. Other calming and potentially mindful games from this studio include *Flower* and *Journey*, as well as their most recent game, *Sky: Children of the Light*, which adorns the cover of this book. In these games, wonder and awe are evoked as players embody a flower, a mystical robed figure, and flying caped heroes, respectively. Like walking sims more broadly, there is never a threat to the player and no fail conditions. Players can pursue goals or elect to glide through ethereal virtual landscapes.

Kind Words: A Game About Being Nice

Set in a floating open-cubed bedroom, *Kind Words (lo-fi chill beats to write to)* is a respite from the noise of the outside world (see Figure 9). In this cozy nook, lo-fi electronic music, scored by composer Clark Aboud, plays. There is a character in the room that sits at a desk facing an open window. Shelves are adjacent to the bed, holding knick-knacks and a stereo.

Paper airplanes fly across the bedroom. Clicking on them unfold notes. One I opened read, "You are doing great! We are proud of you and what you can accomplish. Remember that the next time you are feeling down."

Kind Words is an online multiplayer video game. The letters I read are real, not computer-generated. Actual players send and receive anonymous notes of kindness, gratitude, and encouragement to and from others. It is wonderful!

The more I play, the more stickers I collect. Stickers can be used to decorate the bedroom. Additional music for the stereo can also be unlocked.

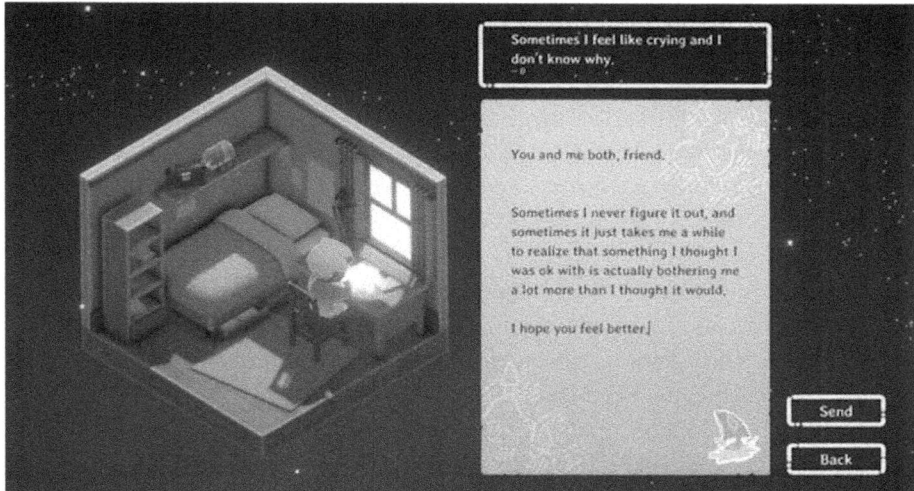

Figure 9. Floating bedroom in *Kind Words*. Source: Popcannibal Games. Reprinted by permission of the publisher.

Writing letters is a guided process led by Ella the Female Mail Deer. She recommends positivity and empathy. She lets me know that sometimes listening and validating are enough, and that everyone's problems are not always solvable. Mental health resources from MentalHealth.gov, a suicide prevention lifeline, and two gaming community resources—CheckPoint and Take This—are linked.

I spoke with *Kind Word*'s designer, Ziba Scott, several times during the summer of 2020. We chatted over Zoom, the videoconference tool that helped so many of us maintain a sense of connectedness while locked in our real-world bedrooms. In the first year of release, more than 2.5 million letters were sent on *Kind Words*. My first question to Scott was forthright: "Are we—all of humanity—that little character stuck home alone in a floating bedroom, yearning for human connection?" "No," he quickly replied. Well, of course not—the game was published months before the pandemic crisis took hold. But, Scott did understand my interpretation, as he too was working from home.

Actually, *Kind Words* was created as a reaction to the divisiveness of the times, where fear, exclusion, and xenophobia were rampant. "We made this in America, during Republican politics under the Trump administration," Scott said. "We wanted to make a game where players could have an opportunity to exercise and understand hard parts of their own psyche and other people's lives."

Scott sometimes analyzes word usage in the letters that players send. Since launch, he expected to read phrases like, "I'm stressed about the environment," or, "I am worried about our government." "I went through the backend and did some analysis on the frequency of words," he said. Rather than generalized worries, players tended to write about what was specifically happening to them personally. Anecdotally, "anxiety," "fear," and "scared" were commonly used.

Did the COVID-19 crisis affect the content of letters? As it happened, there was a spike in the frequency of words like "quarantine," "COVID-19," and "sick." "By far, those were still not the most common words," Scott said. "The words that still mattered most to players were, 'friend,' 'relationship,' 'boyfriend,' 'girlfriend,' and 'family.'"

Kind Words is authentic and humanistic. In short, the experience is real—it's not escapism, nor is it fantasy. "You are literally and actually being nice to other players," Scott said. "People appreciate the feedback to requests because [other players] are volunteering their time."

Is *Kind Words* a video game or is it a nicer form of social media? "*Kind Words* is, sort of, a bad email client," he joked. "What was important to us was that *Kind Words* was *presented* as a game, in the language of gaming, in the space of gaming because of the attitudes, beliefs, and approaches people would then have when they come to it."

Kind Words does not run in a web browser or on a small mobile screen. Instead, it is a full sensory experience—"a full takeover of your computer," Scott explained. "Players anticipate that the game is going to be nice to them. Players are here to have that all-engrossing experience that you get with games. That is why *Kind Words* is a game and not social media."

Unlike Facebook, Twitter, and Instagram, all writing in *Kind Words* is anonymous. Players are forbidden from liking or commenting on letters. The only communication is when others respond to requests (a request is often someone else seeking empathy from another). Once a player responds, that conversation ends.

Player anonymity engenders a sense of global connection. When I sent a letter, I felt as if I was shouting to the universe. Reading a response is equally powerful: the universe (other anonymous players) listened, and cares. "There are plenty of sites where you can be anonymous, but you still have a persistent identity between your messages, a persona that you inhabit on that site," Scott explained. "In *Kind Words*, you are not permitted that. Here, you are not required to be consistent with your messages. And I've seen a lot of players take advantage of that."

Scott and [game artist] Luigi Guatieri monitor letters shared in the game. But they don't ban players. Instead, they "selectively filter." "When people bring their best selves, we can respond to them properly," Scott continued. "Then, there is no barrier for them to mood switch from how they are going to face the world."

Scott and Guatieri mainly rely on the community to report on inappropriate or toxic players. According to Scott, only about 3% of messages get flagged by either the system or other players. "We encourage people to hit the report button for anything, positive or negative. We want people to use the report button often." Curse words are deemed acceptable in this space—"depending on the context, of course," Scott said. "We started filtering curse words in the beginning, but that was useless. This is a game about strong emotions, and people may be here to express strong emotions."

So, what would *Kind Words* look like in a classroom? Can its systems of kindness, compassion, and empathy be harnessed to teach adolescents SEL skills? As it happens, Zachary Hartzman, a high school teacher in New York City, uses the game as a practice space to deepen SEL with his students (he previews letters first). Lessons are framed around reflective discussion questions, asking students questions, like "What advice did you give to another player?" His lesson plan is linked at the end of this chapter.

In addition to responding to letters, Hartzman asks students to consider why this game exists in the first place. Much like analyzing literary fiction, students consider why artists make and share creative works. Students then talk about mental health and the importance of saying nice things (see Figure 10).

Modeling prosocial behaviors is something clinical psychologist and game designer Kelli Dunlap does in her Psychology of Video Games course at American University. "I first showed the class a letter that I had shared, back when I was having a hard time last year when I was trying to figure out what was going on with my life," she began. "Then, we found a letter that someone had posted in my inbox."

The letter was from someone who was struggling academically. The author scored good grades in high school but now struggled in college. Dunlap seized on this opportunity as a teachable moment, crafting a response together with her class. "This was hard to do," she said. "It became Therapy 101."

In therapy, clinicians are trained to validate feelings before offering support. "If someone is complaining about their grades and is feeling overwhelmed, the last thing you want to say is, 'They're just grades!'"

In Brené Brown's viral 2013 YouTube video on empathy (over 15 million views as of this writing), she remarked, "Rarely—if ever—does an empathic response begin with 'at least.'" Here, Brown is contrasting the nuances of empathy and sympathy. "At least you have a marriage," as a response to someone in a failing marriage is not empathy; it is sympathy (Brown, 2013). Empathy is feeling how others feel (Brown, 2013).

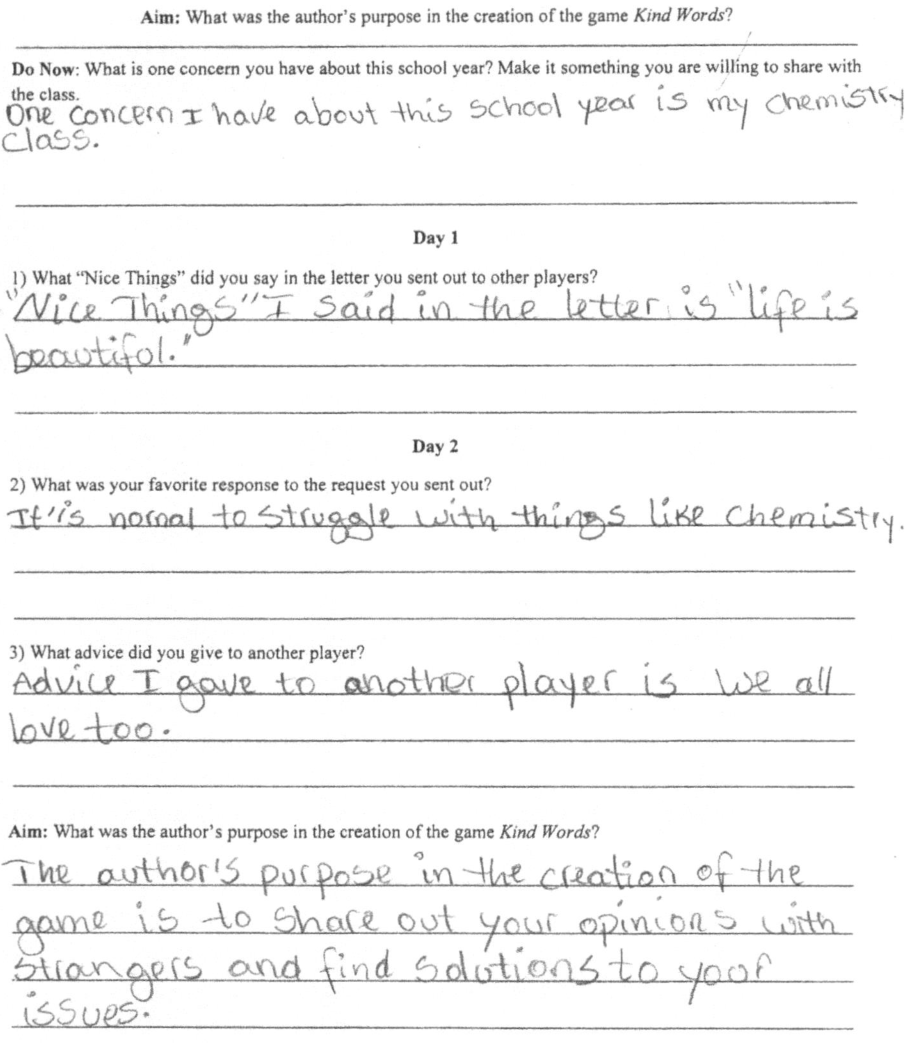

Aim: What was the author's purpose in the creation of the game *Kind Words*?

Do Now: What is one concern you have about this school year? Make it something you are willing to share with the class.

One concern I have about this school year is my chemistry class.

Day 1

1) What "Nice Things" did you say in the letter you sent out to other players?

"Nice Things" I said in the letter is "life is beautiful."

Day 2

2) What was your favorite response to the request you sent out?

It's normal to struggle with things like chemistry.

3) What advice did you give to another player?

Advice I gave to another player is we all love too.

Aim: What was the author's purpose in the creation of the game *Kind Words*?

The author's purpose in the creation of the game is to share out your opinions with strangers and find solutions to your issues.

Figure 10. Student Reflection After Playing *Kind Words*. Source: Zachary Hartzman, founder of Hey Listen Games. Reprinted by permission of the author.

Empathizing with others requires a cognitive pause, reflecting on someone else's understanding of a situation. In Dunlap's course, *Kind Words* was used to model how to listen, offer hope, and give support. She shared her class-authored response to the anonymous academically struggling student with me. It read:

> I'm so sorry to hear that; it's super frustrating to feel like this. Big changes, like from high school to college, are really hard. Grades can feel like the most important thing

in the world, especially if you're used to getting As and Bs. Grades are important, but they don't define your worth. You're doing the best you can with what you've got, and that's enough. Good luck in school, and know you're not alone. Take time for yourself. We're cheering for you.

Instead of offering empty sentiments of encouragement, like, "You'll be fine!" Dunlap taught her students how clinicians listen, empathize, and validate feelings. Take This clinical director Raffael Boccamazzo dubs this approach "EVOO." "It's easy to remember if you cook because it is extra virgin olive oil!" he said. In this context, EVOO stands for "Empathy, Validation, and Offer Options." "It is in that order for specific reasons. When you offer options right away to someone, it is minimizing. For example, if someone is experiencing body dysmorphia, responding, 'Have you tried kale?' or, 'Why don't practice yoga?' subtly messages, 'Well I can figure it out, why can't you?'"

If empathy is the *what*, validation is the *why*. "It doesn't mean agreeing with or condoning; it just means you can reflect back the other person's perspective on things," Boccamazzo continued. "It might be something as simple as labeling their emotion as specifically as possible. You might respond stating, 'It sounds like you are feeling overwhelmed.'"

It is not enough to ask children to be kind or to show empathy. Obvious to some, there are steps, and these may not come naturally for children—or people, more generally. The potential transformative power of using video games to teach SEL is that they often break things down into procedural steps (Bogost, 2007, 2008). With the guidance of thoughtful teachers like Hartzman and Dunlap—and Ella the Female Mail Deer—games like *Kind Words* can make the world a nicer place.

SEL in the Game of School

Classcraft is a game-based approach to classroom learning that uses systems common in role-playing games (RPGs) to boost student engagement and motivation. In the game, students are given roles (e.g., guardians, healers, mages) and then are grouped into teams. As they play, they can level-up, unlocking real-world powers as they progress. Real-world powers are privileges that range from using notes during tests to snacking in class. Student players can also earn rewards by demonstrating positive behaviors toward peers.

Central to the *Classcraft* experience is that the teacher is the "Game Master," the person pulling the pulleys and levers throughout a learning experience. Instead of slaying dragons or defeating orcs, in *Classcraft*, students work together to achieve academic and SEL goals. Game Master tools include the Volume Meter, a visual timer that measures noise level using the microphone input on a computer, and the Wheel of Destiny, a random player picker. The Volume Meter is handy when paired with student-centered learning practices, which can get noisy. As students work in teams on projects, they can self-regulate and self-manage their loudness. The Wheel of Destiny is based on "no hands up" research, as spinning the wheel can limit a teacher's unconscious bias from mainly calling on extroverted students (Eastman, 2019). There are also Random Events, including moments for spontaneous applause.

Classcraft has "behavior presets" that align with several SEL frameworks and large-scale programs schools adopt to promote a positive school climate, like Positive Behavior Interventions and Supports (PBIS) and Multi-Tiered Support Systems (MTSS). Behavior presets give teachers and PBIS and MTSS coordinators a tiered intervention approach that is uniform, schoolwide.

When students show respect, demonstrate empathic concern, or use appropriate strategies for managing stress, they earn experience points (XP). Accumulating XP means that students can unlock more skills and in-game abilities. For teachers, XP data helps to identify students who are succeeding, as well as those at-risk who may require interventions. Of *Classcraft*'s alignment to SEL, Maurice J. Elias, director of Rutgers University's Social-Emotional and Character Development Lab, wrote,

> *Classcraft* is not a program but rather an "approach." It is not a self-contained system for teaching SEL skills, but it affords a viable, systematic way in which educators can create a climate within which SEL can thrive, and within which specific SEL skills can be emphasized, practices, and further developed. (Elias, 2018, p. 1)

Competencies in CASEL's SEL Framework should be demonstrated by children. Ultimately, SEL competencies are desired behaviors. "So much of SEL is when 'the rubber meets the road,'" founder and CEO Shawn Young explained. "How can you get students to exhibit these behaviors and competencies in real life situations? For example, with self-awareness, are students setting goals and working towards it? With self-management, are they exhibiting self-control, or are they acting impulsively? About interpersonal skills, are they respectful or unkind?"

As it presents school as a game with rules, *Classcraft* can make the complex situation of school less complicated. In some ways, it is the opposite of typical school experiences. Through a game designer's lens, school is poorly designed (Schell, 2020). For many, school is an inequitable system with poor feedback mechanisms. It is also driven by extrinsic incentives—outside motivators that come mainly from adults, like test scores, grades, and sports trophies (Schell, 2020). Reading logs, which can demotivate struggling readers (Pak & Weseley, 2012), are an example of an extrinsic incentive. The act of reading—like learning itself—should be fulfilling and pleasurable.

Self-determination theory (SDT) describes the innate human need to feel a sense of autonomy, relatedness, and competence (Deci & Ryan, 1985, 2000; Ryan & Deci, 2018). In the context of school, autonomy is when students see themselves "as the primary locus of control" in a learning environment (Aguilar et al., 2018, p. 46). Relatedness is the social feeling of connectedness we feel with others (e.g., peers, teachers) (Deci & Ryan, 1985, 2000; Ryan & Deci, 2018). Competence describes how we feel when new skills or concepts are just within our grasp (Csikszentmihalyi, 1990/2008; Ryan & Deci, 2018).

Many people play video games because it meets our needs for autonomy, relatedness, and competence (Ryan & Deci, 2018). Games afford agency to players, "the satisfying power to take meaningful action and see the results of our decision and choices" (Murray, 2017, p. 159). Good games keep players in the *flow channel*, where skill and the difficulty increase just enough to make players feel competent (Csikszentmihalyi, 1990/2008; Ryan & Deci, 2018). Games are also social, as many feature communities where players converge to share experiences (Ito et al., 2018).

Let's use skill trees in RPGs as an example of SDT in action. As an RPG, *Classcraft* has skill trees, a visual map that tracks player progression. As the name implies, skill trees have branches that relate to ways a character can level-up or get stronger from experiences. In a *Tomb Raider* game, players unlock and accumulate skill points, which can be used to boost Lara Croft's skills. A *Tomb Raider* game's skill tree may have one branch for health, another for weapons, and one for fighting abilities.

Being able to visualize progression in school may help students feel competent and in control over their experiences. "Skill trees are a great example of SDT because you can see the possibilities," cognitive psychologist Celia Hodent told me. "Players can see that there is something that they want down the line. They also have autonomy because they can typically choose their specialization. Skill trees give clear feedback on competence and progression toward that goal."

Kudos is a peer gratitude feature in *Classcraft* that can engender a sense of relatedness. Like *Kind Words* but not anonymous, students send messages of kindness to classmates. Before getting published and shared, Kudos are first sent to teachers for approval. Teacher approval ensures appropriateness and affords teachable moments to give feedback on writing notes of gratitude.

As it is part of a game, students who send and receive Kudos earn XP. "Pedagogically, what better way to develop your competencies than to identify positive behaviors in other people," Young remarked. "For many kids, peer recognition and peer feedback are more important than top-down feedback." In the first six weeks after *Classcraft* added this feature, 75,000 Kudos were approved by teachers. "Kids are taking time out of their day to write kind notes to other kids, which is pretty powerful," Young said.

Kudos can be shared in classrooms but also schoolwide. Teachers can export a full-screen scrolling presentation that can be displayed in school hallways. "This shares the culture of prosocial encouragement beyond the teacher. When you see your Kudos in the hallway, that adds even more meaning and importance."

Kudos may be incentivizing gratitude, but it also connects to *Classcraft*'s SDT motivational framework. Ultimately, students have the opportunity to be prosocial with people whom they actually know. After all, to kids, school is not a game—it's their real life.

Compassion Games: Survival of the Kindest

Compassion Games is a real-world multiplayer game that can take place in any setting—from schools to academic conferences to entire cities. Like *Kind Words* and *Classcraft*, it incentivizes prosocial behaviors through game mechanics. To date, versions have been played by more than one million volunteers in 40 countries (Compassion Games, 2020).

I had the opportunity to play the *Compassion Games* at a UNESCO MGIEP conference in India. Jon Ramer, the designer, introduced the rules in his opening keynote. His short-term goal was everyone to connect, to forge new relationships and friendships. The long-term objective was a call to action for like-minded folks to promise to collaborate on future prosocial projects.

There are many editions of the *Compassion Games*, including a school-friendly one. The version I played was the result of a collaboration between MGIEP and Compassion Games International, known as the "TECH Compassion Games." Guidebook, a mobile app used to track conference sessions, was the hub to follow the self-paced missions. The instructions read:

> We play to establish authentic trust among the attendees and create the results needed to achieve the conference objective of a call for action to mainstream SEL in education systems. This game will be fun, enriching, engaging, and interactive. We will synergize to create Brave. Kind. Fun. Results. The game will empower us to experience the values we share, inspire us to act together, find courage in each other, and hope in our solidarity. (TECH Compassion Games, 2019)

The first mission was called Bridging Our Differences: Befriend the Other. The stated objective was, "Look for people to connect with whom you might not otherwise approach." Attendees mingled, then scored themselves by completing a Google Form survey. The ultimate goal beyond the call to action was to amass a database network of "DreamKeepers"—teams of people to join the Peace on Earth by 2030 initiative, a plan to create global harmony based on principles started by social change activist David Gershon.

Ramer's story is interwoven with the history of the game. Originally from Brooklyn, New York, he moved to Seattle following the terrorist attacks on September 11, 2001. "I decided to no longer stay on the sidelines," Ramer told the crowd at TECH.

In 2008, Ramer met His Holiness the Dalai Lama while at Seeds of Compassion, a five-day event in Seattle. "I then became the executive director of the Compassion Action Network," he told me. "The goal of the Compassion Action Network was to ensure that compassion would continue onward in a meaningful way once the event had ended."

Ramer was also influenced by the 2008 TED Prize winner, Karen Armstrong. In her TED Talk, Armstrong spoke about scaling the Golden Rule, the ethical principle of treating others as you would want to be treated. The Golden Rule is an ethic of reciprocity, a "moral dictum" found in many religions (Parrott, 2018, p. 1). It appears as "love your neighbor as yourself" in the Hebrew Bible and the New Testament. In Islam, the Golden Rule is part of the teachings of Prophet Muhammad. The Hindu text Mahabharata Shānti-Parva states, "Make dharma your main focus, treating others as you treat yourself." If so many world religions preach this creed, Armstrong wondered, why isn't all of humanity following it?

The Dalai Lama's and Armstrong's messages resonated with Ramer. "These beliefs weren't an ideology or philosophy," he said. "They were a way to turn empathy into action." Ramer put his empathy into action when he helped launch the International Campaign for Compassionate Cities movement in 2009. "There are 450 cities that took it on as a nonprofit," Ramer explained. One of those cities was Louisville, Kentucky, whose mayor, Greg Fisher, sent Ramer a letter proclaiming that they were the most compassionate city in the world—and would be so until proven otherwise.

"I went to the mayor and city council of Seattle and proposed a game that would later have 1,500 people sign on to play." That game was the *Compassion Games: Survival of the Kindest*. First played by cities in 2012, the game is "a community engagement experience that invites people around the world to inspire one another to reveal and promote acts of compassion that better our lives, our communities, and all life on Earth" (Compassion Games, 2020, para. 1). Ramer calls it a *coop-etition*, a portmanteau of "cooperation" and "competition." "You are cooperating to compete with—not against—each other," he said. "We are culture hacking the idea of kindness and service. The goal is not victory, but fulfillment, and continual improvement." Befriending others and doing kind acts and services evoke feelings of compassion and love. "When you do something for someone else, or something kind for yourself, it is powerful."

Children can get in the *Compassion Games*, too. Ramer shared a Google Doc (see the end of this chapter) of kid-friendly compassionate acts. Examples include tutoring, calling a sick friend, drinking more water, riding a bike, volunteering at animal shelters, and cleaning up litter. Acts of compassion can be documented on an interactive Compassion Report Map on the *Compassion Games*'s website. Clicking on digital pins reveals player metrics, such as who volunteered for service, who benefitted from service, and hours of service. There is also the *Teachers Compassion Games Guide*, a school-based adaptation developed by Rahbin Shyne. When your students play, keep in mind that the goal is *coop-etition*, a moonshot of compassion built from everyone's contributions through shared acts of kindness.

Extra Life and the Children's Miracle Network

Each year, my university's esports club hosts an Extra Life event. Students play games like *Rocket League, League of Legends, Counter-Strike: Global Offensive*, and *Overwatch* for hours while raising money for charity. "We usually have a buy-in of $2 per tournament, with half the money going to Extra Life and the other half split among the winners of that tournament," the club president at the time explained. "We also stream the tournaments on Twitch and project it in the room so people can participate even if they aren't at the event in person."

What exactly is Extra Life? Extra Life is part of the Children's Miracle Network, a network of 170 Children's Hospitals in the United States and Canada. Its slogan is, "Play games, heal kids."

Like many, my personal interactions with the Children's Miracle Network was from donating Miracle Balloons at our local Dairy Queen and Rite-Aid (among many other retail partners). Miracle Balloons are paper balloons sold for $1 that hang in restaurants and stores.

The Children's Miracle Network was co-founded in 1983 by Marie Osmond (of Donny and Marie fame). In the 1980s, Osmond, along with actor John Schneider (from TV's *The Dukes of Hazzard*), hosted telethons—live variety shows where viewers called in and donated money. Raising money on a live television broadcast seems like an outmoded concept these days, so Miracle Balloons are where many donations currently emanate. Over $5 billion have been raised over the years for its network of children's hospitals.

The origin story of Extra Life is separate and distinct from the Children's Miracle Network. It began in 2008 when Jeromy "Doc" Adams, a video game podcaster and on-air radio personality, visited a Children's Miracle Network hospital in Houston, Texas, for a radiothon (a telethon on the radio). There, he met an energetic, 11-year-old girl named Victoria (Tori) Enmon, who was at the hospital receiving leukemia treatment. Her prognosis was initially hopeful, but then she and her family found out that her hospital stay would be extended—she needed a second bone marrow transplant. Thinking about how Enmon would occupy her time away from home for so long, Adams asked Enmon if she liked playing video games—which, of course, she did. Adams then reached out to his audience on his Sarcastic Gamer podcast, asking them to donate games. The response was overwhelming; Enmon wound up with so many games that she decided to share with other young patients in the hospital.

Unfortunately, due to an infection as a result of leukemia, immunocompromised Enmon passed away. Inspired to do something in her memory, Adams started Extra Life. At first, it was a fundraiser specific to the gaming community, with the first event held in 2008. In 2010, Extra Life became part of the Children's Miracle Network.

Extra Life has grown exponentially as a peer-to-peer fundraising organization. "Extra Life is a network of big-hearted gamers who want to make a change," Lou Adducci, Extra Life's director of community, explained. "The gamer community is familial. We [Extra Life] foster those behaviors in our culture and values. The community then takes up the mantle of being the hero by driving change at the local level." According to Adducci, to date, gamers have raised over $70 million for Children's Miracle Network hospitals.

Extra Life participants connect and converge on gamer-centered social apps, like Discord, which has about 5,000 members on its channel. Twitch, which is owned by Amazon, partnered with Extra Life in 2012. A timely and synergistic fit, Extra Life game livestreams are interactive telethons. In livestreams, viewers watch and donate funds, but also influence how gamers play. "The interactivity between the viewer and the person creating the content is impactful," Adducci said. "I could donate $25 for you to eat a nasty flavored jellybean. For more money, you might dye your hair or shave your head. It becomes a meta-game between the community/audience and yourself as fundraiser/participant/content creator."

In addition to community-organized events, Extra Life hosts date-specific "tentpole" campaigns throughout the year. One tentpole event is on the National Day of Play. On this day, participants play what they want, for as long as they wish. "Our mission is to create the best charity gamers in the industry," Adducci said. "The community is already playing games. We add value through gaming for good."

This gives gamers a mindset to become activists. They can then engage and activate their community to be donors to a cause that means something to them."

Extra Life United is another tentpole event, a gaming tournament hosted each spring in Orlando, Florida, during Children's Hospitals Week. Winners of tournaments have donations made in their name to their local children's hospital.

Adducci concluded by sharing a story. A few years ago, Dominic Rooney was diagnosed with cancer when he was two-years-old. "The disease stunted his growth and progress as a young child," he said. "The Rooney family persevered and decided to come to the United States from Calgary, Canada. They saw an opportunity to receive treatment and visit Walt Disney World in Orlando, Florida. But Dominic wasn't doing well. In Orlando, his health declined. Before they could celebrate, he passed. It was devastating."

One year later, the Rooney family attended Extra Life United in Orlando in Dominic's honor. Dominic's dad, Sean, remains active in the Extra Life community. He considers gaming and charity to be the legacy of his son. "The Rooneys helped us recognize that not all kids are the champions that we get to meet, but they all are champions that we get to fall in love with, and miss."

Links, Lessons, and Games

Karen Armstrong's TED Talks: https://www.ted.com/speakers/karen_armstrong
Classcraft: http://classcraft.com
Center for Healthy Minds's Kindness Curriculum: https://centerhealthyminds.org/join-the-movement/sign-up-to-receive-the-kindness-curriculum
Compassionate Actions is a Google Doc of kid-friendly service projects for the *Compassion Games*: http://bit.ly/CompassionActions
Compassion Games: Survival of the Kindest: http://www.compassiongames.org
Children's Miracle Network: https://childrensmiraclenetworkhospitals.org
Connected Learning Summit keynote, by Tracy Fullerton: https://youtu.be/GznU1mJrYIY
Extra Life: https://www.extra-life.org
Healthy Minds: https://hminnovations.org
Hey Listen Games's walking simulator lesson plans: https://www.heylistengames.org/the-walking-simulator
Kind Words (lo-fi chill beats to write to): https://popcannibal.com/kindwords
Kind Words lesson plans from Hey Listen Games: https://www.heylistengames.org/social-emotional-learning/kind-words
LoFi Hip-Hop Worlds to Study In is a game designed to help students take breaks and return to work feeling refreshed. It was designed and developed by Tracy Fullerton's student, Matthew Hamilton (from the *Walden, a game* curriculum team), with Israel Jones: https://lofiworlds.itch.io/study

The Mindful Knight: https://education.minecraft.net/lessons/the-mindful-knight
Mindfulness in Minecraft: A Journey in Social Emotional Learning: https://education.microsoft.com/en-us/course/bbac7ca1/0
Mindful Schools: https://www.mindfulschools.org
Mind Yeti: https://www.mindyeti.com
Minecraft: Education Edition SEL Content Pack: https://education.minecraft.net/social-emotional-learning
Random Acts of Kindness: https://www.randomactsofkindness.org/kindness-ideas
Sean Rooney: Why I Extra Life: https://youtu.be/gmqTBndvJZI
#SelfCare: https://truluv.ai/selfcare
SuperBetter: https://www.superbetter.com
Take This: https://www.takethis.org
Teachers Compassion Games Guide: http://bit.ly/CompassionTeachersGuide
Tenacity gameplay demonstration: https://youtu.be/N773l0PZyuA
thatgamecompany, developer of *flOw*, *Flower*, *Journey*, and *Sky: Children of the Light*: https://thatgamecompany.com
Walden, a game: https://www.waldengame.com/educators
Well-being is a Skill, talk by Richard Davidson: https://youtu.be/N5GRm2ebPKw

References

Aguilar, S. J., Holman, C., & Fishman, B. J. (2018). Game-inspired design: Empirical evidence in support of gameful learning environments. *Games and Culture, 13*(1), 44-70. doi:10.1177/1555412015600305
Armstrong, K. (2008, February). *My wish: The charter for compassion.* [Video]. TED. https://www.ted.com/talks/karen_armstrong_my_wish_the_charter_for_compassion
Bogost, I. (2007). *Persuasive games: The expressive power of videogames.* MIT Press.
Bogost, I. (2008). The rhetoric of video games. In K. Salen & E. Zimmerman (Eds.), *The ecology of games: Connecting youth, games, and learning* (pp. 117–140). MIT Press.
Brown, B. (2013, December 13). *Brené Brown on empathy.* [Video]. YouTube. https://youtu.be/1Evwgu369Jw
Brown, K. W., & Ryan, R. M. (2003). The benefits of being present: Mindfulness and its role in psychological well-being. *Journal of Personality and Social Psychology, 84*(4), 822–848. doi:10.1037/0022-3514.84.4.822.
CASEL's SEL Framework. (2020). *CASEL.* https://casel.org/wpcontent/uploads/2020/10/CASEL-SEL-Framework-10.2020-1.pdf
Compassion Games. (2020). *Compassion games: Survival of the kindest.* http://www.compassiongames.org
Csikszentmihalyi, M. (2008). Flow: The psychology of optimal experience. Harper Perennial Modern Classics. (Original work published 1990)

Davis, D. M., & Hayes, J. A. (2012, July/August). What are the benefits of mindfulness? *APA Monitor.* http://www.apa.org/monitor/2012/07-08/ce-corner.aspx

Deci, E. L., & Ryan, R. M. (1985). *Intrinsic motivation and self-determination in human behavior.* New York, NY: Plenum.

Deci, E. L., & Ryan, R. M. (2000). Intrinsic and extrinsic motivations: Classic definitions and new directions. *Contemporary Educational Psychology, 25*(1), 54–67. doi:10.1006/ceps.1999.1020.

Eastman, A. (2019). The controversial classroom: Making understanding visible with no hands up. *Barker Institute.* http://www.barkerinstitute.com.au/media/2623/the-controversial-classroom-making-understanding-visible-with-no-hands-up-print.pdf

Elias, M. J. (2018, August 17). Analysis of the alignment of Classcraft's SEL environment and CASEL SEL standards. *Classcraft.* https://files.classcraft.com/classcraft-assets/research/classcraft-sel-alignment-report.pdf

Farber, M. (2015, January 6). Gone Home: A video game as a tool for teaching critical thinking skills. *KQED MindShift.* https://www.kqed.org/mindshift/38968/gone-home-a-video-game-as-a-tool-for-teaching-critical-thinking

Farber, M., & Williams, M. K. (2020). Interests, relationships, and opportunities within the 2018 Global Minecraft Mentor Program. *Connected Learning Summit 2019 Conference Proceedings.* Carnegie Mellon ETC Press.

Forbes, D. (2019, April 16). How capitalism captured the mindfulness industry. *The Guardian.* https://www.theguardian.com/lifeandstyle/2019/apr/16/how-capitalism-captured-the-mindfulness-industry

Fullerton, T. (2019, October 5). *Keynote with Tracy Fullerton: Connected learning summit 2019.* [Video]. YouTube. https://youtu.be/GznU1mJrYIY

Ito, M., Martin, C., Pfister, R. C., Rafalow, M. H., Salen, S., & Wortman, A. (2018). *Affinity online: How connection and shared interest fuel learning.* NYU Press.

Jazaieri, H., McGonigal, K., Jinpa, T., Doty, J. R., Gross, J. J., & Goldin, P. R. (2014). A randomized controlled trial of compassion cultivation training: Effects on mindfulness, affect, and emotion regulation. *Motivation and Emotion, 38*(1), 23–35. doi:10.1007/s11031-013-9368-z.

Kral, T. R. A., Stodola, D. E., Birn, R. M., Mumford, J. A., Solis, E., Flook, L., … Davidson, R. J. (2018). Neural correlates of video game empathy training in adolescents: A randomized trial. *NPJ Science of Learning, 3*(1), 13–10. doi:10.1038/s41539-018-0029-6.

Krause, C. (2019). *Mindful by design: A practical guide for cultivating aware, advancing, and authentic learning experiences.* Corwin.

Lund, N. (2019, January 2). Birding like it's 1899: Inside a blockbuster American West video game. *National Audubon Society.* https://www.audubon.org/news/birding-its-1899-inside-blockbuster-american-west-video-game

Mindfulness in Minecraft. (n.d.). *Microsoft Education Center.* https://education.microsoft.com/en-us/course/bbac7ca1/0

Murray, J. H. (2017). *Hamlet on the holodeck: The future of narrative in cyberspace.* MIT Press.

Pak, S. S., & Weseley, A. (2012). The effect of mandatory reading logs on children's motivation to read. *Journal of Research in Education, 22,* 251–265.

Parrott, J. (2018). The golden rule in Islam: Ethics of reciprocity in Islamic traditions. *NYU Faculty Digital Archive.* http://hdl.handle.net/2451/43458

Patsenko, E. G., Adluru, N., & Birn, R. M. (2019). Mindfulness video game improves connectivity of the fronto-parietal attentional network in adolescents: A multi-modal imaging study. *Scientific Reports, 9,* 18667. doi:10.1038/s41598-019-53393-x.

Relax with Zen Mode. (2016, June 2). *The Snowman Blog.* https://blog.builtbysnowman.com/post/145301948017/altos-adventure-zen-mode

Roepke, A. M., Jaffee, S. R., Riffle, O. M., McGonigal, J., Broome, R., & Maxwell, B. (2015). Randomized controlled trial of SuperBetter, a smartphone-based/internet-based self-help tool to reduce depressive symptoms. *Games for Health Journal, 4*(3), 235–246. doi:10.1089/g4h.2014.0046.

Ryan, R. M., & Deci, E. L. (2018). *Self-determination theory: Basic psychological needs in motivation, development, and wellness.* Guilford Press.

Iwamoto, S. K., Alexander, M., Torres, M., Irwin, M. R., Christakis, N. A., & Nishi, A. (2020). Mindfulness meditation activates altruism. *Scientific Reports, 10*(1), 6511-6511.

Schell, J. (2020). *The art of game design: A book of lenses.* Elsevier/Morgan Kaufmann.

Singh, N. C., & Duraiappah, A. (2019). *EMC2: A "whole brain" framework for social and emotional learning—the key to human flourishing.* UNESCO MGIEP.

Solnit, R. (2001). *Wanderlust: A history of walking.* Penguin.

Spoon, M. (2019, December 26). Mindfulness video game changes areas of the brain associated with attention. *University of Wisconsin.* https://news.wisc.edu/mindfulness-video-game-changes-areas-of-the-brain-associated-with-attention/

TECH Compassion Games. (2019). *UNESCO MGIEP.* https://mgiep.unesco.org/tech-2019-agenda

Thoreau, H. D. (1854). *Walden; or, Life in the Woods.* Signet.

Thoreau, H. D. (1862). Walking. *The Atlantic.* https://www.theatlantic.com/magazine/archive/1862/06/walking/304674/

Upton, B. (2018). *Situational game design.* Routledge.

Worthen-Chaudhari, L., McGonigal, J., Logan, K., Bockbrader, M. A., Yeates, K. O., & Mysiw, W. J. (2017). Reducing concussion symptoms among teenage youth: Evaluation of a mobile health app. *Brain Injury, 31*(10), 1279–1286. doi:10.1080/02699052.2017.1332388.

Zeidan, F., Martucci, K. T., Kraft, R. A., McHaffie, J. G., & Coghill, R. C. (2014). Neural correlates of mindfulness meditation-related anxiety relief. *Social Cognitive and Affective Neuroscience, 9*(6), 751–759. doi:10.1093/scan/nst041.

CHAPTER SIX

Ethics, Perspective-Taking, and Teen Identity

A runaway trolley without brakes is headed towards five people standing on a rail line. The trolley has no whistle, and there is no way for nearby onlookers to warn them. However, you can. You find yourself near a lever that can cause the trolley to switch tracks. There is just one problem: Someone is standing on the other line. Pulling the lever will kill one person, not five. Is that the right thing to do? Is the problem easier to solve if the five people were older individuals and the one person was a baby? If so, why?

Now, let's say that there is a large man on an overpass. You are now no longer near the lever but behind the man. As he peers over the overpass, you can push him over to stop the trolley before it hits five people. Is it more ethical to push the man over the bridge or to switch the lever?

A classic thought experiment, the dilemma I just described is known as the *trolley problem*. Introduced by Philippa Foot in 1967, it has been reworked, remixed, and updated over the years. In a lifeboat with limited seats, which passengers should be allowed on? When there is a vaccine for a pandemic plaguing the globe, who gets vaccinated first?

Thought experiments do not have concrete solutions; they are open-ended problem sets. In the trolley problem, some people might not push the man over the bridge or pull the lever. However, a utilitarian might argue that saving five lives by sacrificing one is a consistent solution. As Spock stated in *Star Trek II: The Wrath of Khan*, "The needs of the many outweigh the needs of the few or the one."

Let's explore machine ethics of self-driving cars. Can a vehicle be coded to interpret the nuances of who goes first at a four-way stop sign? If a deer is blocking traffic, should that vehicle swerve into oncoming traffic? In a study, Awad et al. (2018) surveyed 2.3 million people from 233 countries and territories about moral choices coded into autonomous technologies like self-driving cars. Results from the Moral Machine survey revealed cultural nuances (Awad et al., 2018). In France, one cluster responded that they would save women over men (Awad et al., 2018). In other cultures, the socio-economic status of those who might get hit affected responses (Awad et al., 2018).

Connected to open-mindedness, critical thinking, and interpersonal reflection, having a set of ethics can help children develop into responsible adults. The capacity to have ethical standards is also part of CASEL's responsible decision-making competency, the capacity "to make caring and constructive choices about personal behavior and social interactions across diverse situations" (CASEL's SEL Framework, 2020, p. 2). This chapter begins with an investigation of several games that model ethical decision-making through procedural play (Bogost, 2007, 2008). Next, the potential games have to transform player beliefs, attitudes, and dispositions is explored.

Can a Video Game Teach Ethics?

The video game *Fable III* features several moral dilemmas similar to the trolley problem. At one point, players have seconds to decide whether to execute their childhood love or to kill a small crowd of townsfolk. Later, players are asked to choose whether to construct a brothel, which will earn them more money, or to be altruistic by building an orphanage. Playing *Fable III* led to a boost in ethical thinking within a college student cohort (Schrier, 2015a, 2015b). In a study from Schrier (2015a, 2015b), participants were observed "interpreting evidence, weighing pros and cons, and reflecting on past decisions" after playing the game (Schrier, 2019, p. 139).

Layoff is another video game that presents difficult choices. Using a similar mechanic as *Bejeweled* and *Candy Crush Saga*, players click on tiles to clear rows. Tiles here are not shiny gems or sugary treats; instead, they are the faces of employees at a downsizing corporation. Minibiographies are on tiles, too, possibly creating "a bond of empathy" between players and potentially fired employees (Belman & Flanagan, 2010, p. 13). Is it ethical to fire someone if the company needs to downsize to survive? Long-term employees may earn more income than newly hired staff but also have families that depend on the company's wages. Whose needs do you consider?

Some video games use ethical quandaries to express political messages. *Bioshock* is an example. A first-person shooter video game, it is set in the seemingly utopian underwater society of Rapture, where all residents are driven by self-interest. Are the politics of self-interest ethical?

Bioshock is actually a statement against *objectivism,* the *laissez-faire* ideology championed by Ayn Rand, author of *The Fountainhead* (1943) and *Atlas Shrugged* (1957). Objectivism is based on four societal tenets proposed by Rand: reality, reason, self-interest, and capitalism (Packer, 2010; Rand, 1943, 1957; Sicart, 2009). Because of adherence to these principles, Rapture has no government restrictions on the right to bear arms, no matter how destructive (Packer, 2010, p. 216). Players experience this firsthand through the game's violent procedural rhetoric (Bogost, 2007, 2008).

Can a video game teach ethics? "Games are just an opening to a conversation," Sherry Jones told me. Jones is a philosopher, rhetorician, and game studies instructor who teaches ethics with video games. "Games can't coach your mind through a problem. It's not that simple. If it were that simple, we could just make art pieces and have people stare at them."

Jones sometimes refers to games as *normative ethical machines.* Normative ethics is "a discipline that considers and defines moral standards that determine whether an act is right or wrong" (Jones, 2018, para. 5). "Games can impose certain ethical rules through game mechanics," she said.

Philosophy education is not about telling students the "right" or "wrong" theories or principles to adopt. When teaching using thought experiments like the trolley problem, students should be asked, What are the theories and principles you are going to abide by? After adopting theories or principles, students can then see if their responses are consistent. Who did you fire in *Layoff*? Why? Were you consistent in your decisions?

Ethics are not the same as morals. "Ethics are a set of moral beliefs that become code," Jones continued. "Morality is one's personal belief about what is right or wrong." Let's consider an animal advocacy television commercial as an example. In it, viewers are shown a montage of sick and abused puppies. These commercials are only effective if viewers share moral beliefs about animal welfare, particularly pets.

Society then codifies ethics into laws. Theft is a good example, as most people believe that it is morally wrong to steal. Because of this shared morality, stealing is typically against the law in most societies.

In games, players understand ethical systems through *procedurality*, where rules are explored through play (Bogost, 2007, 2008). Let's take *Papers, Please* as an example. An award-winning video game set in the fictional communist country of Arstotzka, players take on the role of a border agent at a checkpoint booth. The gameplay is mainly close reading of immigration documents (passports, visas). But some immigrant papers are forged. Players are offered bribes, some from refugees, others from known criminals. Misreading documents results in citations and financial penalties that indirectly affects players. A reduction in income limits the ability to cover necessary monthly expenditures, like rent or heat. A cold apartment will cause illness to the immediate family members who live with the border agent. Lack of funds to purchase medicine leads to deaths.

The ethics of what is right or wrong are not immediately apparent in *Papers, Please*. Should you let a refugee into Arstotzka even though it may result in a citation? Is a citation worth it by denying entry to criminals whose papers are in order? Players may opt to be altruistic (allow a refugee in, deny entry to a criminal), which is morally justified but against the bureaucratic rules of Arstotzka. Through a situational game design lens (Upton, 2018), there is more to *Papers, Please* than clicking a rubber stamp to approve or deny entry through the border. Most of the game is spent challenging players to reflect and contemplate how their moral standards align with these situations.

To better understand the ethics of *Papers, Please*, game design lecturer Nick Fortugno (2014) suggested applying the philosophical frameworks of Immanuel Kant. In *Groundwork for the Metaphysics of Morals* (1785), Kant argued that morally good actions should not be transactional. In other words, prosocial acts should not include expectations that you will get something in return. Instead, moral goodness should be about goodwill—being kind and compassionate for altruistic reasons.

Most video games are designed as transactional systems that reward (or penalize) players who adhere to (or break) ethical rules (Fortugno, 2014). In *Red Dead Redemption 2*, when players assist non-playable characters by performing good deeds (i.e., retrieving someone's runaway horse), they are awarded in-game currency. Conversely, robbing or shooting innocent strangers makes the player "Wanted!" *Papers, Please* subverts transactional gameplay: Complicity to Arstotzka's corrupt system is often rewarded, while altruism is penalized.

Like *Papers, Please*, *Undertale* applies a Kantian framework (Geer & Matthew, 2019; Smalley, 2016). Popular with adolescents, the central dilemma asks players to consider what kind of person they are: warlike or pacifist. (*Fable III* and *Red Dead Redemption 2* also offer this choice to players.) This decision is tested early on when Flowey the Flower, an antagonist, is confronted. At this juncture, players select whether to fight, bribe, or talk their way out of conflict (Geer & Matthew, 2019).

Fallout Shelter is another thought experiment on human nature. The game is set in a post-apocalyptic fallout shelter where non-playable characters are treated as disposable pawns. The tone has dark humor, and sometimes sarcasm (Gandolfi, 2019). Its ethical system equates work with happiness. Jones explained how its rule system embeds ethics that are not necessarily moral. She said,

> I decide who I keep in the shelter and who I kick out. If one of the worker bees in my fallout shelter has reached level 50—basically, old age, where the character no longer can gain any more skills—he can't get me any more points or money. I can then decide to grab that character and throw him out of my shelter, which means death. There is a nuclear apocalypse out there. Well, you're old. That's the rule of the game. For the sake of survival, everyone agrees that we can kick out someone who reaches level 50. In that game, it is ethical, but it does not mean that it is moral.

This War of Mine is a strategy video game similar to *Fallout Shelter* but set in a fictional European war-torn country. In the game, players control a small band of people who try to survive in a bombed-out city by sifting through rubble. Sometimes, players may need to break into homes to steal food, medicine, or toilet paper from non-playable characters to benefit their group. The presentation of ambiguous choice in *This War of Mine* illustrates "the disorientation and difficulties of being a civilian in wartime" (de Smale et al., 2017, p. 388).

Stealing virtual food in *This War of Mine* feels different than reading (or watching) Jean Valjean, the hungry peasant in Victor Hugo's *Les Misérables* (1862), steal bread. Although I may empathize with Valjean and his situation, the palette of emotions I experience is different. Different than other media forms, in video games, players experience the consequences of their actions (Isbister, 2016; Murray, 2017). (A similar scene is presented in the narrative video game *Life is Strange 2*. In one vignette, the main characters—two young brothers on the run—must choose whether to steal bread, mac-and-cheese, hot dogs, and other supplies in a mini-mart or to pay for them with their limited funds.)

Some games implicitly (or explicitly) embed heteronormative ethics in design. In *The Game of Life*, players move a plastic car around a board game track. Versions of rules reward players monetarily if they go to college, have a career, get married, and have children—sometimes in that order! Nintendo's *Super Mario Bros.* series often employs a save-the-princess trope. Actions in the classic arcade game *Space Invaders* represent masculine culture during the Cold War, when "boys, in particular, were socialized to act out symbolic struggles of good against evil, emphasizing a heroic and active conception of masculinity" (Newman, 2017, p. 101).

Queergaming presents a counter-hegemonic discourse (Lajoie, 2018). The award-winning racing game *Sayonara Wild Hearts* is an example. Built on an explicitly queer framework, players control a heroine as she chases enemies on different vehicles (motorcycles, cars, skateboards), all synced to an original pop music soundtrack. The hearts she collects, obstacles she overcomes, and enemies she races are metaphors of her coming out story (Dale, 2019, p. 6).

In 2020, millions of people—children and adults—played Nintendo's *Animal Crossing: New Horizons*. A social simulation game, players begin the game indebted to Tom Nook, an anthropomorphic *tanuki* (Japanese for raccoon dog) character. As I write this, my 10-year-old son owes 98,000 bells (the in-game currency) to Tom for the virtual home he mortgaged!

To many, *Animal Crossing* engendered a sense of social freedom during COVID-19 lockdowns (Khan, 2020). Several high schools and colleges hosted virtual commencements on islands (Groux, 2020), and in Japan, some workers held meetings in the game (Rockett, 2020). Politicians also embraced *Animal Crossing*: Representative Alexandria Ocasio-Cortez tweeted about her gameplay experience (Gordon, 2020), while the Biden-Harris presidential campaign sold signs for digital lawns (Kelley, 2020). (In late November 2020, Nintendo updated guidelines to curtail politics in the game.)

Games scholar Ian Bogost wrote about *Animal Crossing* gameplay as an allegory on capitalism and consumer culture told through *procedural rhetoric* (2007, 2020). He wrote, "By condensing all of the environment's financial transactions into one flow between the player and Tom Nook, the game proceduralizes the redistribution of wealth in a manner even young children can understand" (Bogost, 2007, pp. 269–270). Is *Animal Crossing* pure escapism or is it a "capitalist dystopia" (Rimm, 2020, para. 1)?

Many of the games described in this section are included in *Learning, Education, & Games Vol. 3: 100 Games to Use in the Classroom and Beyond* (2019), a book edited by Karen (Kat) Schrier. Available for purchase or as a free ebook download, it shares discussion starters for game-based educators. In it, Gandolfi (2019) recommends how *Fallout Shelter* can be used in a flipped classroom approach (playing from home) because of its accessibility, ease of gameplay, and multiple platforms that support the game. After playing from home, students can then discuss and debate ethical dilemmas while in class. Euteneuer (2019) similarly shares how *Papers, Please* can be played from home and then analyzed in classrooms.

Next, *Quandary*, also featured in Schrier's book, is explored. Both Schrier and I are *Quandary* advisory board members and use the game in practice. Designed for adolescents, it teaches ethics and perspective-taking through a series of moral dilemmas.

Quandaries, Perspectives, and Dilemmas

Thirty-two light-years away. That's how far Planet Braxos is from Earth. I am the captain, part of its first human colony. As captain, I help resolve internal disputes.

The gameplay begins at the Settlers' Meeting. I am notified that a sheep has gone missing in the settlement. There are visible tracks from a native predator. My role is to consider each colonist's point-of-view and arrive at a solution that will never satisfy everyone.

There are 12 characters on my screen, each presented as if on playing cards. Clicking on cards reveals the name, occupation, and opinion of particular colonists. Some colonists propose setting traps or leaving out poison for native predators. Others have no opinion and are indifferent. The engineer is angry; he argues that traps or poison would be a waste of colonial resources. Dr. Canon points out the medicinal properties in predators' saliva. Mae, the biologist, suggests building a fence.

On the bottom of my screen are blank spaces labeled: Fact, Solution, and Other Opinion. Dr. Canon presents a fact (medicinal properties of the predator's saliva), while Mae recommends a solution (build a fence). But what about the other settlers? Should a farmer's concerns be outweighed by an engineer's or doctor's? Everyone has different perspectives. I sort the cards accordingly.

The playthrough just described is *Quandary*, from the Learning Games Network, a nonprofit spinoff of the MIT Education Arcade. It was designed nearly a decade ago to cultivate ethical decision-making with students through perspective-taking. A social awareness competency, perspective-taking is not quite the same as empathy. Empathy is thinking or feeling how someone else feels (Batchelder et al., 2017; Batson, 2009; Majdandžić et al., 2016); perspective-taking describes the lenses we take when actively considering someone else's "mental states and subjective experiences" (Todd & Galinsky, 2014, p. 374).

Like the classic trolley problem thought experiment, conflicts on Braxos are not easily solvable. "In terms of the game's score, any of the outcomes you choose depend on how well you pay attention to the concerns and needs of people involved in the disputes," Scot Osterweil, a veteran in the field of educational games, explained. Osterweil is the game's creative director and lead designer. "The better you do at listening and understanding other people's perspectives, the better you do at the game."

Quandary does not have obvious heroes or villains. "Although I do love Superman, I generally don't like fiction with all-powerful or all-wise characters," Osterweil continued. "I think it is more interesting to watch people struggle. A game should feel that way too, rather than earning gold stars for doing the 'right' thing."

Free on any device, lesson plans are shared on the *Quandary* website. Lessons are aligned across several curricular areas, making it easy to integrate into existing middle school classrooms. Curriculum shared includes lessons for Earth science and geography, history and social studies, and English language arts classrooms. There are also SEL-specific lessons that focus on in-groups and out-groups in digital spaces.

Quandary can also be played on BrainPOP's learning platform. There, educators can find two additional lesson plans: one on teaching ethics, the other about critical thinking and problem-solving. I asked BrainPOP's Allisyn Levy how she would advise using *Quandary* in a classroom. "Depending on the goal of the teacher, I'd build background first and then watch the BrainPOP movie on ethics," she began. BrainPOP has over 900 animated videos on its website in different content areas, including one on ethics. "This will help teachers to see where kids' ideas overlap and intersect with the content in the movie. I would then introduce the game without any conversation. I would say, 'Hey, I discovered a cool game this weekend, but I am kind of stuck. Please take a look with me and see what you think.'"

This approach aims to pique students' interest and get the class to arrive at the bigger picture of what the game may be teaching. "By bringing the class into the conversation, student ownership of learning is boosted," she continued. "Even if students don't use the word 'ethics,' they might come up with words like 'decision-making,' or 'have to gain consensus,' or 'arguing,' or 'convincing.'" Students should then play in pairs or small groups. One study observed that when played in pairs, *Quandary* became "a catalyst for discussions with complex moral themes" (Ilten-Gee & Hilliard, 2017 as cited in Osterweil et al., 2019, p. 328).

Because there are no completely right or wrong solutions to quandaries, students often have different results. This presents opportunities for pausing the class intermittently for teacher-led debriefs. "It would be fascinating to have groups share their outcomes and how they got there," Levy remarked.

Consider having students journal as they play. Students can also make card-based versions of ethical dilemmas that they have encountered in their real lives. Extensions like these deepen learning, from game-based to project-based.

Awkward Moments and Implicit Biases

"Kids at school have discovered an embarrassing old video of you as a little kid that your dad posted on YouTube," one student reads. Possible reactions to this are written on other cards. One states, "Channel your inner goddess." Another says, "Break into a freestyle rap and express yourself through rhyme." I am the judge, the "Decider." In one round, I consider the most practical reaction. In the next, I choose the funniest.

The game described here is *Awkward Moment*. For three to eight players, gameplay is quick to learn. Commercially available at many retailers, it is a party card game that is also a terrific teaching tool to get adolescents to share strategies for handling uncomfortable situations. The box includes one deck of cards in three suits. Moment cards detail embarrassing yet relatable predicaments. Examples include, "Your teacher calls on you when you haven't done your homework," and, "There is a spider on your wall." Reaction cards share possible responses, from silly to serious, assertive to surreal. Some Reaction cards state, "Hide in a bathroom stall," and, "Say, 'I meant to do that.'" Decider cards are the third suit, a rotating set of guidelines required to win each round. Winning reactions may be for the "Silliest," "Most inappropriate," or "Bravest" responses to Moment cards.

Most Moment cards are general social situations that can happen to anyone at any time. "You write a text to your friend but accidentally send it to your mom," reads one. But some are about gender and social bias. One was inspired by a news headline. It states, "While shopping at the mall, you see a store is selling 'Math is hard!' T-shirts for girls" (see Figure 11). This card was based on a T-shirt sold by J.C. Penney in 2011 that read, "Too pretty to do homework, so my brother has

Figure 11. Image of *Awkward Moment* Cards. Source: *Awkward Moment* by Mary Flanagan and Tiltfactor. Published by Resonym. Reprinted with permission of the publisher.

to do it for me." After a petition and public outcry, the store pulled the shirt and apologized (Richardson, 2011).

Tiltfactor, a research lab at Dartmouth College, created *Awkward Moment* as part of a National Science Foundation grant titled, "Transforming Science, Technology, Engineering, and Math (STEM) for Women and Girls: Reworking Stereotypes & Bias." The game's design was informed by "psychological theory and research on stereotype threat and implicit bias, two powerful psychological obstacles that have been shown to reduce self-efficacy, persistence, and performance among members of underrepresented groups in STEM" (Teachers Guide, n.d., p. 2).

Educators can find out about the game's social impact on the Tiltfactor website, but it is not on or in the box on store shelves. "We found in our research that social impact games work better when the player doesn't know what the impacts are supposed to be—or even that the game is supposed to be impactful," Max Seidman explained. Seidman was part of *Awkward Moment*'s design team at Tiltfactor. "We market games as standalone products because we need to make sure they are fun first. What is the purpose of making an effective game if it is not fun?"

The origin of *Awkward Moment* began with the impact goal of transforming or shifting beliefs about gender bias through gameplay. The design team then did a deep dive into the research on adolescent biases. Next, Moment cards were prototyped and playtested with adolescents. The young playtesters also inspired some of the Moment cards, and they came up with the name *"Awkward Moment."*

In *Awkward Moment*, nothing is presented to jar the player. Players are led to react to biased moments the same way they would to embarrassing situations. Seidman continued,

> It is a delayed reveal. We wanted to make sure that the conversations would not be too heavy; otherwise, people's defense mechanisms go up. *Awkward Moment* is interesting because the discussions are subtle. You get to hear players react to moments, which are the start of discussions. We didn't design the game to start conversations—if the game is designed around the values properly and has the right content and gameplay, it is going to elicit those conversations no matter what.

Embedded design describes the extent to which learning is invisible, or covert, in the player's experience (Kaufman & Flanagan, 2015). "If players know they are playing a game for impact, they will put up psychological defenses, making the game less effective," Seidman observed.

How many impactful moments should a game have? Intermixing was conducted to measure the effectiveness of embedded design—basically, extra Moment cards on gender bias were stacked into some decks (Kaufman & Flanagan, 2015). "Lots of educational games take the 'more is better' approach," Seidman continued. "We did a study comparing the current version of *Awkward Moment* with about 30 biased moments to a stacked version with 90% gender-biased moments." (A control group played *Apples to Apples*, a party card game with a similar mechanic.) Findings suggested that the commercial version was more effective than the overloaded one (Kaufman & Flanagan, 2015).

In a follow-up study, adolescents were shown six characters—three men and three women "with psychologically validated neutral faces," Seidman said. "We told participants, 'Here is a list of professions. Please match the professions to the character.'" Players of *Awkward Moment* tended to match "scientist" to the female characters *after* playing the game more than the control group who did not play the game (Kaufman & Flanagan, 2015).

Playing *Awkward Moment* with adolescents can promote conversation about gender bias and ways to react to imagined situations. In classrooms, students can use the Moment and Reaction cards as writing prompts. Or, they can build expansion packs, sharing and playing their own awkward moments!

iThrive Games and the Teen Brain

iThrive Games is a nonprofit that intentionally uses and designs games to support teen voice while engaging teens through play and design. Susan Rivers is its executive director and chief scientist; Dorothy Batten is the founder and president of its board of directors. She is also the president of the D.N. Batten Foundation.

Professionally, my work has intersected with iThrive several times over the years. I serve on the editorial board of its Journal of Games, Self, and Society, I have co-authored game-based curriculum on youth identity formation (more on that soon!), and we—myself and professor Mia Kim Williams—partnered to host Game Design Studio at my university's campus. Game Design Studio was a multi-session game design program where teens played, created, and shared games based on their lived experiences. This program has evolved into iThrive Studio, a "portable" model that classrooms and schools can adopt.

Prior to iThrive, Rivers co-founded the Yale Center for Emotional Intelligence with Marc Brackett. Brackett, the Center's director, was one of the developers of RULER, the evidence-based approach to SEL shared in Chapter One. Brackett also serves on CASEL's board of directors.

"As a social psychologist, the environment was interesting to me," Rivers recalled, recounting her time at Yale. There, Rivers thought about the adults who did not build up their own social and emotional skills—those who were not emotionally aware. How could that impact the environment where children were learning? "An adult could really help social and emotional skill-building thrive—or, they could thwart it from happening."

Rivers's work shifted to focus on environments that could support SEL. "What are the informal things you need to do—or the formal things to set up—around teaching 'feeling words' [e.g., joyful, angry] or when teaching regulation strategies?" she said. "How do you interweave them both, so it's not, 'Hey, it's Tuesday, and today we are going to talk about emotions? But we won't talk about them any other time.'"

Every encounter should be infused to build, reinforce, and model social and emotional skills; these skills should not be taught in isolation. Schools should not have empathy time or relationship-building class periods divorced from the rest of the day's curriculum. This is evident in CASEL's wheel infographic of SEL competencies (see Figure 3 in Chapter Two). In CASEL's SEL Framework, spokes of competencies are surrounded by the social systems children inhabit (classrooms, schools, families and caregivers, and communities).

Rivers was the lead on an Air Force Research Laboratory grant on human-agent teaming. The objective was to explore how digital systems could be embedded with SEL. "The idea was to create better teams between humans and machines," she said. Through this work, Rivers thought about how teens also spend time in digital spaces. She wondered, How can we intentionally design digital environments that meet teens where they are? Serendipitously, the opportunity to lead iThrive came up. "That is the focus of iThrive: How can we leverage video games to meet teens where they are at, and help them develop strengths to thrive?"

A lot of SEL curriculum tends to focus on early childhood, elementary education, and maybe middle school. "It was sort of assumed that the most critical period [for learning] was in infancy and early childhood," Rivers explained. "Then you suddenly become an adult! But, it turns out that the growth and the fine-tuning of the brain in adolescence is the second most critical period of development."

Adolescent brains' neural connections that are used more frequently strengthen, while pathways used less can get pared away (Griffin, 2017). In high school, I learned how to drive a car, which I still do with a degree of automaticity. I also briefly learned the trombone but quit during my freshman year. Without much cognitive effort, I can still drive; I have no idea how to play the trombone (don't tell my parents!).

Because the cognitive centers of the adolescent brain mature faster than structures that relate to emotion, the adolescent brain experiences neuroplasticity in different ways than young children or adults (Delalande et al., 2019; Kral et al., 2018; Patsenko et al., 2019). Although able to quickly process and store information, the teen brain is still building the architecture to regulate emotions deftly

(Steinberg, 2011). The teen brain is also prone to risk-taking behavior, especially in the presence of peers (Steinberg, 2011). "Adolescent abilities to regulate stress, to regulate powerful emotions, and to make decisions in the face of strong social pulls won't process in the same way as adults," Rivers remarked.

In adolescence, learned and practiced emotional regulation and stress management skills can impact adulthood in important ways. If a teen learns to take deep breaths and build up stress tolerance to control frustration, sadness, or anger, it may become more automatic in adulthood. A teen who does not build up a stress tolerance or ways to manage stress will not build that pathway and may struggle in adulthood. The window for supporting social and emotional growth can't close after elementary school. Rivers continued,

> "By the time they get to be teenagers, it's too late." I hear that so many times. I also often hear, "Let's put the money in the early years because that is what is going to matter most." Yes, it matters a ton there, but adolescence also matters because the brain is going through another significant developmental phase. If we are not nourishing that to understand physiologically and socially what is going on for teens—and if we are not designing for that, in the physical classroom, the digital classroom, and the games that we are creating—then we miss a huge opportunity to support the developmental needs of adolescents.

Two of the game-based learning curricular units published by iThrive, *Museum of Me* and *Sam's Journey*, relate to *identity formation* in adolescence—when teens figure out who they are. "Some of the literature shows that if kids in adolescence don't do the work of identity formation—if they don't work to integrate who they are at home, who they are at school, who they are at the soccer field, or at their job—their sense of self becomes disjointed," Rivers said. That is a problematic way to go through life. You continuously have to code switch, being different for different people in your world. "To some extent, if your identities are closely aligned, it is not as big of a deal. But when they are separate, it becomes a developmental issue with psychological ramifications."

That work of identity formation was top of mind when Paul Darvasi and I suggested designing lessons around the video game *What Remains of Edith Finch*. "We [iThrive] didn't search for a game around identity formation, but the spirits aligned," Rivers recalled. "That game fit the topic. And, we wanted to demonstrate that you could integrate gameplay and SEL into the academic curriculum."

What Remains of Edith Finch is an award-winning narrative video game that tells the story of an 18-year-old girl's possibly cursed family history. Like *Walden, a game* (see Chapter Five), it is a walking simulator: There are no enemies to beat or coins to collect, nor are there clear win or loss conditions. More like a good novel, whether or not the family is actually cursed remains unanswered.

The game begins as Edith returns to her abandoned and expansive childhood home. Locked in each room are objects that reflect the life of family members who inhabited that space. The player-as-Edith examines found items, such as handwritten notes, books, photographs, and other memorabilia of lives now gone. Each room has a journal from a deceased Finch. Interacting with a journal triggers past memories. Once opened, the player is no longer Edith; the player becomes the family member who relives their tragic ends.

What Remains of Edith Finch is filled with opportunities to analyze and explore symbolism, narrative style, magic surrealism, and other concepts traditionally studied in literary fiction classrooms. By examining the Finch family members' rooms and possessions, students are invited to think critically about who and what has constructed their identities.

The curricular unit we developed is named *Museum of Me* because—as the Finches did in life—students curate objects representing who they are. In the classroom, the game is used as a core text, with lessons designed to support it. Rather than a 1:1 computer to student ratio, we recommended a "hot seat" model, where the game is projected on a screen as the class plays and watches together. Lessons around the game include Harkness discussions (similar to Socratic seminars), exit tickets with reflective prompts, and constructionist projects. In one lesson, students create postcards from Finch family members' perspectives that share or hide family secrets. This leads to lessons around students' social media personas.

Following *Museum of Me*, iThrive published *Sam's Journey*, a brief curricular unit around the game *A Normal Lost Phone*. A short, puzzle-based game, players find themselves in possession of a smartphone they explore. In apps, emails, and text messages, a nonlinear narrative unfolds about its owner. *Sam's Journey* was developed by a group of students in Gabrielle Rappolt-Schlichtman's Emotions in Development and Learning course at the Harvard Graduate School for Education. "I posted ten games, with the prompt: 'Pick one and write a unit about it for high school,'" Rivers recalled. "One group picked *A Normal Lost Phone* based on its storytelling—how can we tell the stories of our lives?" iThrive then curated the ideas put forth by the students to publish a three-lesson unit.

What's notable about *A Normal Lost Phone* is that it is not a linear story. Comparatively, *What Remains of Edith Finch* is more like a dark ride, a narrative "on rails." "The emotions that are cultivated when you unwrap a nonlinear story and try to put it together give players time and space to think through and unpack some of the details that they may or may not see if it was a linear trajectory," Rivers said. "There is a metaphor about how we understand ourselves and who we are is a mystery. There are little pieces, clues and hints as we build ourselves together."

The iThrive website freely shares SEL-aligned game-based content. In addition to *Museum of Me* and *Sam's Journey*, there is the *iThrive Sim*, a tech-supported role-playing scenario for experientially learning civics. iThrive also publishes Game Guides to prompt joint media engagement and discussions between teens and their parents, educators, and caregivers. iThrive's Game Design Kits guide youth and designers of all ages in creating games around themes, like growth mindset, cooperation, kindness, and gratitude.

Can Video Games Transform Behavior?

Decisions That Matter is a video game for incoming freshman at Carnegie Mellon University about preventing sexual assault on campus. The game has an interactive fiction structure, like a playable graphic novel, where players choose text bubbles to advance the story. The game begins by asking for the player's first name, which is inserted into dialogue—literally putting the player into the narrative.

In one scene, a friend is cat-called by a passerby. Do you step in and say something? Each time I played, the interaction ended poorly. When I interjected, the friend said, "Hey, I can fight my own battles!" When I replayed, I refrained from doing anything. This time, the friend said, "I wish you would've said something."

"Video games are excellent at disequilibrating players, throwing people off balance," game designer Jesse Schell remarked. Schell is the founder of Schell Games and is a professor at Carnegie Mellon. His studio did not design *Decisions That Matter*; students from another professor's course did.

In games, players are placed into situations, which can then be used to generate discussion. "Games can create teachable moments," Schell continued. "Before, you weren't teachable. But after playing the game, you are teachable. People come out of games ready to think about those issues." (*Decisions That Matter* has a content warning and a "trigger button." At any point, players can exit the experience.)

Over the years, Schell Games has developed transformational games applying Sabrina Culyba's transformational framework (2018), a set of design principles for social impact and educational games. Culyba's book, *The Transformational Framework* (2018), available for purchase or as a free ebook download, shares tips for educators who seek to use games to transform student thinking. (See the link at the end of this chapter.)

Transformational games do more than teach rote facts; they are designed to shift player attitudes and beliefs (Culyba, 2018; Schell, 2020). Let's take a hypothetical civics game as an example. To be transformational, it should not quiz players on when and how to vote; instead, players should become civically engaged after playing. After playing a transformational science game, players should want to become citizen scientists. Transformational games about literacy should not just teach fluency; they should evoke positive feelings about reading (Culyba, 2018).

Culyba listed eight "flavors of transformation," different kinds of games that can fit the description of being transformational (2018, p. 18). Flavors of transformation, which are dependent on context and the goal of the game, include:

- *Educational Games/Learning Games*: These labels are usually applied to games targeting students, often children, both in and out of a classroom setting.
- *Serious Games*: This generally catch-all term is used in many different contexts for any game that has a real-world purpose beyond entertainment.
- *Training Simulations/Simulation-based Learning*: Frequently used in reference to programs that train employees on technical skills, industry procedures, or social interactions through simulation and role-play.
- *Behavior Change Games*: This term seems to be used most often in games initiated in part as research, particularly around health-related behaviors.
- *Games for Health*: As the name suggests, this term refers to games aimed at improving health-related behaviors and outcomes.
- *Impact Games/Social Good Games/Games for Change*: These games are often trying to raise awareness about a societal issue or cause.
- *Empathy Games*: This term is sometimes applied to games that focus less on game mechanics and more on storytelling. They are often centered around evoking an emotional response in players.
- *Citizen Science/Crowdsourcing Games*: These are games that allow the masses to contribute to real-world research or data analysis by encoding the task into a game. (Culyba, 2018, p. 15)

Culyba (2018) wrote that transformational games should be both assessable and achievable. By being measurable, the extent of a player's transformation can then be compared to the player's initial state. Phelps and Rusch (2020) critiqued this part of Culyba's (2018) framework, writing that requiring embedded measurements may impede the further design of transformational games. Should transformational games be all-in-one teaching machines?

In her book, Culyba shares some commercial games that teachers have adapted to become transformational learning experiences. One example was Paul Darvasi's adaptation of the walking simulator *Gone Home*, a nonlinear exploration game about a dysfunctional family. Darvasi created lessons around the game, similar to how teachers develop curriculum around books (Culyba, 2018; Farber, 2017).

Some of the best examples of transformational games come from Schell Games's collaboration with Yale University's play2PREVENT lab. The first project was *PlayForward: Elm City Stories*, a series of minigames about reducing HIV infection rates. *Elm City Stories* is not didactic and does not teach right or wrong. Instead, players are put in social situations where they select dialogue choices from peers in different peer groups that sometimes have unexpected consequences. "HIV and STDs [sexually transmitted diseases] often come from risky decision-making—not understanding consequences and not understanding how to connect the dots," Culyba explained. "If you have stronger skills in areas connected to social pressure, you might have less of a chance of contracting HIV."

The narrative in *Elm City Stories* takes place over several school years. Players begin by seeing their character in the future, with a dead-end job, health issues, and impaired family relationships. This glimpse shares the long-term negative outcomes that resulted from a lifetime of poor decision-making. Back in time to the present day, players revisit pivotal points of their character's life, and now (hopefully) make better choices.

Elm City Stories encourages mindset shifts by giving players a space to rehearse how to react to social moments. Players make value judgments on what is important for them both in the long-term and short-term. The game's scoring metric is based on the social cost to accept or reject those invitations. If you invite someone to be close to you and then resist an opportunity to engage in unsafe behaviors that may not align with your long-term goals, it becomes more difficult to befriend that person later. "When you bring someone into your social circle in real life, it is because you are emotionally motivated," Culyba explained. "We show how that works mechanically to help middle school kids build a mental model about why it matters who you hang out with, and why it might be costlier in some situations to say yes or no to social invitations."

Players are privy to the inner thoughts of the character they inhabit, as well as the opinions of parents and teachers. One parent warns, "If you get in trouble, I'm not going to bail you out of jail." A teacher says, "That would really disappoint me." Having multiple perspectives provides input into the value that players place in their decision-making process.

"Players get a vocabulary that can help them to conceptually break down what is typically a learn-on-your-own abstract social skill," Culyba continued. "This affords surrogate reflection on high-pressure situations that they can hopefully leverage when they are actually in a high-pressure situation."

Adolescents helped design the artwork and social situations in the game. "We got together about 12-15 kids and gave them disposable cameras and said, 'Go to your neighborhoods and go to your homes and take pictures of everything important to you,'" Lynn E. Fiellin recalled. Fiellin is a professor of medicine at the Yale School of Medicine and co-founder of play2PREVENT. "We then developed the film and sent it to Schell Games, which formed the game's artwork. It was literally through the eyes of the kids."

smokeSCREEN is a game about shifting risk perception around combustible cigarettes. Developed by Schell Games and 1st Playable Productions for play2PREVENT, it is available for free on most tablet devices. Here, players take on the role of a character who is represented with a cluster of people that visually form their social network. Players then go through a series of challenges where they can practice the mindset and the thought processes one might go through in the real-world.

As it turned out, most adolescents in the lab's study already knew the risk factors from smoking combustible cigarettes. However, this was not the case with electronic cigarettes. "We've done a lot of work around traditional, combustible smoking versus e-cigarettes," Fiellin said. "We found that kids are pretty well-educated on combustible cigarettes. They've heard about the risks forever, which is reflected in the fact that kids are smoking fewer combustible cigarettes. But there is a huge gap in their knowledge around the risks of e-cigarettes."

Like *Elm City Stories*, *smokeSCREEN* is a practice space for navigating peer pressure situations. Results from a pilot study suggest efficacy: *smokeSCREEN* is an intervention that can change risk perception about smoking and vaping amongst adolescents (Pentz et al., 2019).

Links, Lessons, and Games

Animal Crossing: New Horizons: https://www.animal-crossing.com/new-horizons
Awkward Moment, the game and lesson plans: https://tiltfactor.org/game/awkward-moment
Bioshock: https://2k.com/en-US/game/bioshock
BrainPOP's *Quandary* lesson plan: https://educators.brainpop.com/lesson-plan/ethics-lesson-plan/?bp-game=quandary
Decisions That Matter: https://www.andrew.cmu.edu/course/53-610/profile.html
Fallout Shelter: https://bethesda.net/en/game/falloutshelter
iThrive Games: https://ithrivegames.org
iThrive Games's game-based curriculum: https://ithrivegames.org/ithrive-curriculum
Layoff: https://tiltfactor.org/game/layoff
Learning, Education & Games Vol. 3: 100 Games to Use in the Classroom and Beyond, Schrier's (2019) edited book: https://press.etc.cmu.edu/index.php/product/learning-education-games-volume-3
A Normal Lost Phone: https://anormallostphone.com
Night of the Living Debt: http://nightofthelivingdebtgame.org
Papers, Please: https://papersplea.se
play2PREVENT: https://www.play2prevent.org
Quandary: https://www.quandarygame.org

smokeSCREEN: https://www.smokescreengame.org
Sayonara Wild Hearts: https://simogo.com/work/sayonara-wild-hearts
This War of Mine: https://www.thiswarofmine.com
The Transformational Framework, by Sabrina Culyba: https://press.etc.cmu.edu/index.php/product/the-transformational-framework
The Trolley Problem, explained: https://youtu.be/bOpf6KcWYyw
Games for Civics, Karen (Kat) Schrier's companion website for her book, *We the Gamers: How Games Teach Ethics & Civics*: https://gamesforcivics.com
What Remains of Edith Finch: http://www.giantsparrow.com/games/finch

References

Awad, E., Dsouza, S., Kim, R., Schulz, J., Henrich, J., Shariff, A., … Rahwan, I. (2018). The moral machine experiment. *Nature (London), 563*(7729), 59–64. doi:10.1038/s41586-018-0637-6.

Batchelder, L., Brosnan, M., & Ashwin, C. (2017). The development and validation of the empathy components questionnaire (ECQ). *PLoS One, 12*(1), e0169185. doi:10.1371/journal.pone.0169185.

Batson, C. D. (2009). The definition of empathy. In J. Decety & W. Ickes (Eds.), *The social neuroscience of empathy* (pp. 3–16). MIT Press Scholarship.

Belman, J., & Flanagan, M. (2010). Designing games to foster empathy. *Cognitive Technology, 14*(2), 5–15.

Bogost, I. (2007). *Persuasive games: The expressive power of videogames*. MIT Press.

Bogost, I. (2008). The rhetoric of video games. In K. Salen & E. Zimmerman (Eds.), *The ecology of games: Connecting youth, games, and learning* (pp. 117–140). MIT Press.

CASEL's SEL Framework. (2020). *CASEL*. https://casel.org/wpcontent/uploads/2020/10/CASEL-SEL-Framework-10.2020-1.pdf

Culyba, S. (2018). *The transformational framework*. Carnegie Mellon ETC Press.

Dale, L. (2019, December 11). Sayonara Wild Hearts is a coming out story within a female-focused pop music game. *Syfy Wire*. https://www.syfy.com/syfywire/sayonara-wild-hearts-is-a-coming-out-story-within-a-female-focused-pop-music-game

Delalande, L., Moyon, M., Tissier, C., Dorriere, V., Guillois, B., Mevell, K., … Borst, G. (2019). Complex and subtle structural changes in prefrontal cortex induced by inhibitory control training from childhood to adolescence. *Developmental Science*, e12898. doi:10.1111/desc.12898.

de Smale, S., Kors, M. J., & Sandovar, A. M. (2017). The case of This War of Mine: A production studies perspective on moral game design. *Games and Culture, 14*(4), 387–409. doi:10.1177/1555412017725996.

Euteneuer, J. (2019). Papers, please. In K. Schrier (Ed.), *Learning, education & games vol. 3: 100 games to use in the classroom and beyond* (pp. 279–282). Carnegie Mellon ETC Press.

Farber, M. (2017). *Game-based learning in action: How an expert affinity group teaches with games*. Peter Lang.

Foot, P. (1967). The problem of abortion and the doctrine of the double effect. *Oxford Review*, 5, 5–15.

Fortugno, N. (2014, May 1). *G4C14: Nick Fortugno Well Played Series (Papers, Please)*. [Video]. YouTube. https://youtu.be/kQR3xhC9hJA

Gandolfi, E. (2019). *Fallout shelter*. In K. Schrier (Ed.), *Learning, education & games vol. 3: 100 games to use in the classroom and beyond* (pp. 141–144). Carnegie Mellon ETC Press.

Geer, F., & Matthew, F. (2019). *Undertale*. In K. Schrier (Ed.), *Learning, education & games vol. 3: 100 games to use in the classroom and beyond* (pp. 479–484). Carnegie Mellon ETC Press.

Gordon, A. (2020, May 8). Alexandria Ocasio-Cortez joins Animal Crossing. *CNN*. https://www.cnn.com/2020/05/08/politics/aoc-animal-crossing/index.html

Griffin A. (2017). Adolescent neurological development and implications for health and well-being. *Healthcare (Basel, Switzerland)*, 5(4), 62.

Groux, C. (2020, April 21). Animal Crossing inspires teacher to help students graduate in a pandemic. *Newsweek*. https://www.newsweek.com/animal-crossing-new-horizons-teacher-help-students-graduate-pandemic-1498760

Hugo, V. (1862). *Les Misérables*. Signet.

Ilten-Gee, R., & Hilliard, L. J. (2017. Moral reasoning in peer conversations during game-based learning: An exploratory study. *Journal of Moral Education*, 48(1), 1–26. doi:10.1080/03057240.2019.1662775.

Isbister, K. (2016). *How games move us: Emotion by design*. MIT Press.

Jones, S. (2018, August 2). Thought experiment: Teaching normative ethics with digital games. *Slideshare*. https://www.slideshare.net/autnes/thought-experiment-teaching-normative-ethics-with-digital-games-by-sherry-jones-aug-2-2018

Kant, K. (1785). *Groundwork for the metaphysics of morals*. Hartknoch.

Kaufman, G., & Flanagan, M. (2015). A psychologically "embedded" approach to designing games for prosocial causes. *Cyberpsychology: Journal of Psychosocial Research on Cyberspace*, 9(3). doi:10.5817/CP2015-3-5.

Kelley, M. (2020, September 1). Biden campaign launches official Animal Crossing: New Horizons yard signs. *The Verge*. https://www.theverge.com/2020/9/1/21409727/biden-harris-animal-crossing-campaign-new-horizons-yard-signs-election

Khan, I. (2020, April 7). Why Animal Crossing is the game for the coronavirus moment. *New York Times*. https://www.nytimes.com/2020/04/07/arts/animal-crossing-covid-coronavirus-popularity-millennials.html

Kral, T. R. A., Stodola, D. E., Birn, R. M., Mumford, J. A., Solis, E., Flook, L., ... Davidson, R. J. (2018). Neural correlates of video game empathy training in adolescents: A randomized trial. *NPJ Science of Learning*, 3(1), 13–10. doi:10.1038/s41539-018-0029-6.

Lajoie, J. (2018, March 24). What is queer game studies? *Electronic Book Review*. doi:10.7273/zsfx-m331.

Majdandžić, J., Amashaufer, S., Hummer, A., Windischberger, C., & Lamm, C. (2016). The selfless mind: How prefrontal involvement in mentalizing with similar and dissimilar others shapes empathy and prosocial behavior. *Cognition, 157,* 24–38. doi:10.1016/j.cognition.2016.08.003.

Murray, J. H. (2017). *Hamlet on the holodeck: The future of narrative in cyberspace.* MIT Press.

Newman, M. Z. (2017). *Atari age: The emergence of video games in America.* MIT Press.

Osterweil, S., Hilliard, L. J., & Meneses, S. F. (2019). Quandary. In K. Schrier (Ed.), *Learning, education & games vol. 3: 100 games to use in the classroom and beyond* (pp. 325–330). Carnegie Mellon ETC Press.

Packer, J. (2010). The battle for galt's gulch: Bioshock as critique of objectivism. *Journal of Gaming & Virtual Worlds, 2*(3), 209–224. doi:10.1386/jgvw.2.3.209_1.

Patsenko, E. G., Adluru, N., & Birn, R. M. (2019). Mindfulness video game improves connectivity of the fronto-parietal attentional network in adolescents: A multi-modal imaging study. *Scientific Reports, 9,* 18667 (2019). doi:10.1038/s41598-019-53393-x.

Pentz, M. A., Hieftje, K. D., Pendergrass, T. M., Brito, S. A., Liu, M., Arora, T., … Fiellin, L. E. (2019). A videogame intervention for tobacco product use prevention in adolescents. *Addictive Behaviors, 91,* 188–192. doi:10.1016/j.addbeh.2018.11.016.

Phelps, A. M., & Rusch, D. C. (2020). Navigating existential, transformative game design. *Proceedings of the 2020 DiGRA International Conference: Play Everywhere.* http://www.digra.org/digital-library/publications/navigating-existential-transformative-game-design/

Rand, A. (1943). *The Fountainhead.* Signet.

Rand, A. (1957). *Atlas Shrugged.* Signet.

Richardson, S. (2011, September 2). No comment: The sexist t-shirt J.C. Penney didn't remove. *Ms. Magazine.* https://msmagazine.com/2011/09/02/no-comment-the-sexist-t-shirt-j-c-penney-didnt-remove/

Rimm, H. (2020, May 19). Animal Crossing may be a capitalist dystopia, but I'm just here to make friends. *Refinery29.* https://www.refinery29.com/en-gb/2020/05/9824012/animal-crossing-game-friends-connection

Rockett, A. (2020, March 30). Animal Crossing used by Japanese company in work-from-home effort. *Nintendo Enthusiast.* https://www.nintendoenthusiast.com/animal-crossing-work-from-home/

Schell, J. (2020). *The art of game design: A book of lenses* (3rd ed.). CRC Press.

Schrier, K. (2015a). Ethical thinking and sustainability in role-play participants: A preliminary study. *Simulation & Gaming, 46*(6), 673–696.

Schrier, K. (2015b). Emotion, empathy and ethical thinking in Fable III. In S. Tettegah & W. Huang (Eds.), *Emotion, technology, and games.* New York, NY: Elvesier.

Schrier, K. (2019). Fable III. In K. Schrier (Ed.), *Learning, education & games vol. 3: 100 games to use in the classroom and beyond* (pp. 137–140). Carnegie Mellon ETC Press.

Sicart, M. (2009). *The ethics of computer games.* MIT Press.

Smalley, K. (2016). Undertale and Immanuel Kant: Ethics in video games. *Popmatters.* https://www.popmatters.com/undertale-and-immanuel-kant-ethics-in-videogames-2495432738.html

Steinberg, L. (2011). Adolescents' risky driving in context. *Journal of Adolescent Health, 49*(6), 557–558. doi:10.1016/j.jadohealth.2011.10.001.

Teachers Guide. (n.d.). *Awkward Moment.* https://tiltfactor.org/wp-content/uploads2/awkwardmomentteachersguide_20130812.pdf

Todd, A. R., & Galinsky, A. D. (2014). Perspective-taking as a strategy for improving intergroup relations: Evidence, mechanisms, and qualifications. *Social and Personality Psychology Compass, 8*(7), 374–387.

Upton, B. (2018). *Situational game design.* Routledge.

CHAPTER SEVEN

Co-op Play, Teamwork, and Relationship Skills

"I would rather hire a high-level *World of Warcraft* player than an MBA from Harvard," researcher John Seeley Brown once famously quipped (2012, para. 1). Brown's remark was based on the multiplayer online game's guild structure, where players with different abilities self-organize into teams. Skills developed in the game may translate to the real-world, he surmised.

Over the years, many different kinds of multiplayer games have entered classrooms, including *World of Warcraft*, *Minecraft*, a sandbox for learning, making, and sharing, and *Classcraft*, the game layer that turns learning into a team-based experience (for more, see Chapter Five). Team-based escape room games have also become popular in classrooms (Menon & Romero, 2020). Nicholson (2015) defines escape rooms as live-action games where players "discover clues, solve puzzles, and accomplish tasks in one or more rooms in order to accomplish a specific goal (usually escaping from the room) in a limited amount of time" (p. 1). Breakout EDU is an example of a school-based escape room platform. (More on Breakout EDU soon!)

In cooperative ("co-op") games, players do not receive participation trophies just for showing up. Instead, everyone either all wins together, or all players lose. One example is *Keep Talking and Nobody Explodes*, a game about defusing a bomb. Only one player sees and interacts with a bomb, while other players, known as "experts," have access to the Bomb Defusal manual, a printable document of puzzles. As the timer ticks down, experts need to apply critical thinking skills to decipher clues and then communicate solutions to the bomb defuser.

"Many people think games must be competitive endeavors," Matt Leacock told me. Leacock is the designer of *Pandemic*, one of the most popular cooperative tabletop games of all time. We spoke in the spring of 2020, just as an actual pandemic spread around the world. "The thought of co-op seems like a contradiction. In a cooperative game, the game is fighting against you."

A good cooperative game has a rich problem space where players puzzle it out—what Leacock calls "distributed computation." In escape rooms, all players need to collaborate to break out. If players don't work together in *Keep Talking and Nobody Explodes*, then they all fail and virtually explode. "In cooperative games, players look at the problem from their perspective, and then there is some level of argument and rebuttal until a consensus is reached," he continued. "You have this rotation of who is in charge. I find games like that rewarding because of the creative problem-solving when you work on effective teams."

In Leacock's *Pandemic*, players role-play as experts with the mutual goal of stemming diseases from spreading worldwide. Roles attribute abilities or superpowers to players: the medic is the player who can cure an entire infected city; only the dispatcher can move other players to other cities; the quarantine expert is the only one who can prevent outbreaks.

In my middle school social studies class, *Pandemic* experientially modeled the Columbian Exchange for students. The Columbian Exchange was when plants, animals, cultural ideas—and diseases—were purposely and inadvertently exchanged in the 14th and 15th centuries. As children played, they began to understand how disease spread from European nations to the Americas. They also felt a sense of interconnectedness as they worked together to stop diseases from being spread.

When the COVID-19 pandemic began, my family played together to show our son why we were staying home and avoiding crowds. In the end, our disease-fighting team lost; the disease cubes got the better of us. Although defeated in the game, the message was understood: We are all in this together!

Earlier that spring, Leacock contributed an editorial piece to the *New York Times* titled, *No Single Player Can Win This Board Game. It's Called Pandemic* (https://nyti.ms/3bu2Tm2). In it, he recounted how the SARS epidemic, from one decade earlier, had inspired his design. Now, the world was in a real pandemic. He advised readers to think about his game as "a model for us in this time of crisis. We don't all have to be globe-trotting heroes to do our part. We each have special skills and should use them to make the city and statewide lockdowns safer and easier to bear" (Leacock, 2020, para. 13).

In this chapter, games that foster cooperation, companionship, and interdependence are explored. Some are co-op, while others model teamwork and relationship-building mechanically. Emerging research from the fast-growing field of electronic sports, or esports, is also shared. Like other team-based experiences, in esports tournaments, players work together to achieve mutual goals.

Games of Kinship and Interdependence

Way is a two-player video game where one player collaborates with another to overcome obstacles. In one challenge, one of the two players must climb a set of invisible stairs. Later in the game, spikes drop near that player at timed intervals. Players cannot text—the second player needs to figure out gestures as a form of communication. When they successfully communicate, steps can be climbed and falling spikes are evaded.

A side-scrolling platformer, *Way* is presented in split-screen. (For context, the original *Super Mario Bros.* game was also a side-scrolling platformer.) The game can be played in about 20-minutes, making it perfect for classrooms. Players simply sign on and join a server, and then they are randomly connected to someone else. To win, both players need to remain in the experience. After the final challenge, they are rewarded with a digital whiteboard that appears in a shared space. Once there, players can text one another.

An exploratory study of college students was conducted by Schrier and Shaenfield (2016). They noted that anonymity in the game "seemed to enhance the participant's attachment to the partner, as well as their interest in and awareness of one's partner's emotions" (Schrier & Shaenfield, 2016, p. 289). Another theme that emerged was participants' mutual trust afforded through collaborative problem-solving (Schrier & Shaenfield, 2016).

Karen (Kat) Schrier, associate professor and founding director of the Games and Emerging Media program at Marist College and co-author of the exploratory study, continues to use *Way* in her classroom. "I have all of the students sign on, but I don't tell them much about it," she explained. "Because they all join at the same time, they get paired with each other—but they don't realize that at first."

During gameplay, she circulates and asks questions like, "Are you playing with a real person or a computer?" "They get confused whether or not the other player is an actual person," she recalled. "I then ask, 'What makes you think it's a person? What makes you think it might be a computer or a virtual character?'" Anecdotally, there is usually a mix of responses.

The magic happens as pairs complete the game. Most then realize that they were playing with peers in the same room. Some announce it out loud, exclaiming, "Oh wait, we were playing together!" Through the game, her students had a shared experience. "I think there is something about playing together and having to rely on each other, even for just a few minutes," Schrier continued. "They had a kind of intimacy that only they shared. The game does this well—it mimics the kinds of experience you might have in becoming friends, like establishing trust and starting to care about someone else."

Schrier did some preliminary testing with students, asking about their play experience. Some partners wrote, "You're my friend now because we played this game together." "It was nice to see how people connected through a game," she continued. "The reason I think the game does that is that you are so reliant on each other."

Schrier's work suggests that games, even ones with simple interactions, can model kinship and interdependence to players. "You have to listen to know what kind of information the other player is missing. You constantly learn from the other person, but also teach them what to do."

Brothers: A Tale of Two Sons is another game where cooperation is required to achieve a goal. Different than *Way*, it is a single-player experience, a hero's journey set in a fairy tale. In the game, players simultaneously control two siblings as they solve environmental puzzles. The fraternal metaphor is modeled mechanically with the controller: the left thumbstick is mapped to one brother, the right to the other. This can get tricky, as interdependence on the other is required. Let's say there is a heavy object on a path blocking the younger brother. Only half of the controller can be used to manipulate the older brother to remove the obstruction. Can the left work with the right? When combined with an emotional arc, these actions evoke fraternal affection to both avatars that players control (May et al., 2014).

"Couch co-op" is form of cooperative gameplay. As the name implies, these are games played together in one physical location—like on a couch—where everyone has a mutual goal. *Keep Talking and Nobody Explodes* is an example. *Overcooked 2* is another, a frenetic experience where players assemble meals together. In both games, players need to communicate out loud to succeed.

Never Alone (Kisima Ingitchuna), based on an Iñupiat Alaska Native folktale, is an educational couch co-op video game. It can also be played like *Brothers*, with one player controlling both characters, engendering the same feelings of interdependence. Players control Nuna, a young girl on the quest, and her companion, a mystical arctic fox. Each has unique abilities: Only Nuna can climb ladders and ropes, move heavy objects, and throw a bola weapon at targets; the arctic fox can scramble up walls, jump long distances, and fit through small crevices. Mechanics of wind, snow, and ice are used as metaphors for life in a harsh and cold environment (de Vasconcelos Neto & Alves, 2020).

A core aspect of the gameplay in *Never Alone* is "the symbiotic relationship between Nuna and the fox that befriends her" (Massanari, 2015, p. 88). The only way to win is to work together. When players do, "Cultural Insights" are unlocked, documentary video clips from and about the Iñupiat people.

Cooperative games present meaningful learning opportunities where children can play to their strengths. The next section investigates an educational escape room platform. To win, students must work together to puzzle out solutions to standards-aligned challenges. More than winning or losing, success comes from taking a journey together.

"We Broke Out!"

In educational escape room games, students can build self-management and responsible decision-making skills by solving problems together (Dietrich, 2018; Eukel & Morrell, 2020). Sometimes, students shout possible solutions to classmates out loud (Veldkamp et al., 2020). Oracy is just part of the goal-achievement process.

Breakout EDU is a commercially available escape room platform intended for classroom use. There are two versions: A physical kit that includes plastic boxes, hasps, locks, and other tactile components; and a digital platform where teachers can have students play games together online.

In my educational technology courses, students play *Tricky Travel* in small groups, a digital Breakout EDU game aligned to geography standards. The experience is wrapped in a narrative: "Your bags are packed, you are ready to go, but your ticket is locked up! Apparently, before you can take off, you need to tackle a few tricky puzzles to collect that treasured ticket!" Students then have 20-minutes to solve three kinds of combination locks: a directional lock with arrows, a color-coded lock, and a word lock.

First, is the directional lock. On the screen, students see a clue: the front page of a fictional newspaper. Some letters in the headline story are bolded. The bolded letters correspond to state abbreviations (e.g., MI = Michigan, AL = Alabama) (see Figure 12). Once students realize this, they then need to consult a map to see the cardinal directions of those cities, from west to east.

Next is the color-coded lock. Students see a world map with different colors for each continent. There are a series of three letters above the map. These are airport codes, many of which require web searching to figure out where they are; it may not be immediately obvious that "HEL" is Helsinki, Finland or that "LOS" is Lagos, Nigeria. There is one airport code per color-coded continent.

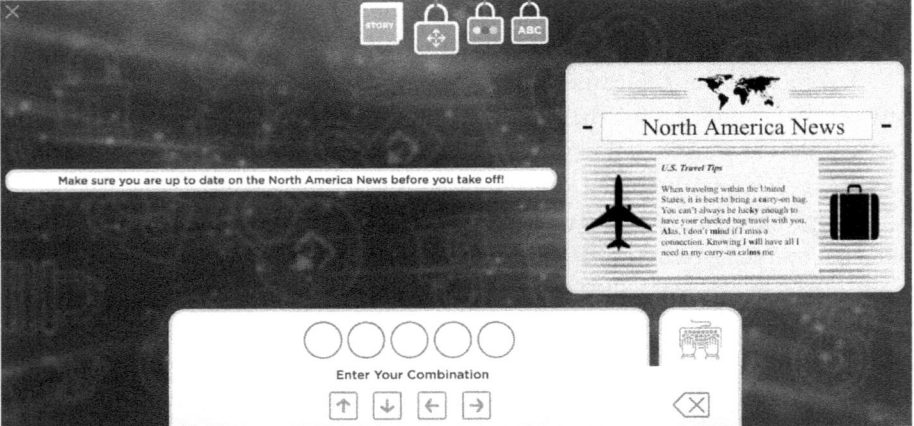

Figure 12. Directional Lock in a Breakout EDU Digital Game. Source: Breakout EDU Platform. Reprinted by permission of the publisher.

The final puzzle is the word lock. An Italian phrase is written above the lock. It reads, "*L'apprendimento è un **viaggio** non una destinazione.*" A quick check on Google Translate reveals the English translation: "Learning is a journey, not a destination." When players realize that the word "*viaggio*" is bolded, they know that "journey" is the solution. As other locks are solved, students often declare, "We broke out!" In all of my years of teaching, I have yet to see students cheer after completing a geography worksheet—hence, the allure of game-based learning!

In addition to *Tricky Travel*, there are more than 1,700 standards-aligned games on the Breakout EDU platform. Games are sorted by teaching discipline: English language arts, math, science, physical education, computer science, the arts, career technical education, and social studies. There are also holiday and team-building games.

Players of Breakout EDU games often fail until they realize how to work together. Generally, the first combination students enter is incorrect. When this occurs, players may backward map their thinking. How far back do they go? Back to the original problem set? "That's the learning, the process of thinking," Adam Bellow, co-founder of Breakout EDU, explained. "There is perseverance to try again. Through failure [the lock won't open], you've been undeniably told you are incorrect. How do you switch gears? What is the thinking process that switches in your head?"

Some user-generated breakouts on the platform tend to resemble trivia games, with combination solutions as the answers to rote problems. Internally, the team at Breakout EDU uses the term "on-the-nose" for puzzles like these. "We are very aware that teachers see numbers in locks as possible solutions to a math problem," Bellow said. "Or, in a color lock, teachers may show an American flag and the solution is red, white, and blue." To guide teachers to design more complex game experiences, Breakout EDU offers lock tutorials, game design worksheets, facilitation materials, and templates. Exemplars of well-designed games are also featured on the homepage.

Most games on Breakout EDU are wrapped in a narrative. "For us, it is about building a story. After all, it's a box or website that has the same locks as last time. How do you make that exciting so kids willingly suspend disbelief and get into the moment?" Bellow shared a game that he designed called *LIFE*, a series of puzzles about a fictional person's life, from birth to death. "Players need to get information from the other players, making this game about interdependence. It also has level design, starting with an easy, 'on-the-nose' lock: the birthdate of the person whose life you are playing."

By proxy, Breakout EDU enables children of all abilities to rise up to challenges. But, there may be some students who try to dominate games. In the tabletop game community, this is known as *quarterbacking*, when a bossy player or personality tries to make all of the group's decisions. It is one thing to play to one's strengths; it is another when that behavior becomes undesirable.

Bellow, a former teacher, suggests classroom management as an intervention. "We don't presume to tell teachers how to structure playing games in classes, but we do give tips," he continued. "We have had teachers assign roles so certain students don't 'hog the box.' One student may become 'the reporter,' the one who takes all of the notes. Another may read the puzzles. They may take turns trying the locks." Breakout EDU games can also give space for introverted students to shine. "We've had anecdotes about students who don't call out in class but were the ones who opened the locks."

Teachers can add constraints to deepen cooperation and interdependence amongst student groups. "We once heard of a class playing very loud, which disrupted the class next door," Bellow recalled. "We workshopped an idea to make it a silent game, where you could only communicate using a shared Google Doc. Then you can also see exactly who contributed and what their contributions were. People have also played breakout games in ASL [American Sign Language]. French classes have played games where students could only communicate in French."

Post-game debriefs can help students build self-awareness by engaging in metacognitive reflection about how and why certain decisions were made and how individual actions affected the team's success or failure. To facilitate reflection, the kit includes a deck of cards with questions and extension activities. One card asks,

"If your group played this game again, what would you change about the approach to solving puzzles?" Other cards prompt students to write game reviews, design additional clues, or create music playlists that can augment play experiences.

Lessons from Recess

"We always have believed in the power of play for play's sake," Elizabeth Cushing told me. Cushing is the president of Playworks, a national nonprofit organization that advises schools and districts on recess. "Play is a developmentally important behavior that has survived millennia of evolution. There must be a value to it."

Since inception, Playworks has served more than 2 million children in 3,000 schools across the United States. Its programs guide schools to provide safe and healthy play experiences for all children. The guidance includes its Great Recess Framework, a vast and inclusive games library, and staff training.

The story of Playworks began in 1996 when founder Jill Vialet was talking with an elementary school principal who expressed how her school's recess was in disarray. Children were being sent to her office repeatedly. Bullying was also a problem, as was conflict on the playground. At that moment, Vialet recalled her childhood, playing at her city's parks and recreation system. A young paid staffer led the games children played and always ensured that she got in the game. She wondered whether she could provide that kind of service to children at schools during recess. Soon after, Sports4Kids was born. A few years later, its name was changed to Playworks.

When we spoke, Cushing described a kind of playground paradox that she has observed. "Children will continue to try to play, even when the game breaks down over disagreements or when there is bullying. That's how much they are intrinsically motivated to play," she said.

What is it about playground play that keeps drawing kids to come back? Why is recess so crucial to childhood development? As it happens, a lot has to do with self-determination theory, our innate human need to feel a sense of autonomy, relatedness, and competence (Deci & Ryan, 2000; Ryan & Deci, 2018). "We have an insight that play is the one activity in the school day where kids actually have mastery, and they know it," Cushing said. "Their levels of mastery, in their minds, are equal to or better than the grown-ups'."

For children to be intrinsically motivated to play, they need to be afforded choice in the games they play and they should never be excluded. Let's look at playground basketball as an example. In a pick-up game self-organized by children, all can likely be part of that experience. But that is not the case with every playground game, like tag or dodgeball. Traditionally, in these games, when an opposing player tags someone with a hand or a ball, the other player must leave the game.

I pondered why so many children are attracted to play *Among Us*. Massively popular, it is a multiplayer video game that uses a similar social deduction mechanic as *Werewolf* and *Mafia*. *Among Us* also blends in elements of *Tag* and *Hide-and-Seek*, albeit digitally. My son plays for hours.

In *Among Us*, crewmates deduce who the imposters are aboard a spaceship. When voted out, imposters do not need to leave the game. Instead, they can remain as ghosts, still participating in tasks. It is an inclusive take on recess play.

How can playground games be remixed to be more inclusive while also engendering children with a playful experience? And how can adults be involved to motivate the adaptation without directing how children play? This is where Playworks's approach comes in. Let's look at *Four-Square*, a recess game where players stand in quadrants while bouncing a ball to other players. The norm of this game is to point at players who miss, possibly jeering them. Playworks's adaptation is more inclusive, having players praise those who are eliminated.

When adults play with children, it signals to them that they have mastery, that play is essential, and that being in a relationship with children is as valuable as knowledge transfer. To this end, Playworks trains its facilitators to join in games and model positive behavior. "By having an adult in a game, the norm and conditions can be set for everyone," Cushing said. "We are not telling the kids, 'You must play or must hit the ball this way.'"

To further guide this facilitation, Playworks has a set of design principles that help ensure that play is inclusive—everyone should get to play. Useful on the playground and adaptable for classrooms or screens, the Six Simple Principles of Play are:

1. Every kid has the opportunity to play every day, from the classroom to the playground, and in the neighborhood.
2. Kids get to choose to play and get to choose games that make them happy.
3. Kids have the right tools to resolve playground conflicts on their own.
4. Adults play alongside kids, modeling and supporting a culture of trust, positivity, and inclusion.
5. Play is not treated as a reward to be revoked.
6. Everyone is welcome to join the game, because playing together is a great way to build community. (Six Simple Principles of Play, n.d.)

In addition to its design principles, Playworks has downloadable game guides. These include curated lists of games to play at home or on the playground. The *Games for Social and Emotional Learning* guide (linked at the end of this chapter) features more than 150 games that promote self-management, teamwork, positive relationship-building, and social awareness. One example is *Rock-Paper-Scissors*, recommended for conflict resolution. The ultimate tiebreaker, it appears throughout the guide. In the *Four-Square* game set-up, instructions state, "Explain that if there is a disagreement about a play, one round of *Rock-Paper-Scissors* resolves the conflict" (Games for Social and Emotional Learning, n.d., p. 68).

About *Rock-Paper-Scissors* and conflict resolution, Cushing said, "Adults say to us, 'But that's arbitrary!' We say, 'Right, exactly!' Children just need a graceful way to resolve disputes." Her response resonated with me: When I taught middle school, *Rock-Paper-Scissors* was written in my classroom's rules and procedures. It was a playful way for most of my students to settle minor disagreements.

In addition to conflict resolution, the *Games for Social and Emotional Learning* guide features activities that promote positive relationship-building. *I Love My Neighbor* is an example. To play, children stand in a circle and then share information about themselves. During the game, commonalities emerge. *Rock-Paper-Scissors* is again recommended as a tiebreaker. Here are the steps to play *I Love My Neighbor*:

- Players stand in a circle where the cone/place marker marks their spot. One player will not have a cone. That person stands in the center of the circle.
- The player standing in the center begins the game by saying "I love my neighbor who …" The player completes the sentence with a fact about themselves. For example,
- "I love my neighbor who likes to play basketball!"; or "I love my neighbor who has brothers and sisters!" The sentence can be anything that the player likes, but must be true for that person.
- Then everyone on the circle who has that in common leaves their spot and runs to any empty spot that is not right next to them.
- The last player who cannot find an open spot changes places with the person in the center and begins a new round of the game by saying "I love my neighbor who …" (Games for Social and Emotional Learning, n.d., p. 94).

Of course, play does not need an explicit SEL goal to be justified. Cushing shared one game designed to be playful just for the sake of being fun. Called *Paparazzi*, in a large group, players silently choose one person to be the celebrity whom they protect and one as the paparazzi photographer who tries to get a picture of that celebrity. "It is essentially running around," she said. "It is silly and hilarious. I bring it up because everyone is a player. Nobody wins or loses. And it has no purpose. For us, that game builds relationships because you demonstrate your more relaxed self."

After *Paparazzi*, players often approach one another, saying, "I was your paparazzi!" People then see each other in a different light. "We use what is attractive about play to bring up a sense of commonality among a group of people."

Playworks also runs developmental sports leagues. "For many kids, this is their first time being on a team or being part of an organized sport," Cushing continued. "We don't keep score. Our rule is, 'Play hard, respect the game, and have fun.' We have to teach adults just to let the kids play for the fun of it. The experience of being on a team is super important."

Research suggests efficacy in Playworks's approach. One study used its Great Recess Framework as an observational tool to assess recess play. In a randomized control trial, Massey et al. (2018) compared children in a Playworks's school to those not using the program. Participant teachers trained by Playworks reported that their students had greater feelings of safety while at school (Massey et al., 2018). What's more, Playworks-trained teachers observed fewer bullying instances (Massey et al., 2018). As it turns out, when we all play together positively and inclusively, we all win!

Scholastic Esports and Cyber Wellness

At the scholastic level, esports leagues of competitive video gaming have emerged. Some are intramural; others function as afterschool clubs. This section focuses on NASEF, the North America Scholastic Esports Federation. There are other scholastic esports organizations, including but not limited to High School Esports League (HSEL), National Federation of State High School Association (NFHS), the National Association of College Esports (NACE), and Liminal Esports. In May 2021, NASEF consolidated and partnered with HSEL and its Middle School Esports League (MSEL).

In the summer of 2020, NASEF, in partnership with the San Diego County Office of Education, published a set of SEL-aligned lessons. For middle and high school students, lessons were co-developed by two NASEF Scholastic Fellows: Chris Aviles and Angelique Gianas. Aviles is a teacher in Fair Haven, New Jersey; Gianas is an English language arts teacher from La Mesa, California (her work on pairing a video game with a novel is featured in Chapter Four).

Both Aviles and Gianas are active on Twitter (search hashtag: #esportsedu) and on Twitch, the game streaming website owned by Amazon. Aviles is also the co-author of *The Esports Education Playbook: Empowering Every Learner through Inclusive Gaming* (2020), a guidebook for educators. He co-founded the nonprofit Garden State Esports and he coaches the FH Knights, the first esports team for middle schoolers in the United States. To Aviles, FH Knights is explicitly a team, not a club; his students compete to be on varsity squads, maintain passing grade point averages, and are required to behave to school standards. For many of his students, this experience is the first time they have ever been coached. "A team is like a family," he tells his students. "You may not always like your family, but you always have to look out for each other."

Each year, Aviles purchases team jerseys adorned with the FH Knights logo. "When you join something and become a part of something, it is bigger than you, and it's not just about you," he told me. Being part of a team affords opportunities to forge new friendships and develop together as a peer group. "I asked the team what they enjoyed the most, and they said it was after the matches, when we go out for pizza together," he continued. "Maybe these kids were gaming by themselves or with strangers online. Now they have a whole new group of friends from school."

Gianas's esports program is different than Aviles's; hers functions more like a club than a coached team. "I started our club about two years ago," she recalled. "It started super small: three kids who met after school to play [Nintendo's] *Super Smash Bros*. There was no bigger goal or leadership yet." Her club has since branched out to meet the needs of students who play casually and those who want to belong to a team.

Esports can attract an underserved school population. Many students on Aviles's and Gianas's respective teams did not have a home anywhere else in school. "They may not be traditional athletes who play sports, and they may not be involved in clubs," Aviles said. "They leave school at the end of the day, go home, and play video games. Esports brings something they love into school, which helps with attendance, grades, and behavior."

The NASEF SEL curriculum they co-developed draws on their shared coaching experiences. Aligned to California's SEL Competencies and the Common Core State Standards, the lessons are shared as prompts on Flipgrid, Microsoft's free video reflection tool. Self-regulation and self-care strategies are recurring themes throughout.

The curriculum is in three modules: *Good Gamer*, *Tactical Teams*, and *Creative Competition*. In *Good Gamer*, youth self-explore their personalities to better understand who they are. Students are first asked, "What type of gamer do you want to be? How can you build positive skills to achieve goals?" Students then reflect on themselves outside of gaming. Next, they are asked to interview peers about their strengths and passions.

Good Gamer lessons also include wellness check-ins intended to help players understand how their mental and physical health affects their gameplay. One topic is "Rage Quit 101." Rage quitting is when gamers abandon gameplay due to player frustration. Other lessons are on tracking sleep schedules, eating habits, and exercise. "As a gamer, you may be eating Cheetos and not sleeping at night," Gianas said. "We have a lesson on how to create a self-care plan."

Next are the *Tactical Teams* lessons. These focus on teamwork, conflict resolution, resilience, and anti-bullying. After all, the dynamic of being part of an esports team is not all that different from traditional athletics. This is explored in the positive role model lesson called "Plus One People." There are also team-building exercises about trust, and more reflective prompts.

Creative Competition is the final module. Here, students are prompted to create their own tournament on any game that they can access. There are lessons on marketing, bracketing, and catering to an audience. Students can also explore gaming in popular culture and research their favorite streamers. "Some kids want to be a streamer or a shoutcaster [esports broadcaster]," Gianas said. "We hit all aspects, so kids understand that esports goes beyond just being good at *Fortnite*. If you are interested in one of these things, there is something out there for you. This meshes SEL and esports opportunities, which are more than being good at an event."

Tilt Malleability and Growth Mindset

Tilt—or tilting—describes the moment when emotions compromise gameplay. When tilt occurs in esports tournaments, players may take unnecessary risks, make flawed calculations, and act out emotionally. Typically, players perceive tilt as unfavorable as it may include negative feelings, like frustration and anger. What's worse, tilt may lead to toxic online behavior. "In esports, tilt is when you make rash decisions that are not logical," researcher Constance Steinkuehler remarked. "Your emotions get jacked up."

Steinkuehler is a professor of informatics at the University of California, Irvine (UCI). Her work in games and learning includes collaborations with Richard Davidson at the Center for Healthy Minds and as a senior policy analyst in the White House Office of Science and Technology Policy. There, she advised the Obama administration on initiatives relating to games for impact. Steinkuehler's current research at the Connected Learning Lab at UCI takes the work from esports ecosystems and connects it to educational goals. When we spoke, she shared new findings on tilt, a construct her lab considers to be the "esports version of self-regulation" (Steinkuehler & Wu, 2020, p. 1).

Steinkuehler's team has been conducting scholastic esports research for more than three years. In the first year, they observed what youth were doing in leagues and clubs by making field observations in six schools. From there, data were coded and then analyzed to see what patterns emerged.

CASEL's SEL Framework guided the research—specifically, constructs around communication and self-management. As her research team refined SEL variables, they decided to dive straight into tilt because that was "the sweet spot." "When you interviewed kids, they repeatedly talked about how they lost patience and temper with their teammates, opponents, and themselves," Steinkuehler said. "Everything then goes haywire because of their emotional response, and the game and the team fall apart." The SEL findings were part of a broader array of variables that the research team explored. Other findings pertained to tilt triggers and tilt resiliency. The overall study also looked at STEM skills, STEM interests, and communication competencies.

The concept of tilt comes from pinball, describing how angry or frustrated players sometimes physically lift and tilt arcade cabinets to get the silver ball to roll where desired (Duncan, 2015). Modern pinball machines have sensors that trigger when a cabinet is lifted or shook, voiding points accumulated during tilted play.

Tilt can affect anyone, whether in pinball, poker, competitive video gaming, or at work. How to handle those emotions is another dimension, one that relates to mindsets. "The idea is that performance can fall apart once players get emotionally worked up and are no longer making sage decisions," Steinkuehler said. "They start tilting, but they are also not quitting."

Steinkuehler's PhD student Minerva Wu was similarly interested in tilt. Both studied tilt by first giving a simple survey with four open-ended questions. Participants (n = 95) were then asked to share words associated with tilt, tilt triggers, tilt responses, and perceptions around tilt malleability (Steinkuehler & Wu, 2020).

"Among the interesting findings were tilt triggers," Steinkuehler said. "The first and biggest response was that opponents did not cause it—they blamed their own team members as the trigger. Some players blamed themselves and their own behavior. They got toxic when they felt they were performing far less than they should have been."

When sensing the onset of tilt, players reported that they exited games about one-third of the time. "Ostensibly, this is a good strategy," Steinkuehler said. "It is what high-stakes poker players recommend."

Self-care strategies came second, such as taking calming breaths and redirecting emotions by smiling. About one-fifth of the findings were decidedly negative: screaming, cussing, flaming out, and smashing desks. "Here is where it gets really interesting," Steinkuehler continued. "We explored whether players could change their behavior." This is *tilt malleability*, the perception that "emotional volatility" could be tempered or self-regulated (Steinkuehler & Wu, 2020, p. 5). Tilt malleability relates to Dweck's (1986; 2006) work on a growth mindset versus a fixed mindset. Students with a fixed mindset believe their abilities are not malleable; they perceive that their intelligence and talents cannot be changed or developed. Having a growth mindset is an understanding of how practice can improve one's abilities. A growth mindset requires self-awareness of one's strengths (Dweck, 2006).

To learn more about players' beliefs around tilt malleability, Steinkuehler and Wu (2020) asked the following set of questions: Does the type of thing that triggers you lead to different responses? Do different types of triggers elicit different responses? Do beliefs about malleability predict positive or negative responses? Steinkuehler explained further,

> Both were strong relationships: You either think tilt is malleable or not. Whether or not you believe tilt is malleable amplifies the valance of the response. If you believe tilt is malleable, your responses shift more towards positive or negative. If you believe in malleability—and that the trigger may just be a bug [a coding issue] in the game, and that there are no emotions in the game's code—then your tilt shifts more towards positive exiting type strategies. When you don't believe in malleability, it shifts more to a negative strategy.

As mentioned, some participants blamed themselves—they saw themselves as the tilt trigger. "Here, it doesn't matter what you believe in malleability," Steinkuehler continued. "In our data, it looked as though the highest valance in responses in self-reactivity was about abusing yourself. There is self-recrimination in toxic behavior with tilt." Of course, self-reproach may also be part of traditional athletics.

In scholastic esports, coaches can intervene when toxic behavior is observed. Instead of lectures, conversations can take place about how tilt hurts the team's performance. This puts self-regulation in context, as players then see immediate results from managing emotions. "Being a good player means being able to hold it together under incredible stress," Steinkuehler said. "In many ways, this is standard coach behavior."

Katie Salen Tekinbaş, also a professor of informatics at UCI, shared the near-peer mentorship model used by coaches in the NASEF program. Tekinbaş is the co-founder of Connected Camps and she is a primary investigator of youth esports with Steinkuehler. "If you can connect kids with a near-peer mentor around a shared interest, it can be life-changing and totally transformative," Tekinbaş began. "These kids are not only getting their interests legitimized, but they are also seeing futures they may not have imagined for themselves via the college kids who are coaching them. They can relate to them. They learn all of the different majors. You can be into esports and anthropology or economics or mathematics. Kids then put those together. It's not to say that kids are doing mathematics within esports, but that those identities can co-exist."

Connected Camps trains its coaches on community norms, known in the sports world as *team charters*. "We work on pausing-and-breathing with our esports players," Tekinbaş continued. This relates to tilt resilience and emotional self-regulation. "We do a lot of work around conflict resolution, too."

The idea is that coaches-as-peers do not swoop in to solve problems. "When there is a problem, coaches try to create a culture where kids are the ones who try to solve the problem. We also do a lot of training around relationship-building, especially in esports, where teams work together. We talk about goal-setting and affirmations and confirmations. These strategies then lead to open conversations, reflections, and journaling."

Why is it important to have happy and well-balanced esports players? From a wellness perspective, understanding what triggers negative emotions—in games and life—can help us cope with stress in modern society. "When you ask kids what they get most out of the NASEF program, again and again, it was that they learned to manage their tilt and that the coach was one of the main vehicles for doing that," Steinkuehler said. "I hope we can add to coaches' work to stop players from being self-abusive when failing in a game."

Games of Love and Self-Discovery

Mission: It's Complicated is a narrative-based superhero game that can be used to teach adolescents about dating and relationships. It covers the complexities of friendships, platonic and romantic relationships, and mental health issues. Superhero characters vary in gender and orientation.

Available for free, gameplay is about "OTP," shorthand for "one true pairing," and "ships," internet slang for "relationships." OTP and ships can be platonic or romantic and describe any fan-favorite pairing, from peanut butter and jelly to Romeo and Juliet to *Star Trek*'s Captain Kirk and Mister Spock.

Mission: It's Complicated is mainly text-based, similar to an interactive graphic novel. As Professor L, players send superheroes on adventures and dates. The game's main interface resembles a text message client, like WhatsApp. Sometimes chats are linear conversations, while at other times, players select responses. There are about 100,000 words of fiction in its narrative; the sheer amount of player-driven reading means that this game can teach both literacy and SEL.

Mission: It's Complicated is sort of like a dating simulator (sim), only it's not. The genre of dating sims began in Japan in the 1980s. These days, there are thousands of dating sims. KFC—the fried chicken franchise—even has one! In *I Love You, Colonel Sanders! A Finger-Lickin' Good Dating Simulator*, players try to win the heart of the famed chicken salesman. (Not only is there a KFC-branded dating sim game, but there are also verified "KFC Gaming" accounts on YouTube, Twitter, and Instagram, with a bio that reads, "Finger Clickin' Good!" Yes, you read that right!)

In a dating sim, the player is one person trying to date other people. *Mission: It's Complicated* is different; the player-as-Professor L is the matchmaker, arranging both superhero missions and dates. Mission success is graded with a report card: A+ or A if successful, B or C if one or both sustain an injury fighting a villain, and D or F for failing. Players are told in the tutorial by Pugsly, a talking pug, that unlike school, failing still results in a D—technically, passing. Completed missions show a "Bond Up" meter, which gradually increases. Once fully bonded, things get, well, complicated.

I spoke with Jesse Schell about the development of the game. His studio, Schell Games, released it on Valentine's Day (February 14th) in 2020. Schell Games also produces Daniel Tiger SEL games (to learn more, see Chapter One). "In the game, you manage multiple parallel relationships," Schell explained. "You get to know these characters over time and how they interact. Players also explore relationships through the constraints in the game's story. For instance, if someone is injured in a mission, they can't go on a date."

Mission: It's Complicated began as a health game, part of a contract Schell Games had with the University of Pittsburgh Medical Center. "The idea was to make virtual health coach software where people would interact on their phones by texting with bots," Schell recalled. That game, *Odyssey*, is a free mobile download with three missions: stress reduction, smoking cessation, and healthy eating and exercise. In *Odyssey*, instead of selecting superheroes, you pick a health coach. "We have 15 potential faces that could be health coaches, but all with the same dialogue," Schell said.

The health coach in *Odyssey* interacts with players using a chat interface. *Mission: It's Complicated* was built on that engine. "We thought about an entertainment game with a texting interface," he continued. "The team came up with this idea of having players give superheroes missions through texting."

The design team next considered relationships, including LGBTQ+ pairings. "We asked, What if the game was about building relationships between characters, partly so they could help each other, but partly because they are exploring their relationships?" Schell recalled. "We also thought about LGBTQ+ relationships because we didn't want to mandate relationships. We didn't want characters to wear their orientation on their sleeves. What if you could pair anybody with anybody?"

Florence is another game about the complexities of dating. It is also one of my "go-to" recommendations for educators who are new to emotional arcs that games can afford. Like other walking sims (see Chapter Five), threat assessment is not part of the experience. Instead, the game is told as an interactive narrative on a mobile touchscreen.

Florence Yeoh is the game's title character, a 25-year-old woman who feels stuck in a routine. She wakes up alone, commutes to work, and swipes dating apps on her phone. Her career is menial, not fulfilling. Then she meets Krish, a cellist whose music and conversation breathes life into hers.

This is a game about falling in and out of love. It is told with mechanics seemingly not aligned to romance, like toothbrushing. In this sequence, players swipe the screen left and right to make Florence brush. At first, she does this by herself. But when she brushes while standing next to Krish, swiping on the smartphone suddenly feels intimate.

On their first date, comic strip speech bubbles appear above each character's head. As players maneuver jigsaw puzzle pieces into the bubbles, the puzzle pieces get larger and easier to fit, suggesting that their conversation metaphorically becomes easier. This is the opposite of most games, where challenges typically increase in difficulty. By having fewer pieces interlock, effortless conversation is visually modeled. Later in the game, the reverse happens: Florence and Krish have fallen out of step; they are no longer a good fit. Jigsaw pieces become smaller and jagged. It is heartbreaking.

Florence: Perspectives and Patterns is an online game-based course developed by UNESCO MGIEP that explores identity and gender through Florence's life and relationships. I spoke with Robin Sharma about the development of the lessons, which are on its Framerspace platform. "The core design was to build curriculum around pause points," Sharma began.

The free course has three modules themed on self-awareness and identity, gender stereotypes, and conflict resolution. "We ran a series of four workshops where we invited students to come in and play the game," Sharma recalled. "We explained to students that the objective of the workshop was for them to identify what they learned from the game."

Workshop participants identified the lack of spoken dialogue in *Florence*. This This observation led Sharma and his team to add a lesson where students guess what Florence and Krish are discussing by using context clues.

Midway through the game, Krish moves in with Florence. As they go about dividing house chores, the course asks students to reflect upon gender roles. "What was your reason behind assigning tasks by gender roles?" the course asks. "What was your thinking behind assigning grocery shopping to a particular character and not to another one?"

Games like *Mission: It's Complicated* and *Florence* model the intricacies of interpersonal relationships. As games, they proceduralize these complexities into manageable steps. What's more, they provide discussion points—conversation starters for teachers to help deepen these experiences, where game-based learning can be transferred from screens to the real-world.

Links, Lessons, and Games

40+ Free Digital Escape Rooms (Plus a Step-By-Step Guide for Creating Your Own): https://ditchthattextbook.com/30-digital-escape-rooms-plus-tips-and-tools-for-creating-your-own

Among Us, social deduction game: http://www.innersloth.com/gameAmongUs.php

Breakout EDU, the educational escape room game platform with more than 1,700 standards-aligned games: https://www.breakoutedu.com

Brothers: A Tale of Two Sons, a video game about fraternal bonds: https://www.hazelight.se/games/brothers

Connected Camps: https://connectedcamps.com

Cyber Wellness, esports curriculum: https://www.nasef.org/learning/cyberwellness

Escape the Room, escape room board game: https://www.thinkfun.com/escapetheroom

Fairplay Alliance, best practices in online gaming: https://fairplayalliance.org

Florence: https://annapurnainteractive.com/games/florence

Florence: Perspectives and Patterns, blog detailing the UNESCO MGIEP course: https://link.medium.com/K0lNQbOLTeb

Keep Talking and Nobody Explodes: https://keeptalkinggame.com

Learn with League, well-being esports curriculum: https://oce.learnwithleague.com/wellbeing

Mission: It's Complicated: https://www.schellgames.com/games/mission-its-complicated

Never Alone (Kisima Ingitchuna), cooperative video game based on an Iñupiat Alaska Native folktale: http://neveralonegame.com

Overcooked 2, cooperative cooking video game: https://www.team17.com/games/overcooked-2

Pandemic, cooperative tabletop game about a global health crisis: https://www.zmangames.com/en/games/pandemic

Playworks's *Games for Social and Emotional Learning* guide: https://www.playworks.org/resources/get-the-sel-game-guide

Tom's Digital Breakouts, free templates for making digital breakout games using Google and Microsoft apps: https://sites.google.com/view/tomsdigitalbreakouts/home

Way, cooperative game: https://makeourway.com

Zoo U, a social simulation game for elementary school children: https://www.centervention.com/zoo-u-sel-game

References

Brown, J. S. (2012, August 6). How World of Warcraft could save your business and the economy. *Big Think*. https://bigthink.com/videos/how-world-of-warcraft-could-save-your-business-and-the-economy-2

CASEL's SEL Framework. (2020). *CASEL*. https://casel.org/wpcontent/uploads/2020/10/CASEL-SEL-Framework-10.2020-1.pdf

Deci, E. L., & Ryan, R. M. (2000). Intrinsic and extrinsic motivations: Classic definitions and new directions. *Contemporary Educational Psychology, 25*(1), 54–67. doi:10.1006/ceps.1999.1020.

de Vasconcelos Neto, H. P., & Alves, M. A. F. (2020). Cultural playing: A videogame case study of Never Alone and the teaching of culture. In T. Ahram (Eds.), *Advances in human factors in wearable technologies and game design*. AHFE 2019. Advances in intelligent systems and computing (Vol. 973). Cham: Springer. doi:10.1007/978-3-030-20476-1_22.

Dietrich, N. (2018). Escape classroom: The leblanc Process: An educational "Escape game". *Journal of Chemical Education, 95*(6), 996-999. doi:10.1021/acs.jchemed.7b00690

Duncan, A. M. (2015). *Gambling with the myth of the American dream*. Routledge Research in Sport Culture and Society.

Dweck, C. S. (1986). Motivational processes affecting learning. The American Psychologist, 41(10),1040–1048. doi:10.1037/0003-066X.41.10.1040

Dweck, C. (2006). *Mindset: The new psychology of success*. Random House.

Eukel, H., & Morrell, B. (2020). Ensuring educational escape-room success: The process of designing, piloting, evaluating, redesigning, and re-evaluating educational escape rooms. *Simulation & Gaming*, 104687812095345. doi:10.1177/1046878120953453

Games for Social and Emotional Learning. (n.d.) *Playworks*. https://www.playworks.org/resources/get-the-sel-game-guide/

Leacock, M. (2020, March 25). No single player can win this board game. It's called pandemic. *New York Times*. https://nyti.ms/3bu2Tm2

Massanari, A. L. (2015). Never Alone: Possibilities for participatory game design. *Well-Played*, 4(3). http://press.etc.cmu.edu/content/volume-4-number-3-diversity-games

Massey, W. V., Stellino, M. B., Mullen, S. P., Claassen, J., & Wilkinson, M. (2018). Development of the great recess framework—observational tool to measure contextual and behavioral components of elementary school recess. *BMC Public Health, 18*, 394.

May, A., Bizzocchi, J., Antle, A. N., & Choo, N. (2014). Fraternal feelings: How Brothers: A Tale of Two Sons affects players through gameplay. *2014 IEEE Games Media Entertainment* (pp. 1–4). doi:10.1109/GEM.2014.7048074.

Menon, D., & Romero, M. (2020). Game mechanics supporting a learning and playful experience in educational escape games. In M. Farber (Ed.), *Global perspectives on gameful and playful teaching and learning* (pp. 143–162). IGI Global. doi:10.4018/978-1-7998-2015-4.ch007.

Nicholson, S. (2015). *Peeking behind the locked door: A survey of escape room facilities.* http://scottnicholson.com/pubs/erfacwhite.pdf

Ryan, R. M., & Deci, E. L. (2018). *Self-determination theory: Basic psychological needs in motivation, development, and wellness.* Guilford Press.

Schrier, K., & Shaenfield, D. (2016). Collaboration and emotion in way. In S. Tettegah & W. Huang (Eds.), *Emotions, technology, and digital games* (pp. 289–312). Elsevier.

Six Simple Principles of Play. (n.d.). *Playworks.* https://www.playworks.org/about/why-play/principles-of-play/

Steinkuehler, C., & Wu, M. (2020). Understanding tilt. *Connected Learning Lab.* https://connectedlearning.uci.edu/wp-content/uploads/2020/02/5013.06_Y3-Tilt-Report.pdf

Veldkamp, A., Daemen, J., Teekens, S., Koelewijn, S., Knippels, M. P. J., & Joolingen, W. R. (2020). Escape boxes: Bringing escape room experience into the classroom. *British Journal of Educational Technology, 51*(4), 1220-1239. doi:10.1111/bjet.12935

CHAPTER EIGHT

How Making Games Supports Self-Awareness

A common misconception about game design is that it is the same as coding. However, the career of a game designer may or may not actually involve writing lines of computer code. A broad field, game design encompasses systems engineering, sound design, narrative design, user experience, user interface testing, environmental design, character art, and, yes, coding. (Of course, like any profession these days, having some proficiency in coding helps!)

"The act of writing code and the process of designing games are different skillsets," Kevin Miklasz told me. Miklasz is on the Global Game Jam board of directors. Over the years, we have worked together on several youth-centered game jam initiatives.

What is a game jam? A game jam is a "rapid prototyping event that typically takes place over a few days or a weekend, where game developers are given a theme and need to develop a game within the time frame" (Schrier, 2019, p. 4). Cooking competition television shows are a good analogy for how game jam events take place. On Food Network's *Chopped* series, chefs open a secret basket of ingredients, then prepare an appetizer, main course, and dessert in a limited time frame. The aesthetics of dishes are then scored using an agreed-upon rubric. Similarly, at game jams, participants are given constraints—time, software, themes—to design a game for someone else to play. Sometimes, game jams are competitive endeavors, while at other times, participants have mutual goals. Examples include social impact game jams, such as ones themed on arctic life, healthy habits, and staying safe during the COVID-19 pandemic. In 2014, the Obama administration hosted a White House Education Game Jam, inviting game developers, teachers, and students to participate.

The game jam model can be adapted to be a form of project-based learning, the pedagogical approach where students learn through making and sharing personally meaningful artifacts that address real-world problems or complex questions (Resnick, 2017). For instance, students can be challenged to make games about recycling by using materials, like index cards, markers, or dice, or with coding applications.

Designing an experience for someone else to play embeds empathy and perspective-taking (Dishon & Kafai, 2020). Participation in game jams may also mean that teamwork is required—game design is often a task that one individual likely cannot complete alone. What's more, game design has multiple entry points; one team member may be interested in narrative design, while others may focus on aesthetics.

At the game jams that I have been involved with, we tended to use "lower bar" tools, including Scratch, the visual block-based coding language from MIT's Lifelong Kindergarten Lab. This approach enabled participants to focus on skills related to rapid prototyping. "For me, it's about the process of design," Miklasz continued. "The idea is for kids to practice essential design skills right away, allowing them to iterate on those skills, rather than get caught up with issues of what I call 'coding grammar.'"

Miklasz is referring to programming languages like JavaScript and Python, where precision in syntax is required. "Coding grammar is thinking about whether a semicolon needs to be here or if this word should be there. Those are valuable skills, but they are technical 'hard skills' that don't necessarily build the social and emotional skills we are aiming for in game jams." "Hard skills" are tacit and concrete, sometimes rote, and are therefore more easily measurable; comparatively, "soft skills" describe SEL competencies, like emotional intelligence, communication skills, and the capacity to be self and socially aware (Baker-Doyle, 2017).

As an adolescent, I struggled when the dreaded "syntax error" message appeared on my Commodore 64 computer screen. It meant failure, and I felt defeated. When I was 13-years-old, I was inspired to learn BASIC programming after playing *Lemonade Stand*, a business simulator where players allocated funds for advertising, set drink prices, and faced random events, like inclement weather. As I played, I thought about a video rental store nearby that recently opened. Could I code a video rental simulator game? I tried but eventually quit in frustration. Syntax errors stifled my desire to be creative.

Decades later, I learned how to remix other people's games on Scratch—including lemonade stand games! I also found out about Twine, a free interactive fiction authoring tool. With Twine, little coding is required to create a choice-based, player-driven experience. My 13-year-old self was excited!

Game design is a multimodal form of expression, a medium for children to create and share artifacts about meaningful topics. In this chapter, several youth-centered constructionist gaming models are explored. It is gaming SEL in creative mode!

The Games for Change Student Challenge

The Games for Change Student Challenge is a competition where middle and high school students design games about real-world topics and issues. There are currently four cities that participate: New York City, Los Angeles, Detroit, and Atlanta, as well as a nationwide competition.

The Student Challenge originated in 2015 from folks within the New York City CS4all (Computer Science for All) team and the New York City Department of Education. They wanted to serve students in the same way that a photography competition or a poetry competition might inspire young photographers or poets. Games for Change, which was already connected to other New York City learning organizations, developed that competition.

Launched in 2004, Games for Change is a nonprofit that brings together game developers, educators, and innovators who seek to harness games and immersive media to be tools for social good. Each year, there is the Games for Change Festival, an international event hosted in New York City. The Festival includes an awards ceremony, keynote speakers, workshops, and panels. There are four Festival tracks: games for learning, civics and social issues, health and wellness, and extended reality. Games for Change president Susanna Pollack sometimes calls the event "the Sundance Film Festival of video games." (The two organizations are not affiliated; however, both are mission-based and host festivals that promote independent storytelling.)

"We had the assumption that students would already know how to make games," Games for Change's senior program coordinator Tania Hack recalled when we spoke. That turned out to be an incorrect assumption. Just because many children play games does not mean that they are literate in design. "If we were going to launch a competition, we realized we needed to launch all of the infrastructure around it to help students learn how to create games—in particular, social impact games."

What exactly are social impact games? Reading this book, you have likely encountered several. Games set in war-torn countries, experiences about marginalized people, and games that transform player beliefs and attitudes are considered social impact games. Examples include *GRIS*, which is about grief and acceptance, *Bury Me, My Love*, the interactive fiction story about Syrian refugees, and *Quandary*, the perspective-taking and ethics game. Regarding youth who design for impact, Hack said, "We hope to see students make games that demonstrate a solution to a real-world problem or an outlook that can change the minds, hearts, and actions of people who play their games."

Students can enter their games into the Student Challenge between February and April. They may work by themselves or in teams of up to four people. The submission process is relatively straightforward: complete a form and include the game's URL, the weblink where the game can be played online. Games must be created using a free and open platform, like Scratch or Unity for Education. Once entered, there is an internal review to ensure that submitted games address the topic themes and that the weblinks function. Next, games are sent to three rounds of jurors.

The Student Challenge has grown exponentially. Over the program's history, more than 32,000 students across the United States have participated, making over 3,000 social impact games. The 2020 professional development cohort included nearly 450 teachers. "Last year, it involved 150 judges," Hack said. "We received 2,000 games that year." Students have the opportunity to win prizes, too. The grand prize is a $1,000 scholarship. Entrants can also win technology, games, and experiential prizes related to either the themes or the game industry.

The awards ceremony is the culminating event where winning games are celebrated. At the event, all of the student finalists and their families are invited to showcase their games. Past ceremonies were held at the Museum of the Moving Image and the Intrepid Museum, in New York City.

Each year's Student Challenge begins long before the entrant's submission date in February. The process starts with teachers at training sessions that take place at the start of each school year. "We recruit student cohorts in each of the Challenge's cities," Hack explained. "This year [2020], we are working with over 100 teachers in New York City, almost 100 in Los Angeles, and 50 or 60 in Atlanta and Detroit. We train those teachers at the start of the school year on how to teach impact game design."

After training, teachers bring the curriculum back into their classrooms. Throughout the school year, they receive support from Games for Change's mentors—individuals in the game development industry, or folks from related design or technology fields. In a typical year, mentors are sent into classrooms to work with students directly. Mentors share about their careers in the industry and provide feedback on students' games. "We often hear stories about their excitement working with teachers, and that they continue those relationships," Hack said.

As a whole, the program focuses more on design than it does on the hard skills of coding. The learning outcomes that are measured align more to 21st century skills (e.g., collaborative problem-solving, critical thinking, creativity) than the skills needed to get students ready to take a computer science exam.

In addition to lessons, there are daylong hosted events—game jams that relate to the different social impact themes. These begin with an icebreaker activity and an introduction to the theme. "We do this in the morning so students can start thinking about them right away," Hack said. Next is an analog game jam activity, where students prototype with physical materials. After a pizza party break, the afternoon is spent digitally designing the games prototyped in the morning's analog phase. The mentors, as well as staff from the Games for Change team, help facilitate. The goal is to have digital prototypes of games to share by the end of the day.

Themes often align with SEL competencies. Recent topics included *A Clean and Happy Earth*, an anti-smoking and vaping theme, *Get the Party Started*, which was about launching new political parties, *Resilience Through Games*, about social distancing, and *Build a Better World*, a challenge about celebrating diversity. *Inclusive Play: Designing Games for All*, sponsored by AT&T, was a theme that resonated with Hack. Using universal design for learning (UDL) resources, students added accessibility features to games. "Students really understood how to introduce the theme in a meaningful way and how to incorporate that theme into their mechanics," she remarked.

The *Benefits of the Human-Animal Bond* theme, sponsored by the Wallis Annenberg Pet Space, an animal rescue shelter in Los Angeles, challenged students to explore the relationships people have with pets. "This theme touched on how animals support our emotional well-being and how they are important companions for human beings," Hack said. "We saw some beautiful games. A middle-schooler created one about an emotional support animal. From the dog's perspective, you help a human who needs emotional support." (That game, *Pickle's Quest for Happiness*, can be played here: https://scratch.mit.edu/projects/357436772.)

The Student Challenge's website is a trove of flexible teaching materials that can support project-based learning and SEL. "We see a huge range of middle school and high school educators who teach math, English language arts, social studies, science, and special education in the Challenge," Hack said. "That is largely due to the themes and the different entry points they afford. Games as a tool for communication and expression are very powerful."

Global Game Jam NEXT: A Global Game Jam for Youth

In 2016, I was part of a team awarded a Hive Digital Media Learning Fund Catalyst Grant by the New York Community Trust. With Games for Change, we then facilitated a series of "Moveable Game Jams" in multiple locations around New York City—daylong events that encouraged youth to invent, adapt, and reimagine the rules of different games. Kevin Miklasz, who co-founded the original vision, Sara Cornish, Games for Change's project director at the time, and I led it. Tania Hack also helped to facilitate events on Games for Change's behalf.

Because our Moveable Game Jams were coordinated with Games for Change, we shared the same themes as that year's Student Challenge. Those themes were: *Future Communities*, sponsored by Current by GE; *Climate Change*, from NOAA and NASA; and *Local Stories and Immigrant Voices*, supported by a separate grant from the National Endowment for the Humanities. Events were hosted at different locations throughout New York City, including a community center in the Bronx, Brooklyn Community College, the Museum of the Moving Image, and the Jefferson Market branch of the New York Public Library.

Each game jam began with an icebreaker followed by a hands-on lesson on that day's theme. After lunch, participants self-selected to join one of four game design stations, each facilitated by a partner organization (e.g., CoderDojo NYC, Global Kids, the Institute of Play). After one hour, participants rotated to a second station. The events concluded with a group share. Often, parents and caregivers were in attendance for these presentations.

Miklasz, Cornish, Alex Fleming (formerly of Mouse, a STEM nonprofit), and I documented all of our Moveable Game Jams in a free ebook, *Game Jam Guide*, linked at the end of this chapter. The guide features over 20 lessons and activities created by learning organizations in the Hive New York City network. Now, anyone can replicate a Moveable Game Jam!

In the fall of 2017, I gave an Ignite talk at the Digital Media and Learning Conference on our experience. Afterwards, I was approached by game design veteran Michael "MJ" John, who had just met with Miklasz. John asked us if we would be interested in connecting with Susan Gold and Ian Schreiber, two founders of Global Game Jam, an international game jam organization. As it happened, Gold and Schreiber were organizing GGJ NEXT, a global game jam for youth. Of course, we both agreed.

Different from the Student Challenge, Global Game Jam is not a competition. Instead, it is an annual event designed to stimulate collaborative teamwork amongst creators. Founded in 2008, each year, there is a keynote speaker and a theme. Past themes have been one-word prompts, like *Deception, Extinction, Repair, Waves*, and *Transmission* (Global Game Jam History, 2020). Themes can manifest in any part of designed games. *Transmission*, for example, could be interpreted as a mechanic where players transmit information to one another, or it could be construed as making a game about radio waves or automotive transmissions.

Similar to Global Game Jam, GGJ NEXT would have keynote speakers and themes. It would also have local sites hosted internationally. But rather than a target audience of college students and game design professionals, GGJ NEXT participants would range from ages 12-17.

With a team of collaborators, Miklasz and I designed a robust curriculum for site organizers. Our goal was to ensure they had the guidance they needed to support youth jammers. The curriculum considered cognitive (e.g., logical thinking, problem-solving) and SEL outcomes, such as teamwork (Arya et al., 2019).

The first year's theme was math-based: *Fractals*. Year two was *Inconvenient Superpowers*, a theme that mapped well to self-awareness competencies. In 2020, during COVID-19 social distancing measures, the curriculum and events were adjusted for youth to engage remotely. That year's theme was *Connection*.

Laila Shabir, founder and CEO of Girls Make Games, led the inaugural keynote. "Anyone with ideas can make games," she told the young jammers. She then advised participants to keep a growth mindset. "When frustrated, power through, because a journey with friends to make games is powerful and meaningful." Agnes Larsson, a senior gameplay developer at Mojang Studios, maker of *Minecraft*, was the second year's keynote speaker. Celia Hodent, the psychologist and game UX consultant who worked on *Fortnite*, led the third year's keynote.

Unlike one-off game jams that need to be organized on a site-by-site basis, GGJ NEXT was immediately scalable. Annual events occur at nearly 50 locations worldwide, almost simultaneously—at least, within the same month. Most of the initial sites were coding clubs and camps, built on Global Game Jam's existing network. We also spent a lot of time scaffolding how to run events for children, which meant consent forms for site hosts and participants.

As game jams are a form of project-based learning, we knew the curriculum should be modular for potential classroom use. With that in mind, we coded the curriculum using letters. On the website, "JM" means "jam" and "GD" stands for "game design." JM modules introduce how jams work; GD is about design skills, but not technical coding skills. JM and GD are then divided into smaller, discreet elements. JM has materials on logistics—running all-day game jams may involve lots of pizza for hungry young jammers! GD includes modules about how youth interact when practicing game design skills. Other parts get into more niche topics; although Scratch and analog game tools are used, some participants may want to learn more about Unity, C++, or GameMaker: Studio.

Rather than a prescribed scope and sequence, the goal was to give facilitators agency to access lessons based on their local needs. The GGJ NEXT website also features video lessons from professional game designers. The entire curriculum can be freely accessed here: https://ggjnext.org/curriculum. Hopefully, after reading this, you head to ggjnext.org to sign up as a potential future site host!

Anti-Defamation League Game Jams

Karen (Kat) Schrier, associate professor at Marist College, served as a Belfer Fellow for the ADL Center for Technology and Society from 2018-2019. As part of her fellowship, she co-organized—and studied—game jams on identity and bias reduction.

ADL is the Anti-Defamation League, an anti-hate nonprofit organization founded in 1913 in response to rising anti-Semitism and bigotry worldwide. Today, its mission continues: combating hate, extremism, and bias, while standing up for social justice and human rights. The ADL is as essential now as it was one century ago.

Daniel Kelley, associate director of the ADL Center for Technology and Society, focuses on bringing the ADL into initiatives like Raising Good Gamers, which seeks to reduce online harassment while supporting digital citizenship. In the past several years, this work has included ADL-aligned game jams. "The idea was to explore whether game jams could be used as a form of training to educate game developers about anti-bias issues," Kelley said.

The first ADL-sponsored jam was themed on *Being an Ally*. A collaborative event between ADL Education, the ADL Center for Technology and Society, and the Museum of Art and Digital Entertainment, the jam took place in October 2017. The winning game was *Ali Tale*, "an anti-bullying game about a high school student who meets a magical cat that grants the power to understand people better" (Fogel, 2018, para. 4). Participants used ADL's Six Ways to Be an Ally to guide design. The steps, which share how to be an ally to targets of name-calling and bullying, are:

1. Support targets, whether you know them or not.
2. Don't participate.
3. Tell aggressors to stop.
4. Inform a trusted adult.
5. Get to know people instead of judging them.
6. Be an ally online. (Six Ways to Be an Ally, 2020)

Game jams themed on *Identity* followed in 2018. Hosted by the ADL Center for Technology and Society, Global Game Jam, and Game Jolt, an independent games community, it was led by Schrier. Her work resulted in the downloadable *ADL Mini-Guide to Identity, Bias, and Games* (https://www.adl.org/media/12529/download), making it replicable for classrooms, educational workshops, and out-of-school spaces (i.e., museums and libraries). It shares ready-to-use ideas on how to run game jam events, as well as questions and prompts that cultivate empathetic thinking around identity with participants.

"The focus of game jams came from anti-bias education programs in schools in the United States," Kelley recalled. "We have a cadre of anti-bias facilitators across the United States affiliated with every regional office. They do anti-bias training in communities."

In the *Being an Ally* game jam, anti-bias trainers gave a presentation to participants before the allotted time for game design. "There is a tension between what kind of training and how long," Kelley said. Perhaps, embedding anti-bias trainers on the game design teams could help the process be more organic? "In the second year [*Identity*], we brought in anti-bias trainers as team members. When the team iterated on what to make, they collaborated and discussed with a skilled and trained anti-bias educator. It was no longer, 'Here's some stuff to put in your game.' Having both on a team could be a net positive."

When studying game jams, researchers can analyze the artifacts that participants produce (e.g., game prototypes, designer diaries) or they can assess the participants' experience. "Some people look at the games that are made and analyze those, which we could do," Schrier explained. "But we wanted to know if the experience of the game jam—the journey, the process—was changing people's identity or perspectives, making them more open and empathetic to others." Kelley concurred. "The odds that we would get a really good empathy game out of a game jam is extremely small," he said. "The focus should not be on outputs."

The *Identity* jams were piloted at Marist with about 70 students. "We were interested in game-making as a potential perspective-taking process," Schrier recalled. "As a game developer or designer, you have to think about other people—the audience, people on your team—to create that experience with them. We surveyed before and after the game jams to see if there were any changes in those aspects."

After the pilot, game jams were hosted online and in-person at ADL's regional offices in the United States. "There were detailed instructions at each location, with surveys to collect data," Schrier said. "I was at the New York one."

In addition to the *ADL Mini-Guide to Identity, Bias, and Games*, Schrier authored *Designing Ourselves: Identity, Bias, Empathy, and Game Design*, a report on her findings. It presents an overview of what game jams are, as well as games to play that support empathy and perspective-taking. These include *That Dragon, Cancer*, about a family whose young son has terminal cancer, *Liyla and the Shadows of War*, a game set in the Gaza Strip, and *When Rivers Were Trails*, about the Anishinaabeg in the 1890s who were displaced from Fond du Lac, Minnesota. These games serve as models or mentor texts to inspire jam participants.

Many of the *Identity* games are available to play at http://jams.gamejolt.io/adljam. "They were all different," Schrier said. "One was on interracial dating. Another used sound, where players listened in on other people's conversations. The theme was *Identity*, so some people made detective games, ones with secret identities, or games on their own identities."

Findings were mixed: "Among all the participants in the study, perspective-taking and empathic concern did not increase significantly from before to after the event. And, the measure of biased attitudes overall did not change" (Schrier, 2019, p. 33). "We didn't find all of that," Schrier said. "Maybe because the experience wasn't that long, or maybe because we divided the sample into three conditions, or maybe game jams do not do that. But we found some directional indications." Participants did report feeling safer from the process. They also felt more secure and at ease through working together. "We found that they talked about other people's identities and thought about others' perspectives. They were also more confident in their abilities as game developers. And they also had fun and felt it was inspirational."

Interestingly, a small but significant percentage of participants were resistant to the theme and anti-bias education, more generally. "They didn't want to talk about this kind of stuff," Schrier said. "If our goal is to reduce bias and to increase equity in companies or games themselves, we need to reach the people who are the most resistant."

Some folks are already connected to ideas around identity, bias reduction, social justice and inclusion. How can we reach those who are most resistant? Are game jams the right answer to reach those people? Perhaps. Or, maybe it is a combination of approaches, a concert of ideas across different media that may also include game design.

Autopathographical Game Design

Autopathographies are autobiographical narratives on illness, disease, or disability. A portmanteau of "autobiography" and "pathology" (Couser, 1997), there are lots of examples in the memoir book genre. Autopathographical books include Elizabeth Wurtzel's *Prozac Nation* (1995), Paul Kalanithi's posthumously published *When*

Breath Becomes Air (2016), Susanna Kaysen's recount of her mental illness, *Girl, Interrupted* (1994), and Jill Bolte Taylor's *My Stroke of Insight: A Brain Scientist's Personal Journey* (2009).

In addition to written memoirs, autopathographies are in the visual arts. A notable example is Frida Kahlo's self-portraiture series of physical disability (Crosby, 2006). Today, we see visual autopathographies in internet-shared self-portraits, or "selfies." Hospitalglam, hosted on Tumblr, is a website where patients share selfies taken at hospitals (Hospitalglam, n.d.). Its tagline is, "Taking the shame out of being in treatment one selfie at a time" (Hospitalglam, n.d., para. 1). Of Hospitalglam, researcher Tembeck (2016) wrote, "The dramaturgical thrust of such imagery is to convey both the centrality of medical experiences in the subjects' lives and their specific desire to be publicly identified as persons living with illness" (p. 9).

Blogs are another form of digital autopathography. Cancer blogs—online journals written and published by patients receiving chemotherapy—are one example (Nesby & Salamonsen, 2016). The medical information website WebMD includes cancer blogs, as well as autoethnographic narratives on anxiety, heart health, and pain management.

Game design tools can also be used to share and self-express illness narratives (Danilovic, 2019). Profound and deeply personal, *That Dragon, Cancer*, mentioned earlier, is an example. Other autopathographical games include *Depression Quest* and *Fractured Minds*, experiences that reflect their designer's struggles with social anxiety disorder and depression.

Psychologist Kelli Dunlap spoke to me about game design as *expressive therapy*. Like art therapy and play therapy, the act of making games can be therapeutic. "Each is a valid approach for people to manage and overcome their traumas," she said. Dunlap then spoke about Emily Mitchell, who rapidly prototyped *Fractured Minds* at a game jam when she was 17-years-old. "This girl [Mitchell], who suffers from significant anxiety and depression, was able to put her experience into a game. That then connects with others who play it, who then see themselves represented. But, it was also therapeutic for her, as the designer."

Why would someone choose to play a autopathographical game? "We are all fascinated with life and death, illness and disease," Sandra Danilovic explained. "These are existential topics that have significance and meaning. Regardless of gender, race, and immutable characteristics, illness, disability, and disease are universal. We will all go through them, one way or another." Danilovic then quoted playwright Susan Sontag who published the treatise, *Illness as Metaphor* (1978/2001). Sontag wrote, "Illness is the night-side of life, a more onerous citizenship. Everyone who is born holds dual citizenship, in the kingdom of the well and in the kingdom of the sick" (1978/2001, p. 3).

Danilovic is an assistant professor of game design and development at Wilfrid Laurier University in Ontario, Canada. A multimedia artist, photographer, and social issue documentary filmmaker, her current work centers on game design for health and well-being, interactive illness and trauma narratives, autobiographical games, abstract games, computational literacy, and maker cultures. When we spoke for this book, she was writing a book on autopathographical game design based on her dissertation research.

Often reflective and contemplative, autopathographies afford the author and the reader/viewer/player space to make sense and meaning of life, death, illness, and disability. "We all have loved ones who have been sick and died and have gone through these experiences," Danilovic continued. "Sometimes, it's about figuring out a way to reach acceptance, which can be therapeutic. It can alleviate fear when we confront difficult emotions."

We are not immortal; there is always the possibility of us getting sick. Making and playing autopathographical games enables us to build resilience and insight into what it means to be human. "We actively seek to understand how other people have gone through illness so we can understand it indirectly. Often, illness can be overcome, which helps us build our resources and natural desire not just to accept but to exert control over our destiny."

Sometimes, those who write autopathographies have explicit objectives. They seek curative possibilities or use the medium as an opportunity to journal to help them process and understand. Others are created to leave a legacy. Danilovic continued,

> To me, an autopathography is an exploration of the mind, a meditation on selfhood. It is part of a quest for self-discovery. By writing them, you take experience and trauma that can be incoherent and rife with chaos and tension, and then you 'order it' through language and words—you impose control on it. And the same with games. Games are interesting as a medium, as game design can be a rigid and methodological approach in ordering. You impose a structure on an experience, which can then provide a sense of relief—the perception that you can take control of your illness.

Danilovic shared her work in mental health autopathographies, where people designed experiences based on their invisible disabilities. Symptoms of invisible disabilities, which can be physical, mental, or neurological, are hidden. In her study, participants created games on bipolar disorder, anxiety, attention deficit hyperactivity disorder (ADHD), color blindness, post-traumatic stress disorder (PTSD), shyness, grief, and insomnia (Danilovic, 2019). Some participants' games had "an echo of *Depression Quest* where they withdrew player agency, and the player got jolted," she said. In *Depression Quest*, players see some written choices as crossed out, a metaphor for the author's social anxiety disorder (Farber & Schrier, 2017; Schrier & Farber, 2019).

Autopathographical games are not necessarily "empathy games." Nor are they "disability simulators" (e.g., a blindness game that uses a blindfold). Autopathographical games typically share an author's personal experience—they do not necessarily invite players to *become* the game's author (Danilovic, 2019). Instead, they are playable art pieces that promote an understanding of illness, disease, or disability. "Frequently, authors may be marginalized and stigmatized, so it comes down to freedom of artistic expression—to create something as cathartic," Danilovic remarked. "You then offer it to someone as an option to play."

At the autopathographical game jam she hosted, Danilovic invited but didn't mandate the theme. They all took her up on it. "They craved the chance to do this at other game jams," she recalled. "It became an opportunity to make the games they always wanted to make."

Comparing autopathographical game design to writing in a personal journal or diary, Danilovic encouraged a "no-holds-barred" approach. This gave participants the liberty to freely express. "You can write anything in a diary," she said. "And at some point, people may engage with it."

Her participants' autopathographical games sometimes metaphorically symbolized illness, disease, and disability. One was designed about bipolar disorder, challenging players to balance the highs of mania with the lows of depression. But some had no explicit autopathographical content. However, they were all informed and based on the author's disability narrative. "These are powerful rhetorical devices in transforming narrative. It is a literal transformation in terms of how it is a mirror of the designer—the designer is trying to transform themselves."

Following the game jam, Danilovic conducted interviews with participants. She asked about the metaphors in the games, as well as the design decisions of the rules, mechanics, graphic design, and visual symbols. She then did a phenomenological reading, which drove a data-driven theorization of literary analysis (Danilovic, 2019).

The conceptual framework in her dissertation was what she calls the *Tetrad of Therapoiesis* (Danilovic, 2019). In more simple language, it is a tetrad, or group of four, that describes the process of therapeutic making. The first of the four dimensions, or components, is *sociopoiesis*, or collective making (Danilovic, 2019). This explains the game jam as a social event. "*Sociopoiesis* describes the encounters and the ways the designers communicated and interacted with each other at the event." Social interactions included the process of sharing, playtesting each other's games, "as well as simple gestures like small acts of openness to each other. There was a sense of community that developed over the game jam. It was akin to a therapy support group. Except it wasn't—it was pseudo, but that was how they experienced it."

The second dimension of the *Tetrad* is *autopoiesis*, or self-making—the autobiography and autopathography in practice (Danilovic, 2019). As designers confront their own emotions, they can become self-aware. "This can be regenerative because it is a self-inquiry—a self-study, essentially," she said.

Next is the metaphorical symbolic-making, or *fabulopoiesis*, when designers transition from concentrating on the self to focusing on the world and others (Danilovic, 2019). *Fabulopoiesis* is the positive reinterpretation of experiencing illness and then reconceiving oneself through character, story, metaphor, and symbolism. "They reinvent themselves through metaphor and analogy," she said. "They come up with alter egos and characters." One participant made a game about obsessive-compulsive disorder. "He created a hyper-analytical detective character who had to solve a crime at a murder mystery dinner, like *Clue*."

Logopoiesis describes the fourth dimension of the *Tetrad*, the computational thinking and logic that undergirds games-as-systems (Danilovic, 2019). *Logopoiesis* affords game designers an opportunity to gain distance from their illness, disease, or disability experience (Danilovic, 2019). "*Logopoiesis* allowed participants to take their experiences and put it into chunks of rigid numbers and values. They distilled their emotional experiences through software code. This is procedural literacy."

When children design games, write poems, journal, or draw about their lives or lived experiences, they may include trauma. When we hosted a game design summer program for high school youth in 2019, one team designed a horror game that included arguing parents (Farber et al., 2020). In their culminating presentation, the group remarked, "It happens all the time" (Farber et al., 2020, p. 63). Was this a self-expression of a lived experience? Or, was this pure fiction?

Family stressors, divorce, death, bullying, discrimination, or other personal trauma, can manifest in anything children produce. "I've been doing game design work with kids for a long time," Katie Salen Tekinbaş told me. "The very early lessons are that kids make games about their lives."

Tekinbaş is a professor of informatics at the University of California, Irvine. She was the co-founder of the Institute of Play, a partner organization in our Moveable Game Jams. Tekinbaş shared an anecdote about a sixth-grade student,

> One of the games a kid in a workshop made was about his father going to the airport. His father was an immigrant and it became really clear that there was this issue of his father leaving all the time. But the game was just about going to the airport. The kid said, "I want to make this game about going to the airport, and there is luggage." When you dig into it, it was a deeply personal story. The kid didn't realize he was revealing something; it was his life at the moment. And lots of stuff comes out.

Game design is a mechanism for young people to develop self-awareness and knowledge about the systems that they inhabit. Introspective, the process can be self-therapeutic and reparative.

When children make games, they think about their own thinking, a central tenet that undergirds project-based learning. As education and technology theorist Seymour Papert famously wrote in *Mindstorms: Children, Computers, and Powerful Ideas*, "In teaching the computer how to think, children embark on an exploration about how they themselves think. The experience can be heady: Thinking about thinking turns the child into an epistemologist, an experience not even shared by most adults" (1993, p. 19).

Links, Lessons, and Games

ADL Mini-Guide to Identity, Bias, and Games: https://www.adl.org/media/12529/download
Depression Quest: http://www.depressionquest.com
Fractured Minds: https://store.steampowered.com/app/688740/Fractured_Minds
Game Design Kits from iThrive Games: https://ithrivegames.org/resources/game-design-kits
Games for Change Student Challenge Resources Hub: http://gamesforchange.org/student challenge/g4c-resources-hub
Game Jam Guide, free curriculum ebook: https://press.etc.cmu.edu/index.php/product/game-jam-guide
Girls Make Games: https://www.girlsmakegames.com
Global Game Jam: https://globalgamejam.org
GGJ NEXT: https://ggjnext.org
Six Ways to Be an Ally poster: https://www.adl.org/media/2124/download
Scratch: https://scratch.mit.edu
That Dragon, Cancer: http://www.thatdragoncancer.com
Twine, a free interactive fiction authoring tool: https://twinery.org
White House Education Game Jam: https://obamawhitehouse.archives.gov/blog/2014/10/06/white-house-education-game-jam

References

Arya, A., Gold, S., Farber, M., & Miklasz, K. (2019). GGJ NEXT: The global game jam for youth. *Proceedings of the International Conference on Game Jams, Hackathons and Game Creation Events* (pp. 1–4). doi:10.1145/3316287.3316289.

Baker-Doyle, K. (2017). *Transformative teachers: Teacher leadership and earning in a connected world*. Harvard Education Press.

Couser, G. T. (1997). *Recovering bodies: Illness, disability, and life-writing.* University of Wisconsin Press.

Crosby, M. (2006). Frida Kahlo's illustrated autopathography: A voice of disability. *A/B: Auto/Biography Studies, 21*(2), 161–175. doi:10.1080/08989575.2006.10815161.

Danilovic, S. (2019). Game design therapoetics: Authoring the computer game autopathography. *Meaningful Play 2018 Conference Proceedings* (pp. 218–232). Carnegie Mellon ETC Press.

Dishon, G., & Kafai, Y. (2020). Making more of games: Cultivating perspective-taking through game design. *Computers & Education, 148,* 103810.

Farber, M., & Schrier, K. (2017). *The strengths and limitations of using digital games as "empathy" machines.* UNESCO MGIEP.

Farber, M., Williams, M. K., Mellman, L., & Yu, X. (2020). Systems at play: Game design as an approach for teen self-expression. *Journal of Games, Self, and Society, 2*(1), 40–84. Carnegie Mellon ETC Press.

Fogel, S. (2018, October 15). Anti-Defamation League to host second annual game jam this weekend. *Variety.* https://variety.com/2018/gaming/news/adl-game-jam-2018-1202980435/

Global Game Jam History. (2020). *Global Game Jam.* https://globalgamejam.org/history

Hospitalglam. (n.d.). *Hospitalglam Tumblr.* https://hospitalglam.tumblr.com/

Kalanithi, P. (2016). *When breath becomes air.* Random House.

Kaysen, S. (1994). *Girl, interrupted.* Vintage.

Nesby, L., & Salamonsen, A. (2016). Youth blogging and serious illness. *Medical Humanities, 42*(1), 46–51. doi:10.1136/medhum-2015-010723.

Papert, S. (1993). *Mindstorms: Children, computers, and powerful ideas* (2nd ed.). New York, NY: Basic Books.

Resnick, M. (2017). *Lifelong kindergarten: Cultivating creativity through projects, passion, peers, and play.* MIT Press.

Schrier, K. (2019). ADL's designing ourselves: Identity, bias, empathy, and game design. *Anti-Defamation League.* https://www.adl.org/media/13011/download

Schrier, K., & Farber, M. (2019). Full paper: Open questions for games and empathy. *Connected Learning Summit 2018 Conference Proceedings.* Carnegie Mellon ETC Press. doi:org/10.1184/R1/7793804.v1.

Six Ways to Be an Ally. (2019). *Anti-Defamation League.* https://www.adl.org/media/2124/download

Sontag, S. (2001). *Illness as metaphor.* Picador. (Original work published 1978)

Taylor, J. B. (2009). *My stroke of insight: A brain scientist's personal journey.* Penguin.

Tembeck, T. (2016). Selfies of ill health: Online autopathographic photography and the dramaturgy of the everyday. *Social Media + Society, 2*(1), 205630511664134. doi:10.1177/2056305116641343.

Wilensky, U. (2016). Designing computational thinking for mathematics and science classrooms. *Journal of Science Education and Technology, 25*(1), 127–147. doi:10.1007/s10956-015-9581-5.

Wurtzel, E. (1995). *Prozac nation: Young and depressed in America.* Mariner.

Index

A

ABC News 83
Aberlin, Betty 16
Abbott, Eleanor 60
Aboud, Clark 114
Adams, Jeromy "Doc" 125
Adducci, Lou 125–126
ADL Center for Technology and Society 182–183
ADL Education 182
ADL Mini-Guide to Identity, Bias, and Games (curriculum guide) 183
Adventureland (Disneyland) 68
Affective empathy 84–85, 91
Affordances 5, 61–62, 76, 93, 99, 110, 112
Age of Enlightenment, Jr. 9
Air Force Research Laboratory 142
Allstate Foundation 35
Alto's Adventure (video game) 114
Altruism 52, 134
Amazon 125, 163
American Samoa 9
American University 117
Among Us (video game) 4–5, 46–47, 68, 71, 161
Amsterdam 95
Anaheim, California 66
Animal Crossing: New Horizons (video game) 4, 27–28, 60, 64, 111, 136
Anne Frank House VR (virtual reality experience) 95
Anthropomorphic 88, 136
Anticipatory play 74–75, 84, 112
Anti-Defamation League (ADL) 182–183
Anxiety, xii 25, 37, 75, 84, 88–89, 116, 185–187
Applied Statistics and Research Methods 42
Apples to Apples (card game) 141
Apple Watch 105
App Store 105
Armstrong, Karen 123
Arrival (film) 27

Arsenal Center 18
The Art of Failure (book) 3
Assassin's Creed (video game) 64
Assemble with Care (video game) 29
Association for Supervision and Curriculum Development (ASCD) 36
Atlas Shrugged (book) 133
AT&T 179
Attention deficit hyperactivity disorder (ADHD) 186
Audubon Society 111
Auschwitz 96
Autonomous sensory meridian response (ASMR) 15–16
Autonomy 29, 64, 121, 160
Autopathographies 184–186
Autopoiesis 188
Aviles, Chris 163–164
Awkward Moment (card game) 138–141

B

BAFTA 75
Balanced design 62
BASIC (programming language) 176
Bastion (video game) 85–86
Batten, Dorothy 141
Beall, Mike 85
Beckett, Samuel 66
Behavioral activation 26
Bejeweled (video game) 132
Bellow, Adam 158–159
Biden-Harris presidential campaign 136
Big Bird 10
Bill & Melinda Gates Foundation 35
Bioshock (video game) 133
Bipolar disorder 186–187
Bitmoji (app) 70
Bloom's Taxonomy 13, 20
Blume, Judy 9
Boccamazzo, Raffael 119
Bogost, Ian 136
Borst, Grégoire 47

Bostwick, Elizabeth 12
Brackett, Marc 25, 38, 48, 141
Brain Games 44–46, 52
BrainPOP (website) 13, 138
Braithwaite, Brenda 96
Braunfeld, Daniel 90, 93–96
Brazelton, T. Berry 18
Breakout EDU 153, 157–159
Breathe (app) 105
Bronfenbrenner's ecological systems theory model 40
Brothers: A Tale of Two Sons (video game) 156
Brooklyn Community College 180
Brooklyn, New York 72, 123
Brown, Brené 117
Brown, John Seeley 153
Buckleitner, Warren 14–15
Buffett, Warren 35
Bury Me, My Love (video game) 75, 178

C

C++ (programming language) 181
Calgary, Canada 126
California's SEL Competencies 164
Call of Duty (video game) 63
Calm (app) 105
Campbell, Joseph 75
Cancer 62, 88, 126, 184, 185
Candy Crush Saga (video game) 132
Candy Land (board game) 59–60, 71
Carnegie Mellon University 145
Casablanca (film) 66
CASEL's SEL Framework xii, 19, 35, 37–40, 48, 50–52, 120, 142, 166
Catharsis 3, 27–28
Catcher in the Rye (book) 88
Celeste (video game) 2–4
Center for Healthy Minds 85, 105–106, 165
Chan Zuckerberg Initiative 35
Character Lab 44
Character education 36, 52

CheckPoint 115
Chen, Jenova 75, 114
Chess (board game) 59, 64
Child, Julia 15
Children's Hospitals Week 126
Children's Miracle Network 124–125
Children's Museum of Pittsburgh 21
Children's Television Workshop 10
Chocolate-covered broccoli 62
Chopped (television show) 175
Cigarettes 148
Civilization (video game) 64, 74
Classcraft (game) 119–122, 153
A Class Divided (documentary film) 93
Climate change 180
CNN 83
CoderDojo NYC 180
Cognitive affordances 61
Cognitive behavioral therapy (CBT) 26
Cognitive empathy 84–85, 91
Cognitive load theory 46
Cold War 135
Coleridge, Samuel Taylor 66
Collaborative for Academic Social, and Emotional Learning (CASEL) 10, 35–37, 40–42, 44–45, 48, 132, 141
    See also CASEL's SEL Framework
Color blindness 186
Columbian Exchange 154
Committee for Children 109
Commodore 64
The Common Book of Baby and Child Care (book) 17
Common Core State Standards 164
Common Sense Education 89
Compassion xii, 28, 37, 38, 40, 47–51, 106–107, 117, 123–124
Compassion Action Network 123
Compassion Games (game) 122–124
Competence 29–30, 121, 160
Conflict resolution 162, 165, 170
Connected Camps 167–168
Connected Learning Lab 165
Connected Learning Summit 74, 112

Content warnings 87–89, 145
Cooney, Joan Ganz 10
Cooperation 85, 123, 145, 155–156, 159
Cooperative games 154, 157
Core mechanic 86, 110
Cornish, Sara 180
Coronavirus 60
Cortana 69
COVID-19 xv, 4, 13, 29, 37, 60, 70, 116, 136, 154, 176, 181
Co-viewing 10–11
Couch co-op 156
Counter-Strike: Global Offensive (video game) 124
Crayola 16
Creative Competition 164–165
Critical inquiry 48–51
Crossy Road (video game) 29
Crystals of Kaydor (video game) 85–87
Cultural appropriation 95
Culyba, Sabrina 22, 145–147
Current by GE 180
Cushing, Elizabeth 160–163

D

Dairy Queen 124
Daniel Tiger 15, 20–22, 169
Daniel Striped Tiger 10, 16, 20
Daniel Tiger's Grr-ific Feelings (app) 21
Daniel Tiger's Neighborhood (television show) 14, 20–21
Daniel Tiger's Neighborhood Ride 21
Daniel Tiger Stop & Go Potty (video game) 22
Danilovic, Sandra 185–187
Dark rid 68–69, 144
Darling-Hammond, Linda 35
Darvasi, Paul 143, 146
Davidson, Richard 85–86, 105, 165
Davis, Angela 93
Decisions That Matter (video game) 145
Depression Quest (video game) 84, 185–186

Designing Ourselves: Identity, Bias, Empathy, and Game Design (report) 183–184
DiAngelo, Robin J. 90
Differentiated instruction 13
Digital Media and Learning Conference 180
Disability simulators 187
DiSalvo, Betsy 113
Discord 125
Disney+ 87
Disneyland 60, 65–69
Disneyland Railroad 66
Disney Pixar 23, 25, 88
Disney, Walt 66
Donohue, Chip 12–14, 18–19, 22, 41
Doom Buggy 68–69
Dora the Explorer (television show) 15
D.N. Batten Foundation 141
The Dukes of Hazzard (television show) 124
Dumbo (film) 88
Dumbo (theme park ride) 67
Dunlap, Kelli 89, 117–119, 185
Duraiappah, Anantha xi–xii, 48–50
Dysgraphia 108
Dyslexia 108

E

Earthrise: Bearing Witness to Our Planet (lesson plan) 53
Ebert, Roger 95
Eco, Umberto 67
Ecological Approaches to Social Emotional Learning (EASEL) Laboratory 43–46, 52
Educational television 10–11, 13–14
Ekman, Paul 23–25, 86
Electric Company (television show) 10
Elias, Maurice J. 36, 120
Elliot, Jane 93–94
Emotional Intelligence: Why It Can Matter More than IQ (book) 36

Emotions Revealed: Recognizing Faces and Feelings to Improve Communication and Emotional Life (book) 24
Emotion scientists 25, 26
Empathy xii, 4, 21, 26, 37–38, 40–41, 47–51, 62, 83–86, 89–92, 95–97, 106–107, 115–119, 123, 132, 137, 142, 176, 183–184
Empathy games 85–99, 146, 187
Empatico 48
Encouraging Prosocial Actions in Students (lesson plan) 53
Entertainment Software Ratings Board (ESRB) 3, 88
Epic Games 63
Equity in Learning with BrainPOP: Fostering Access and Impact for All (publication) 13
Erikson, Erik 17–18
Enmon, Victoria (Tori) 125
Environmental storytelling 110
Eudaimonic 27, 28
European Renaissance 94
Esports 124, 155, 163–165, 167–168
Ethics 40, 52, 132–136, 138, 178
Eye of the Storm (documentary film) 93
Experience points (XP) 120
Explore SEL 44, 107
Extra Life 124–126

F

Fable III (video game) 132, 134
Fabulopoiesis 188
Facebook 116
Face the Future: A Game about the Future of Empathy (curriculum) 90
Facial Action Coding System (FACS) 24, 86
Facing History and Ourselves 90, 93, 95–97
Fallout Shelter (video game) 135–136
False empathy 51
Fantasyland 68
Feelings Wheel 23
FH Knights (esports team) 163–164

Fiellin, Lynn E. 147–148
Fisher, Greg 123
Fleming, Alex 180
Flight to Freedom (video game) 92
Flipgrid 48, 164
Florence (video game) 170–171
Florence: Perspectives and Patterns (curriculum) 170
flOw (video game) 114
Flow channel 121
Flower (video game) 114
For Crown or Colony (video game) 91
Food Network 175
Four-Square (game) 161–162
Fractured Minds (video game) 185
Framerspace 170
Framework for 21st Century Learning 48
Free to Be… You and Me (song) 9
Fred Rogers Center for Early Learning and Children's Media at Saint Vincent College 12, 14–15, 19, 41
Fred Rogers Productions 20–21
The French Chef (television show) 15
Freud, Anna 17
Focus (game) 45
Foot, Philippa 131
Fort Collins, Colorado 65
Fortnite (video game) 28, 46, 63–65, 68, 165, 181
Fortugno, Nick 134
The Fountainhead (book) 133
Frank, Anne 95
Frogger (video game) 29
Fruit Ninja (video game) 106
Fullerton, Tracy 67, 73–76, 109–114
Functional affordances 61–62
Functional magnetic resonance imaging (fMRI) 85, 106

G

Game-based learning 143, 158, 171
Game Design Studio 141
Game Developer Conference 69
Game feel 62–65
Games for Change 75, 90, 146, 177–179, 180
Games for Change Festival 83, 89
Game jams 175–176, 179–185
Game Jam Guide (book) 190
Game Jolt 183
Games for Social and Emotional Learning (curriculum) 162
The Game of Life (video game) 135
Game Innovation Lab 109
GameMaker: Studio 181
Gandhi, Mahatma 53
Garcia, Courtney 28
Garden State Esports 163
Garrett, Joseph Mark 16
Gaynor, Steve 110
Gear Learning 85
Gee, James Paul 65
Generation Z 15
Generosity 52, 85
Georgia Tech 113
Gerstein, Jackie 23
Gershon, David 123
Ghost Host 69
Gianas, Angelique 97–99
G.I. Bill 71
Girl, Interrupted (book) 185
Girls Make Games 181
Global Game Jam 175, 180–181, 183
Global Game Jam (GGJ) NEXT 180–182
Global Kids 180
Goff, Harper 65–66
Golden Rule 123
Go Goals! (board game) 71
Gold, Susan 180
Goleman, Daniel 36
Gone Home (video game) 69, 110, 146
Good Gamer 164
Google Doc 124, 159
Google Form 123
Gratitude 20, 52–53, 107, 114, 121–122, 145

Gratitude for Our Food (lesson plan) 53
Great Depression 71
Greater Good in Education 48, 52
Greater Good Science Center 52
Great Recess Framework 160, 163
Green, Ryan 88
Green, Amy 88
Greenberg, Mark T. 36, 45, 48
Grief 1, 4, 25, 29, 88, 178, 186
GRIS (video game) 1–4, 25, 178
Grover 10
Groundwork for the Metaphysics of Morals (book) 134
Growth mindset 2, 40–41, 43, 145, 165–167, 181
Guardians: Unite the Realms (video game) 26
Guatieri, Luigi 116–117

H

Hack, Tania 177–180
Hackathons 108
Hamilton, Matthew 110–111, 113
Hanks, Tom 14
Halo (video game) 69
Happy Salmon (card game) 73
Hard skills 36, 176, 179
Hartzman, Zachary 2, 117, 119
Harvard Graduate School of Education 43, 144
Haunted Mansion (theme park ride) 66, 68–69
Headspace (app) 105, 113
Head Start 9, 44
Hedonic 27–29
Healthy Minds (app) 105
Hellblade: Senua's Sacrifice (video game) 88
Hemingway, Ernest 7
Henson, Jim 10
Hebrew Bible 123
Hey Listen Games 118
Hide-and-Seek (game) 71
High School Esports League (HSEL) 163

Hindu 123
Hirsh, Emile 110
His Holiness the Dalai Lama 123
Historical empathy 90–92, 95
HIV 146–147
Hive Digital Media Learning Fund Catalyst Grant 180
Hodent, Celia 46, 62–65, 121, 181
Holden Caulfield 88
Holocaust 90, 96
Hoovervilles 71
Hospitalglam 185
Howdy Doody (television show) 10, 15
How Games Move Us: Emotion by Design (book) 75
Heuristics 74
Hugo, Victor 135
Huizinga, Johan 67–68
Human flourishing 48–49, 51

I

I Can Problem Solve (ICPS) (curriculum) 36
iCivics 93
Identity formation 141, 143
Idlewild Park and Soakzone 21
Illness as Metaphor (book) 185
Imagineers 67
Immersive Reader 108
Immigrants and Border Patrol (board game) 71–72
Indigenous cultures 95
Insomnia 186
Institute of Play 108, 180, 188
I Love My Neighbor (game) 162
I Love You, Colonel Sanders! A Finger-Lickin' Good Dating Simulator (video game) 169
In-groups 84, 138
Inner Resilience Program 52
Inside Out (film) 23–25
Instagram 116, 169
Institution of Education Sciences 35

Institute for the Future 90
Interdependence 155–156, 159
International Campaign for Compassionate Cities 123
Interstellar (film) 27
Into the Beautiful North (novel) 97
Into the Wild (film) 110
Intrepid Museum 178
Iñupiat 156–157
Invisible disabilities 186
iPad 4, 106
iPhone 29
Islam 123
iThrive Games 48, 141–144
It's a Small World (theme park ride) 69

J

Japanese-American internment camps 91
JavaScript (programming language) 176
J.C. Penney 139
Jennings, Patricia 48
Jigsaw puzzle 60, 170
Jim Crow laws 96
John, Michael "MJ" 180
Johnson, Lyndon B. 9
Joint media engagement 10–13, 21, 25, 145
Jones, Stephanie M. 43–46
Journey (video game) 75, 114
Journeys in Film 111
Joy of Painting (television show) 15
Jungle Cruise (theme park ride) 67
Jurassic World: The Ride (theme park ride) 68
Juul, Jesper 2–3

K

Kahlo, Frida 185
Kahoot! 48
Kalanithi, Paul 184
Kamenetz, Anya 14

Kamp, David 9
Kant, Immanuel 134
Kaysen, Susanna 185
Keep Talking and Nobody Explodes (video game) 153–154, 156
Kelley, Daniel 182
Keltner, Dachner 24
Kendi, Ibram X. 90
Kennedy, John F. 9
Kindness xii, 17, 20, 37, 53, 107, 114, 117, 121, 123–124, 145
Kindness Buddy (lesson plan) 53–54
Kind Words (lo-fi chill beats to write to) (video game) xii, 114–119, 121–122
King Friday XIII 16
King, Jr., Martin Luther 53, 93
King, Maxwell 18
KIPP charter schools 36
Kitil, Jennifer 48
Knott's Berry Farm 68
Koster, Raph 59–60
Kowert, Rachel 27, 29–30
Krause, Caitlin 113

L

Lady Aberlin 16
Lakitu 65
Lara Croft 121
L'arrivée D'un Train en Gare de La Ciotat (The Arrival of a Train at La Ciotat Station) (film) 28
Larsson, Agnes 181
Layoff (video game) 132–133
Leacock, Matt 154
League of Legends (video game) 124
Learning, Education, & Games Vol. 3: 100 Games to Use in the Classroom and Beyond (book) 136
Learning Games Network 86, 137
LEGO 44
Lemonade Stand (video game) 176
Les Misérables (book) 135

Leukemia 125
Level Up: The Guide to Great Video Game Design (book) 65
Levy, Allisyn 13, 138
Lewis, John 53
LGBTQ+ 169
LIFE (breakout game) 159
Life Is Strange (video game) 88
Life is Strange 2 (video game) 135
Life's Little Lessons 21
Liminal Esports 163
The Limits and Strengths of Using Digital Games as "Empathy Machines" (working paper) 95
The Little Prince (book) 17
Liyla and the Shadows of War (video game) 184
Llama piñatas 63
Logopoiesis 188
Loneliness (video game) 72–73
Lootboxes 62
Louisville, Kentucky 123
Lunch with Soupy Sales (television show) 10

M

Mafia (card game) 4, 161
The Magic Garden (television show) 9
Magnetic resonance imaging (MRI) 47, 85, 106
Main Street, U.S.A. 65–67
Marceline, Missouri 66
Mario Kart 8 Deluxe (video game) 29
Marist College 155, 182
Maslow's Hierarchy of Needs 20
Master Chief 69
Max Caulfield 88
McFarland, Margaret B. 17–18
McGonigal, Jane 90, 105
Mechanics, Dynamics, Aesthetics (MDA) Framework 73
Medicaid 9
Meehan, John 69–70

Meier, Sid 74
Mental transport 60, 66, 84
Merchant, William 42
Microsoft 23, 107–108
Microsoft Education 107, 109
Microsoft Edge 108
Microsoft Research 108
Mightier (video game) 26
The Migrant Trail (video game) 97–99
Miklasz, Kevin 175–176, 180–181
Milgram experiment 94
Milgram, Stanley 94
Milk, Chris 95
Milton Bradley 60
The Mindful Knight xii, 107–109, 113–114
Mindfulness 44, 47–53, 70, 105–114
Minecraft Atlas 107
Minecraft 5, 12–13, 16–17, 26, 64, 107–109, 111, 153, 181
Minecraft: Education Edition (video game) xii, 113–114
Miracle Balloons 124
Mission: It's Complicated (video game) 168–169
Mission Lab 108
Miyamoto, Shigeru 65
Monopoly (board game) 70–71
Millennium Falcon 67
Mirror neurons 50, 85
Mission US 91
Mr. McFeeley 19
Mister Rogers 9, 15–18, 22
Mister Rogers' Neighborhood (television show) 14–21
Mitchell, Emily 185
MIT Education Arcade 137
MIT's Lifelong Kindergarten Lab 176
MIT Media Lab 26
Mojang Studios 181
Molly of Denali (television show) 12
Montessori, Maria 19
Mood management theory 26–30
Mood Meter 25–26
Morals 133

INDEX | 199

Moral Machine survey 132
Mortality salience 66
A Mortician's Tale (video game) 29
Mouse 180
Moveable Game Jams 180, 188
Multimodal 3, 97, 99
Multi-Tiered Support Systems (MTSS) 120
Muppets 10
Museum of Art and Digital Entertainment 182
Museum of Me (curriculum) 143–144
Museum of the Moving Image 178, 180
My Stroke of Insight: A Brain Scientist's Personal Journey (book) 185

N

NASA 180
National Day of Play 125
National Endowment for the Humanities 111, 180
National Science Foundation (NSF) 140
National Association of College Esports (NACE) 163
National Federation of State High School Association (NFHS) 163
Nazi Germany 94
Nearpod 23
Neighborhood of Make-Believe 14, 16–18, 66, 68
Neuromotion Labs 26
Neuroplasticity 42, 47, 50, 106, 142
New Deal 71
New Delhi, India 47
New Testament 123
New York Community Trust 180
New York Public Library 180
New York State Regents exam 2
The New York Times (newspaper) 24, 60, 93, 154
Never Alone (Kisima Ingitchuna) (video game) 156–157

Night in the Woods (video game) 88
Nightmare: Malaria (video game) 63
Nintendo 4, 60, 68, 135–136, 164
Nintendo Switch 29
NOAA 180
No Child Left Behind 37
A Normal Lost Phone (video game) 144
Normative ethical machines 133
North America Scholastic Esports Federation (NASEF) 163
Nostalgia 67
NoVo Foundation 35

O

Obama administration 165, 176
Objectivism 133
Ocasio-Cortez, Alexandria 136
Odyssey (app) 169
Omnimover 69
The Oprah Winfrey Show (television show) 93
The Oregon Trail (video game) 97
Orlando, Florida 126
Osmond, Marie 124
Osterweil, Scot 137
Out-groups 84, 92, 138
Overcooked 2 (video game) 156
Overwatch (video game) 64–65, 124

P

Paciga, Kathleen 12, 15–19
Pac-Man (video game) 29
Paired texts 97–99
Pandemic (tabletop game) 154
Paparazzi (game) 162–163
Papers, Please (video game) 134, 136
Paradox of failure 2–3
Parasocial relationships 15, 19
Paris Descartes University 47, 65
Participate 48

Passive constraints 74, 84, 112
Paul Ekman Group 24–25
PBS KIDS 12, 22
PeaceMaker (video game) 92
Peace on Earth by 2030 123
Pear Deck 23
Peekapak 23–24
People Who Made a Difference (lesson plan) 53
Permission to Feel (book) 25
Perspective-taking 26, 37, 41, 50, 96, 107, 136–137, 176, 178, 183–184
Physical affordances 61
Peter Pan (film) 88
Phillips, Cole 108
Piaget, Jean 38
Pirates of the Caribbean (theme park, ride) 67, 69
Pittsburgh, Pennsylvania 17, 21
Plants vs. Zombies: Battle for Neighborville (video game) 27
PlayForward: Elm City Stories (video game) 146
Playing History 2: Slave Trade (video game) 91
Playing Sandcastle (video game) 22
play2PREVENT lab 146–148
Playworks 160–162
Plutchik's Wheel of Emotions 23
Polio 60
Pollack, Susanna 177
Positive Behavior Interventions and Supports (PBIS) 120
Positive Greetings at the Door 20
Post-traumatic stress disorder (PTSD) 186
Pratham's Life Skills Framework 48
Prisoner in My Homeland (video game) 91
Proceduralize 4, 171
Procedural play 132
Promoting Alternative THinking Strategies (PATHS) (curriculum) 36, 45
Promoting Social and Emotional Learning: Guidelines for Educators (book) 36
Prophet Muhammad 123
Prosocial 5, 39–40, 50, 52–53, 85, 117, 122, 134
Prozac Nation (book) 184
Public Broadcasting System (PBS) 10, 93, 98
Puppet Pals (app) 16
Python (programming language) 176

Q

Quandary (video game) 136–138, 178
Quarnstrom, Deirdre 107–109
Quarterbacking 159
Queergaming 136
Quest to Learn 69, 108
Quinn, Zoë 84

R

Raising Good Gamers 13, 182
Ramer, Jon 122–124
Rand, Ayn 133
Rappolt-Schlichtman, Gabrielle 144
Red Dead Redemption 2 (video game) 68, 111, 113, 134
Red Light, Green Light (game) 45
Refugee camp 95
Reid, Stephen 107
Relatedness 4, 29, 64, 121, 160
Relationship-building 52, 142, 155, 162, 168
Remember (game) 45
Rethinking Learning: A Review of Social and Emotional Learning for Education Systems (publication) 5, 48
Responsible decision-making 37, 38, 132, 157
Ricard, Matthieu 48
Rite-Aid 124
Rivers, Susan E. 48, 141–144
Rockefeller Foundation 35
Rockefeller Growald, Eileen 35

Rocket League (video game) 124
Rock-Paper-Scissors (game) 162
Rogers, Fred 14–23, 41, 49, 51, 74
Rogers, Scott 65, 69
Role-playing games (RPGs) 84–85, 96, 113, 119
Rooney, Dominic 126
Roosevelt, Franklin D. 71
Ross, Bob 15
RULER Approach 25, 38, 48
Rutgers University 120

S

Sam's Journey (curriculum) 143–144
San Diego County Office of Education 163
Sarcastic Gamer (podcast) 125
Sayonara Wild Hearts (video game) 136
Schell, Jesse 21–22, 145, 169
Schell Games 21–22, 145–148, 169
Schrier, Karen 95, 132, 136, 155–156, 182–184
Schoolhouse Rock! (television show) 9
Schneider, John 124
Scott, Ziba 115–117
Scratch (coding app) 176–178, 181
Screen Therapy (YouTube channel) 28
Sea of Solitude (video game) 25, 63
Seeds of Compassion 123
Seidman, Max 140–141
Selective empathy 51, 84
Self-care 23, 70, 105, 164–166
#SelfCare (app) 105
Self-determination theory (SDT) 29, 64, 121, 160
Self-management 37–38, 43, 120, 157, 162, 166
Self-regulation 38, 40–41, 43, 45–47, 59, 109, 164–165, 167–168
SEL Kernels 44–47, 52
Sendak, Maurice 9
Sensory affordances 61
Serious Games Interactive 91

Sesame Street (television show) 9–10, 14
Sesame Workshop 10, 44
Schonert-Reichl, Kimberly A. 38, 41–42, 48
Schreiber, Ian 180
Shabir, Laila 181
Shapiro, Arana 89
Sharma, Robin 170
Sheinman, Nimrod 48
Shriver, Sargent 9
Shriver, Timothy P. 10, 35, 42
Shure, Myrna 36
Shyne, Rahbin 124
Shyness 186
Signifiers 61
Silly Stories (game) 45
Simon Says (game) 45
Singh, Nandini Chatterjee 48–51
Situational game design 74–75, 84, 134
Six Feet Under (television show) 29
Six Principles of Learning Readiness 17–20, 49–50
Skill trees 121
Sky: Children of Light (video game) 68, 114
Slave Tetris (video game) 91
Sleeping Beauty's Castle 60, 68
smokeSCREEN (video game) 148
Snakes and Ladders (board game) 71
Social and emotional learning (SEL) xi, 2, 14, 18, 35–53
Social-Emotional and Character Development Lab 120
Sociopoiesis 187
Soft skills xi, 36, 176
Solis, Rick 86
Solnit, Rebecca 112–113
Sonic the Hedgehog 63
Sontag, Susan 185
Space Invaders (video game) 135
Special Olympics 35
SPENT (video game) 83–84
Spiritfarer (video game) 29
Spock, Benjamin 17
SpongeBob SquarePants (television show) 29
Sports4Kids 160

Stages of Grief 1, 4, 25
Stampy Cat 16–17
Star Trek (television show) 168
Star Trek II: The Wrath of Khan (film) 132
Steam 91
Steinkuehler, Constance 165–168
STEM 140, 166, 180
Stroop Test 46
Stop-and-Think (game) 45
Stop Light (game) 45
Stop-Signal-Task 46–47
Student Challenge 177–178, 180
Sunny Days (book) 9
SuperBetter (app) 105
Super Mario Bros. (video game) 1, 59, 155
Super Mario 64 (video game) 65
Super Smash Bros. (video game) 164
Suspension of disbelief 66, 159
Sustainable Development Goals (SDGs) 47–48, 71
Sympathy 117
Systemic SEL (publication) 39

T

Tacoma (video game) 110
Tactical Teams 164–165
Tag (game) 71, 161
Takei, George 91
Take This 27, 119
Taxonomy Project 43
Taylor, Jill Bolte 185
Tea Party (video game) 21–22
Teachers Compassion Games Guide 124
TeachSDGs (website) 48
Teaching Strategies (TS) GOLD 42
Technology in Early Childhood Center at the Erikson Institute 12
TED Talk 95, 123
Tekinbaş, Katie Salen 13, 167–168, 188
Telltale Games 84
Tenacity (video game) 106, 112
Tetrad of Therapoiesis 187–188

Tetris (video game) 91
That Dragon, Cancer (video game) 62, 88, 92, 104–105
thatgamecompany 75, 114
A Theory of Fun for Game Design (book) 59
Theory of mind 50, 97–98
They Called Us Enemy (book) 91
This War of Mine (video game) 135
Thought experiment 131, 133, 135, 137
Thoreau, Henry David 70, 74, 109–113
3 Cs 63–65
3-2-1 Contact (television show) 10
Tie Fighters 67
TikTok (app) 16
Tilt, tilting 165–168
Tiltfactor 139–140
Tilt malleability 166–167
Tilt resilience 166, 168
Train (tabletop game) 96
Tomb Raider (video game) 64, 121
Tomorrowland 68
The Transformational Framework (book) 145
Transformers: The Ride (theme park ride) 68
Transportation theory 66
Trauma 88–89, 92, 94–96, 185–186, 188
Tricky Travel (breakout game) 157–158
Trigger warning 87–88, 99
Trolley problem 131–133, 137
Tumblr 185
20,000 Leagues Under the Sea (film) 66
Twine 177
Twitch (website) 15, 124–125, 163
Twitter 116, 163, 169
2001: A Space Odyssey (film) 27

U

UCI Esports 165, 167
Undertale (video game) 134
The Undocumented (documentary film) 98

UNESCO Mahatma Gandhi Institute of Education for Peace and Sustainable Development (MGIEP) 5, 75, 89, 95, 122, 170
UNESCO MGIEP's EMC² Framework for Social and Emotional Learning xii, 47–52, 106
UNICEF 44
United Nations 71
United Nations Educational, Scientific and Cultural Organization (UNESCO) 49
Unity 181
Unity for Education 178
Universal design for learning (UDL) 13, 179
Universal Studios Hollywood 68
University of California, Berkeley 52
University of California, Irvine 165, 188
University of Houston 93
University of Illinois, Chicago 35
University of Northern Colorado 42
University of Pittsburgh Medical Center 169
University of Southern California 73, 109
University of Wisconsin, Madison 85, 105
Up (film) 88
Upton, Brian 74–75, 113
Urban Ministries of Durham 83
Urrea, Luis Alberto 97–99
US Civil War 96
Utilitarian 131–132

V

Vialet, Jill 160
Virtual Reality (VR) 91, 95

W

Waiting for Godot (play) 66
Walden, a game (video game) 74, 109–114, 143

Walden; or Life in the Woods (book) 110
Walden Pond 74, 110
Walking (essay) 112
The Walking Dead (video game) 84
Walking simulators / walking sims 110–114, 143, 146, 170
Wallis Annenberg Pet Space 179
War on Poverty 9
Way (video game) 155–156
The Way Things Work (curriculum) 69
WebMD (website) 185
Weimar Republic 96
Weins, Adam 86
Weissberg, Roger P. 35, 42
Well-being 3–5, 20, 27, 30, 38, 48–49, 51–52, 67, 90, 107, 179, 186
Werewolf (card game) 4, 70–71, 73, 161
WETA 11
WNET/Thirteen 91
WhatsApp (app) 168
What Remains of Edith Finch (video game) 143–144, 69, 89
When Breath Becomes Air (book) 184–185
When Rivers Were Trails (video game) 184
Wilfrid Laurier University 186
White House Education Game Jam 176
White House Office of Science and Technology Policy 165
Whole Child 17
Wilcox, Gloria 23
World Health Organization (WHO) 44, 60
World of Warcraft (video game) 153
World's Largest Lesson 48
World War II 71
Wu, Minerva 166
Wurtzel, Elizabeth 184

X

Xbox Adaptive Controller 108
Xenophobia 115

Y

Yale Center for Emotional Intelligence 21, 25, 48, 141
Yale University 35, 83, 146
Yang, Robert 95
Young, Shawn 120
YouTube (website) 15–16, 28–89, 106, 117, 138, 169

Z

Zakrzewski, Vicki 48, 52–53
Zelda: Breath of the Wild (video game) 68
Zimmerman, Eric 3–4, 73
Zinn Education Project 92
Zinn, Howard 92
Zombie 3, 84
Zone of proximal development 59–60
Zoom 115

www.ingramcontent.com/pod-product-compliance
Ingram Content Group UK Ltd.
Pitfield, Milton Keynes, MK11 3LW, UK
UKHW022239230426
12048UKWH00018BA/1344